Women's Suffrage

Other Books in the Turning Points Series:

Turning | Points
IN WORLD HISTORY

Women's Suffrage

Brenda Stalcup, *Book Editor*

David L. Bender, *Publisher*
Bruno Leone, *Executive Editor*
Bonnie Szumski, *Editorial Director*
David M. Haugen, *Managing Editor*

Greenhaven Press, Inc., San Diego, California

Every effort has been made to trace the owners of copyrighted material. The articles in this volume may have been edited for content, length, and/or reading level. The titles have been changed to enhance the editorial purpose.

No part of this book may be reproduced or used in any form or by any means, electrical, mechanical, or otherwise, including, but not limited to, photocopy, recording, or any information storage and retrieval system, without prior written permission from the publisher.

Library of Congress Cataloging-in-Publication Data

Women's suffrage / Brenda Stalcup, book editor.
    p.   cm. — (Turning points in world history)
    Includes bibliographical references and index.
    ISBN 0-7377-0326-1 (lib. : acid-free paper) —
  ISBN 0-7377-0325-3 (pbk. : alk. paper)
    1. Women's rights—United States—History. 2. Women—
Suffrage—United States—History. 3. Women in politics—United
States—History. 4. Prohibition—United States—History. 5. Anti-
slavery movements—United States—History. 6. United States.
Constitution. 19th Amendment—History. I. Stalcup, Brenda.
II. Series.

HQ1236.5.U6 W65 2000
305.42'0973—dc21   99-055609
                                                     CIP

Cover photo: FPG International
Library of Congress, 15, 31, 35, 38

©2000 by Greenhaven Press, Inc.
P.O. Box 289009, San Diego, CA 92198-9009

Printed in the U.S.A.

Contents

the fears of the southern states, this unfortunate development actually sped up the adoption of suffrage, but it did so at the cost of the moral integrity of the movement.

Chapter 4: The Antisuffragists

Chapter 5: The Final Push for Women's Suffrage

ratification of the Nineteenth Amendment by thirty-six
state legislatures.

Chapter 6: The Impact of the Nineteenth Amendment

Foreword

Certain past events stand out as pivotal, as having effects and outcomes that change the course of history. These events are often referred to as turning points. Historian Louis L. Snyder provides this useful definition:

> A turning point in history is an event, happening, or stage which thrusts the course of historical development into a different direction. By definition a turning point is a great event, but it is even more—a great event with the explosive impact of altering the trend of man's life on the planet.

History's turning points have taken many forms. Some were single, brief, and shattering events with immediate and obvious impact. The invasion of Britain by William the Conqueror in 1066, for example, swiftly transformed that land's political and social institutions and paved the way for the rise of the modern English nation. By contrast, other single events were deemed of minor significance when they occurred, only later recognized as turning points. The assassination of a little-known European nobleman, Archduke Franz Ferdinand, on June 28, 1914, in the Bosnian town of Sarajevo was such an event; only after it touched off a chain reaction of political-military crises that escalated into the global conflict known as World War I did the murder's true significance become evident.

Other crucial turning points occurred not in terms of a few hours, days, months, or even years, but instead as evolutionary developments spanning decades or even centuries. One of the most pivotal turning points in human history, for instance—the development of agriculture, which replaced nomadic hunter-gatherer societies with more permanent settlements—occurred over the course of many generations. Still other great turning points were neither events nor developments, but rather revolutionary new inventions and innovations that significantly altered social customs and ideas, military tactics, home life, the spread of knowledge, and the human condition in general. The developments of writing, gunpowder, the printing press, antibiotics, the electric light, atomic energy, television, and the computer, the last two of which have recently ushered in the world-altering information age, represent only some of these innovative turning points.

Each anthology in the Greenhaven Turning Points in World History series presents a group of essays chosen for their accessibility. The anthology's structure also enhances this accessibility. First, an introductory essay provides a general overview of the principal events and figures involved, placing the topic in its historical context. The essays that follow explore various aspects in more detail, some targeting political trends and consequences, others social, literary, cultural, and/or technological ramifications, and still others pivotal leaders and other influential figures. To aid the reader in choosing the material of immediate interest or need, each essay is introduced by a concise summary of the contributing writer's main themes and insights.

In addition, each volume contains extensive research tools, including a collection of excerpts from primary source documents pertaining to the historical events and figures under discussion. In the anthology on the French Revolution, for example, readers can examine the works of Rousseau, Voltaire, and other writers and thinkers whose championing of human rights helped fuel the French people's growing desire for liberty; the French *Declaration of the Rights of Man and Citizen*, presented to King Louis XVI by the French National Assembly on October 2, 1789; and eyewitness accounts of the attack on the royal palace and the horrors of the Reign of Terror. To guide students interested in pursuing further research on the subject, each volume features an extensive bibliography, which for easy access has been divided into separate sections by topic. Finally, a comprehensive index allows readers to scan and locate content efficiently. Each of the anthologies in the Greenhaven Turning Points in World History series provides students with a complete, detailed, and enlightening examination of a crucial historical watershed.

Introduction

While the status of women has varied widely throughout history, in most places and eras women have had few legal, political, or economic rights. The early United States was no exception: American women were not allowed to vote, sit on a jury, or run for political office. Any property a woman brought into marriage fell under her husband's control, and married women who worked had no right to keep their own wages. Very few girls received a thorough education, and no colleges would admit female students.

As early as the colonial days, some individual Americans—both men and women—raised questions concerning the unequal status of women. However, a concentrated feminist movement did not begin until 1848, when the first convention on women's rights was held at Seneca Falls, New York. This new movement for women's rights focused on a number of issues, including married women's property rights, equal pay for working women, liberalized divorce laws, dress reform, and education. Suffrage—the right to vote—was one of the first and foremost demands of the movement.

Initially, suffrage was a controversial subject even within the women's rights movement. Many feminists worried that the demand for women's suffrage was too extreme; they feared that asking for such a radical change would decrease the likelihood that the movement would be taken seriously on any issue. Without the right to vote, however, women only had a few means by which they could attempt to directly affect politicians and laws, such as sending petitions to Congress. The feminists discovered that petitioning and the other measures available to them required an inordinate amount of time and energy, yet had little influence and very rarely had positive results. As women realized that the right to vote would enable them to bring about other reforms more quickly, suffrage became the driving cause of the movement.

Women also wanted the right to vote in order to gain political equality with men. Many women felt it was unjust that as American citizens they should not have the right to vote, to have a personal say concerning laws that affected them and their families. If the United States really was founded on the ideals of equality and liberty, they argued, then in all fairness women should not be forbidden to cast their ballots alongside men in free and open elections. As historian Marjorie Spruill Wheeler writes, the suffragists believed that "enfranchisement . . . was essential both as a symbol of women's equality and individuality and a means of improving women's legal and social condition."

Supporters of suffrage—including moderate and radical feminists, temperance workers, and social reformers—all hoped that women's use of the ballot would usher in numerous changes in women's status and in society at large. However, suffrage also affected American women and society in ways that the early suffragists could never have predicted. Once women were enfranchised, it was not long before they started to take active roles in other political and legal arenas, such as serving as jurors or congressional representatives. Moreover, the suffragists' larger goals of full equality and freedom for women laid the foundation for the resurgent feminist movement that began in the 1960s and furthered the advancement of women's rights.

The articles contained in *Turning Points in World History: Women's Suffrage* explore the birth of the suffrage movement, its divisions and achievements, and its enduring legacy. Selected for readability and content, these articles present a variety of views concerning women's suffrage, as well as an examination of the theories and tactics of the antisuffragists. Each reading begins with an introduction that summarizes the author's main points and supplies historical context. This volume also includes an appendix of primary source documents, providing a sample of the arguments made for and against suffrage throughout the long history of the movement. In addition, the historical essay that begins this volume and the detailed chronology both serve to highlight the most significant events discussed in the articles and documents.

Unfortunately, many U.S. history books still gloss over the suffrage movement, stating that Congress gave women the right to vote without mentioning the thousands of women and men who actively campaigned for the Nineteenth Amendment. The intent of this volume is to shed light on the remarkable struggle for women's suffrage and the lasting impact of that hard-won victory.

A Brief History of the Women's Suffrage Movement

The Nineteenth Amendment to the U.S. Constitution, which gave American women the right to vote, officially became law on August 26, 1920. The passage of the amendment marked the end of a seventy-two-year struggle for women's suffrage in the United States. Most historians date the beginning of the suffrage movement from the 1848 women's rights convention in Seneca Falls, New York, where for the first time a group of women publicly demanded the right to vote. Of the sixty-eight women at Seneca Falls who signed a resolution calling for women's suffrage, only one—Charlotte Woodward, then nineteen years old—lived long enough to see the passage of the amendment in 1920. The founders and foremost members of the movement—Elizabeth Cady Stanton, Lucretia Mott, Susan B. Anthony, Lucy Stone, and many others—devoted years of hard work to achieve a victory that would not be realized in their lifetime. As Carrie Chapman Catt and Nettie Rogers Shuler wrote shortly after the Nineteenth Amendment was adopted,

> Hundreds of women gave the accumulated possibilities of an entire lifetime, thousands gave years of their lives, hundreds of thousands gave constant interest, and such aid as they could. It was a continuous, seemingly endless, chain of activity. Young suffragists who helped forge the last links of that chain were not born when it began. Old suffragists who forged the first links were dead when it ended.

The goal these suffragists worked for was a simple one, yet incredibly profound in its impact on society: They sought enfranchisement and political equality for half the citizens of the United States.

The Origins of the Movement

Although the United States was founded on the precepts of freedom and equality, these principles did not apply to American women, who were not allowed to vote, serve as jurors, hold political offices, or even attend college. Married women were specifically restricted by the legal concept of coverture,

Susan B. Anthony and Elizabeth Cady Stanton were friends, colleagues, and founders of the women's suffrage movement.

which stated that a wife's legal identity and rights were sub-sumed by her husband. Under coverture, a married woman had no legal control over her own personal property or any wages she earned. She could not buy or sell property, sign contracts, or make a will without her husband's consent. In the case of her husband's death, she had no automatic right to the custody of her children. While single women were not bound by coverture and theoretically had more rights, in practice they were often required to turn over their earnings and control of their legal affairs to their male relatives.

Women were also expected to follow strict social rules: They were to cultivate a modest and docile personality, center their lives around their children and domestic tasks, and obey their husbands in all matters. For single women, there were only a few avenues for respectable employment, and even fewer that paid well. The jobs open to them—school-teacher, seamstress, maid—typically involved domestic or child-centered duties. Furthermore, women were not al-lowed a public voice: Most churches and other social insti-tutions forbade women from speaking during services or meetings, and women were not supposed to publicly air their opinions on the important issues of the day.

Throughout the colonial and Revolutionary eras, there were scattered protests against the social and political dis-abilities of women. However, it was not until the early nine-teenth century that discontent over women's situation reached the boiling point, and one of the main irritants was that women could not speak publicly. In the early 1800s, America experienced a wave of social change; several reform movements arose, including temperance and abolitionism. Women were interested in taking part in these movements, but they encountered a great deal of resistance to their in-volvement. Many men felt that it was improper for women to take an active interest in controversial matters such as slav-ery. Some reform organizations, such as the American Anti-Slavery Society, refused to accept female members; other groups allowed women to join but required them to remain silent during meetings. Despite such treatment, most female reformers were determined to participate in the movements.

When they were barred from joining male-run organizations, they formed their own groups, such as the Philadelphia Female Anti-Slavery Society, and coordinated their own meetings and petition drives. And then a few of these reformers took the crucial step of giving public lectures.

By the standards of the day, this was a daring and radical move. As author Miriam Gurko explains, "In the early nineteenth century, women simply did not address a public group. It was considered not only beyond their capacities, but was frowned upon as improper, indecorous, unfeminine, irreligious, against both God and nature." It was bad enough for a woman to go on a lecture tour and speak in public auditoriums to other women, but it was unheard of for a woman to address a "mixed" or "promiscuous" audience of both men and women. Nevertheless, a handful of abolitionist women began to do just that. The two who created the most commotion were Sarah and Angelina Grimké, the daughters of a slave owner from South Carolina. Sarah and Angelina became Quakers, moved to the North, and joined the anti-slavery movement. Initially, the sisters only intended to speak to small groups of women, but their lectures attracted overwhelming crowds, and so many men tried to attend their presentations that they soon found themselves addressing large mixed audiences wherever they went. In July 1837, Angelina even went so far as to publicly engage in a debate with two men.

The Grimké sisters' flaunting of conventional customs caused an uproar, and they were roundly condemned as immoral. One particularly hostile attack came from the Massachusetts Congregationalist clergy, who issued a statement declaring that female reformers were "unnatural" and liable to "fall into shame and dishonor." Sarah and Angelina both responded directly to their critics, defending women's right to a public forum. As they formulated their arguments, they began to consider other discriminatory attitudes about women. In her *Letters on the Equality of the Sexes*, for example, Sarah Grimké not only addressed the topic of public speaking but also declared that women should receive the same educational opportunities as men and be paid equal wages for equal work. The sisters also started to draw parallels between slavery and the status of women; in her *Letters to Catherine Beecher*, Angelina Grimké wrote, "The investigation of the rights of the slave has led me to a better understanding of my own. . . . Woman was . . . the first victim of power. In all heathen nations, she has been the slave of man, and Christian nations have never acknowledged her rights." The sisters' writings on women's rights were widely read and discussed. In 1837, Angelina noted, "The whole land seems aroused to discussion of the province of woman, and I am glad of it. [Sarah and I] are willing to bear the brunt of the storm, if we can only be the means of making a break in that wall of public opinion which lies right in the way of woman's rights."

Three years later another important event occurred, again within the anti-slavery movement and again concerning women's right to have a public voice. In 1840, a number of American abolitionists sailed to England to attend the World Anti-Slavery Convention in London. Among them were several women who had been elected to represent their respective organizations as delegates to the convention. On the first day of the convention, however, many of the men objected to allowing women to serve as delegates, insisting that it was improper and unseemly for women to participate in the convention. Other male delegates rose to the women's defense, and soon a furious debate broke out over whether to admit the female delegates. Not allowed to defend their own case, the women sat in frustrated silence as the men spent hours arguing. Despite the impassioned arguments of the women's supporters, the majority of the men voted against admitting the female delegates. The women were allowed to stay and listen to the convention proceedings, but they were compelled to sit in the gallery behind a curtain, where they could be neither seen nor heard.

The experience was terribly humiliating for the women, both those who had been chosen as delegates and those who had come as attendees. One of the banned delegates was Lucretia Mott, a prominent abolitionist who was accustomed to speaking freely in public venues. During the convention,

Mott befriended Elizabeth Cady Stanton, the wife of one of the American delegates. "After the sessions," writes historian Eleanor Flexner, "the two women walked the London streets together . . . , talking about the anomaly of devoted workers in the anti-slavery cause being denied any voice in its deliberations simply because they were women." The more Mott and Stanton discussed the legal and social disabilities of being a woman, the more convinced they became that a reform movement was needed, and they agreed to hold a convention on women's rights when they returned home.

The First Women's Rights Convention

Eight years passed by before Mott and Stanton were able to follow through with their decision to hold a women's rights convention. Over those years, the two had stayed in touch through letters, and neither had lost their interest in improving women's situation. Although Mott had been busy with her abolitionist work, she had also started to write and speak about women's condition. Stanton was occupied with her growing family, but she had found time to lobby for a state law in New York that strengthened the property rights of married women. Still, Mott and Stanton wanted to do more. When they met again in July 1848 at a small tea party in Waterloo, New York, they and the other three women present began discussing their discontent with women's lot in life. By the end of the day, they had decided to hold a two-day convention on women's rights the following week in the nearby town of Seneca Falls, where Stanton lived.

They hurriedly planned the meeting during the next few days, forming an agenda and lining up speakers. They also decided to write a declaration stating their beliefs about women's rights, similar to the declarations that were often presented at abolitionist conventions. Stanton was the primary author of the Declaration of Sentiments and the list of resolutions that accompanied it, which the convention attendees were to vote on. Among the twelve resolutions, she included a demand for the right to vote. The other organizers worried that the resolution on suffrage was too radical and extreme; they tried to convince her to remove it. But

Stanton appealed to Frederick Douglass, a former slave and a leader in the abolitionist movement, who she knew through her anti-slavery work. Douglass understood what it meant to be disenfranchised; as a black man, he was also unable to vote. He encouraged Stanton in her determination to present the suffrage resolution and promised to support the measure at the convention.

The turnout on the first day of the convention was far greater than anyone had expected: Approximately three hundred people arrived, including about forty men. By and large, the convention proceeded smoothly—surprisingly so, considering that it had been hastily organized around a novel and controversial topic and that most of the women presenters had no experience in public speaking. Eleven of the resolutions—supporting women's right to speak in public, equality in marriage, and so on—passed quickly and unanimously. However, as Mott and the others had feared, the suffrage resolution provoked far more controversy. Most of those who objected to the resolution did not believe that women should never have the right to vote; rather, as Gurko explains, they "argued that so excessive a demand would arouse such antagonism and derision that the movement would be killed before it even got under way." Stanton countered that if women had the right of suffrage, they could use the power of their votes to achieve their other goals more rapidly and easily. Then, as he had promised, Douglass took the floor and voiced his support for women's suffrage. According to historian Doris Weatherford, Douglass "insisted that without this fundamental right to participate in government, the principle of equality for women would never be taken seriously." After much debate, the resolution carried by a small margin, and one hundred men and women affixed their names to the Declaration of Sentiments.

Reactions to the Convention

As the second day of the Seneca Falls convention drew to a close, the participants—still excited about all the new ideas that they had been discussing—enthusiastically agreed to meet again two weeks later, in the larger town of Rochester,

New York. This second convention, which was more heavily advertised than the one at Seneca Falls, attracted an overflowing crowd of interested participants. Women's suffrage was again among the issues debated, and this time the resolution passed by a wider margin.

The organizers had been pleasantly surprised by the number of local residents who attended the Seneca Falls and Rochester conventions. The reaction of the national press was also a surprise, and far less pleasant. At most, the women had expected a few local newspapers to run short articles on the conventions; they underestimated the newsworthiness of such an unusual and shocking event. The major newspapers in New York City quickly picked up on the story, and soon the entire nation was reading about the women's rights conventions. Very few of these articles and editorials were favorable: Most made fun of the women, while others condemned their actions as appallingly unnatural. Nevertheless, as distressing as Stanton found this wave of negative publicity, she realized that it would also ultimately serve the cause by spreading the news faster and farther than she and her colleagues could have done on their own. When the *New York Herald* printed the Declaration of Sentiments in its entirety in order to ridicule it, Stanton was pleased. "Imagine the publicity given to our ideas by thus appearing in a widely circulated sheet like the *Herald*," she wrote. "It will start women thinking, and men too; and when men and women think about a new question, the first step in progress is taken."

Stanton's assessment proved to be correct. During the next year, women across the United States discussed the issues raised at Seneca Falls, published articles on feminist topics, and made preparations for several more conventions. In 1850, four women's rights conventions took place in Ohio alone, and the First National Woman's Rights Convention was held in Massachusetts, with delegates arriving from as far away as California. The national convention became an annual event, and regional meetings occurred frequently in states throughout the North and the Midwest.

It is important to note that not all women supported the

movement; in fact, the early feminists were a distinct minority. The South was particularly resistant to the idea of women's rights, which was linked closely with abolition, and the early movement did not take hold among the women of the southern states. Nevertheless, the women's rights movement grew and spread throughout the 1850s, attracting many new members. Among those who joined the movement during this period were two women who became prominent leaders: Lucy Stone and Susan B. Anthony.

At the time of the Seneca Falls convention, Lucy Stone was employed as a lecturer for the Massachusetts Anti-Slavery Society, but she had also begun to speak on women's rights. Although she did not attend the earlier conventions, Stone was one of the principal organizers of the First National Woman's Right Convention in 1850, where she delivered an impassioned speech to a captivated audience and established herself as an important new leader. Susan B. Anthony came a little later to the cause. Anthony's parents and sister attended the 1848 Rochester convention and signed the resolutions, but Anthony was too preoccupied with her teaching career and her participation in the temperance movement to give much thought to women's rights. However, she changed her mind during 1852 and 1853, when she was forbidden to speak at two temperance meetings and a teachers' association convention because she was a woman. Once Anthony had dedicated herself to working for the women's movement, according to Weatherford, she "set aside temperance, abolition, and other reforms to place singular value on women's rights—and within that area, she would spend her life aimed like an arrow on the vote."

The Character of the Early Movement

In the beginning, however, the movement as a whole was not aimed on the vote; suffrage was just one of many demands in a broad campaign for women's rights. As the movement progressed during these early years, the internal opposition to asking for suffrage died down, and most feminists came to see the right to vote as an essential goal. But the movement also concentrated on issues such as expanding married women's property rights, reforming the divorce laws, and opening the doors of higher education and the professions to women. The various regional and national women's rights conventions remained the primary venues through which these measures were discussed and advanced. During the first few years of the burgeoning women's rights movement, the feminists were almost solely occupied with formulating their ideas on the different issues that concerned them. The frequency of the conventions "led to the charge that the women did nothing but talk," Flexner writes, "[but] at this stage, there was not much else they could do." She continues:

> Having stated their dissatisfaction with things as they were, they had to agree on what they wanted to achieve, and to develop an ideology which would serve to refute their critics and win them new adherents. What *was* the proper condition of married women? What should be woman's place in the church, the community, the professions, the state? On what basis should divorce be permitted . . . ? From the gatherings where these issues were thrashed out there emerged a body of thought, new and dedicated leadership, wide publicity, and new recruits.

To a lesser extent, this discussion was also carried on in some abolitionist newspapers that were sympathetic to women's rights and in the feminist periodicals that the women began to publish for themselves.

The conventions remained important for another reason: The women of the fledgling movement were resistant to the idea of formal organization. While some small feminist groups did arise in New England, the Middle Atlantic states, and the Midwest, attempts to form a national women's rights society floundered during the 1850s. Most early feminists feared that a permanent national organization would be cumbersome and restrictive; instead, they preferred an informal grassroots approach. In Weatherford's words, "That was the way the movement would proceed until after the Civil War: without any bylaws, headquarters, official publication or other accoutrements of formal organization, the cause would carry on."

The Effects of the Civil War

The Civil War and its aftereffects changed the women's rights movement immeasurably. When the war broke out in the spring of 1861, the leaders of the movement had to decide how best to react. Anthony believed that the women should continue on as usual, holding their conventions and engaging in their political activities regardless of the war. They could not afford to place the campaign for women's rights on hold during the hostilities, she maintained; any break in the movement's momentum could only work against them. However, none of the other prominent leaders agreed with Anthony. First of all, they felt that persisting in political agitation during a time of national crisis would be irresponsible and unpatriotic. But they also hoped that if they devoted all their energy to the war effort, they would be rewarded with suffrage by a grateful government. Historians Elizabeth Frost and Kathryn Cullen-DuPont explain that the movement's leaders viewed the temporary abandonment of their cause "as a tactical move;" they believed that if they concentrated on aiding the war effort, their "contributions as citizens would make it clear that they were entitled to the vote."

Anthony had grave doubts about the wisdom of this tactic, but since she was alone in her misgivings, she reluctantly agreed to shelve her work for women's rights during the course of the war. From 1861 to 1865, no women's rights conventions were held, and all other political work—such as the circulation of petitions concerning suffrage—ground to a halt. Instead, the feminists dedicated themselves to fundraising, nursing, and relief work. In 1863, Anthony and Stanton founded the Women's National Loyal League, which Stone and many other prominent women's rights leaders joined. The league's main goal was to advocate the abolishment of slavery in every state, including those slave states that had not joined the Confederacy.

Over a period of fifteen months, in a national petition drive that was larger and more ambitious than any the feminists had organized before, the Loyal League collected nearly four hundred thousand signatures in support of complete emancipation of the slaves. This impressive number of petitioners helped to convince Congress that the proposed Thirteenth Amendment, which would abolish slavery nationwide, had a significant amount of grassroots approval. Moreover, the intensity and scope of the petition drive gave the league's leaders valuable experience that they would carry over into the women's rights movement. The drive enabled them to develop a network of two thousand petition gatherers, as well as records of the names and addresses of other potential supporters of women's rights. Additionally, as Flexner notes,

> One of the most far-reaching effects of the League's work was to accustom the women themselves to the value of organization as a means to accomplish their ends. Their experience in the League, fortified by the many other activities they carried on during the war, acted as a powerful solvent to changing their earlier views that organization could only be constricting and harmful.

The revitalized women's rights movement that emerged after the Civil War would benefit immensely from the skills that the feminists acquired during their work for the league.

The leaders of the league applied their new organizational expertise to the cause of women's rights almost immediately following the end of the war. The South surrendered in April 1865, and shortly thereafter, Congress began discussing an amendment designed to protect the freed slaves' civil rights, including the right to vote. One of the congressmen, a sympathizer to the cause of women's rights, forwarded a draft of the proposed Fourteenth Amendment to Stanton and other former officers of the Loyal League, who were horrified to discover that its wording specifically excluded women. Stanton and her colleagues had long supported the goal of black suffrage, but they had expected that the proposed amendment would also grant suffrage to women, both white and black. Instead, they realized, if the Fourteenth Amendment were adopted as written, it would introduce the word "male" into the U.S. Constitution, blatantly disenfranchising women. Stanton and Anthony immediately swung into full activist mode, distributing petitions and firing off letters to newspaper editors and congressmen. They also started planning the Eleventh National Woman's Rights Convention, the first to be held since before the Civil War.

Controversy and Division

The convention met in May 1866, a month after the Fourteenth Amendment had been officially proposed in Congress, its gender-specific language still intact despite intense lobbying by women's rights advocates. The convention was attended by many members of the now-obsolete American Anti-Slavery Society. Mott, Stanton, and Anthony all urged the abolitionists and feminists to continue working together to secure the rights of both African Americans and women. At the convention's close, the participants voted in favor of forming a new organization called the American Equal Rights Association, dedicated to universal suffrage regardless of race or sex.

The stinging betrayal represented by the Fourteenth Amendment had galvanized the feminists to transform what had been a wide-ranging reform movement into a focused suffrage campaign. However, the coalition created by the American Equal Rights Association proved to be an uneasy one. A number of abolitionist men refused to join the association and opposed its work. The idea of suffrage for black men was already controversial, they maintained; adding women's suffrage to the proposed amendment would make it even more controversial, thus jeopardizing the passage of a measure desperately needed to protect the rights of the newly freed slaves. The members of the association also began to differ over the same issue: Though they agreed that universal suffrage was their ultimate goal, some felt that the association should put the issue of women's enfranchisement on hold until black men's voting rights were secured, while others believed they should fight against any legislation that did not grant suffrage to both groups. The association—which was comprised of men and women of both races—did not divide on this question strictly along race or gender lines. For instance, some African Americans, including the famous lecturer Sojourner Truth and abolitionist Robert

Purvis, repeatedly argued that neither group should obtain suffrage at the expense of the other. Nevertheless, the debate over whether to support or obstruct the Fourteenth Amendment drove a wedge into the American Equal Rights Association almost from its very conception.

During these years, the suffragists increased their political activity in numerous arenas. In the fall of 1866, for example, Stanton declared her intent to run for a seat in the U.S. House of Representatives "as a rebuke to the dominant [Republican] party for its retrogressive legislation in so amending the National Constitution as to make invidious distinctions on the ground of sex." Her eligibility as a candidate was not challenged, and she therefore became the first woman to run for Congress, although she received only twenty-four votes. Then in 1867, the Kansas legislature announced a referendum on whether to remove the word "male" from the state's voting requirements. "It was the first time that woman suffrage had come up for a political test," Flexner writes, "and the woman leaders . . . put their best efforts into it." Stone, Stanton, Anthony, and other suffragists traveled to Kansas and campaigned all across the state in support of the measure. Although they were sorely disappointed when the measure was defeated at the polls, the Kansas campaign provided them with useful experience for similar state referendums in the future.

The suffragists' efforts to remove the word "male" from the Fourteenth Amendment also failed, and the amendment was officially added to the Constitution in July 1868. A few months later, the Fifteenth Amendment was introduced into Congress; it stated that the right to vote could not be denied "on account of race, color, or previous condition of servitude." Again, Stanton and Anthony objected to the phrasing of the amendment, arguing that they could not support it unless the word "sex" was added to it. Once more, other prominent suffragists—most notably Stone—disagreed; while they were not happy about women's exclusion from the amendment, they could not in good conscience attempt to block the passage of a measure intended to protect the rights of black men. The May 1869 convention of the American Equal Rights Association erupted into a heated debate over the Fifteenth Amendment, as old friends and colleagues bitterly split into two factions. It would be the last meeting of the American Equal Rights Association, and the beginning of a twenty-year divide in the suffrage movement.

Two Different Approaches to Suffrage

Immediately following the disastrous last meeting of the American Equal Rights Association, Stanton and Anthony organized the National Woman Suffrage Association (NWSA), with membership initially restricted to women. Stone countered a few months later by forming the American Woman Suffrage Association (AWSA), which was open to both men and women. Quite predictably, NWSA opposed passage of the Fifteenth Amendment, while AWSA supported it. But although the disagreement concerning the Fifteenth Amendment was the straw that broke the camel's back, the two factions of suffragists also differed over other important issues. The leadership of AWSA focused solely on winning women's suffrage; they avoided issues such as divorce reform or women's labor unions, which they believed were too controversial and would reflect badly on the suffrage movement. In addition, AWSA concentrated on gaining suffrage state by state. On the other hand, NWSA continued to address a broad spectrum of women's rights issues, and its principal aim was the passage of a national suffrage amendment. Of the two, NWSA was by far the more revolutionary group, whereas AWSA appealed to the mainstream. As Flexner points out, "The reason for the split between women once so closely united and with the same basic aims . . . lay in deeply opposing social viewpoints—the conservative and the radical—which clashed, not on whether women should vote, but on *how* that goal could be won."

Ironically, during the same time that the suffrage movement was busy tearing itself in two, the legislature of the Wyoming Territory quietly passed a bill that granted women the franchise. In the words of author Bill Severn, "When the news reached the East suffrage leaders were overjoyed. The first clear victory had come so unheralded they were astounded." However, the news did herald the beginnings of a distinctive trend: Of the states and territories that gave women the right to vote before the passage of the federal suffrage amendment, the vast majority were in the West. According to historian Marjorie Spruill Wheeler,

> Historians differ as to the reason why the West was so precocious in its adoption of woman suffrage. One theory was that frontier conditions undermined traditional gender roles and that women, having proven their ability to conquer difficult conditions and do "men's work," were rewarded with the vote. Another theory was that the politicians hoped that women voters would help to "civilize" the West. Most historians stress political politics as opposed to advanced ideology as the explanation, arguing that western politicians found it expedient to enfranchise women for a variety of reasons.

Regardless of the reasons, the passage of women's suffrage in the Wyoming Territory and other parts of the West provided suffragists with actual proof that allowing women to go to the polls on election day would not automatically result in chaos.

The New Departure

After the Fifteenth Amendment was ratified in 1870, the NWSA suffragists altered course: It was true that they had failed to block the passage of the Fourteenth and Fifteenth Amendments, but they thought that perhaps they could now use those amendments to their advantage. They noticed that although the second section of the Fourteenth Amendment referred to "male citizens," it was only in the context of the possible denial of suffrage to men. Nowhere did the wording explicitly bar women from voting. Conversely, the first section of the amendment stated that "all persons born or naturalized in the United States" were citizens. The suffragists realized that this clause could be interpreted to mean that women were citizens and therefore had the right to vote. This legal strategy and similar ones based upon the Fourteenth and Fifteenth Amendments became known collectively as the New Departure.

A number of suffragists decided to put this interpretation to a practical test; in 1871 and 1872, approximately 150 women attempted to vote in ten states and the District of Columbia. Most of the women were not allowed to register as voters, or if allowed to register, they were turned away at the polls. If they did manage to vote, their ballots were usually discarded without being counted. Anthony was among the women who went to the polls during the November 1872 elections. She was permitted to cast her ballot—and was promptly arrested for voting illegally. Anthony was more than prepared to go to jail; she was determined to take her case to the U.S. Supreme Court if necessary. However, due to gross irregularities in her trial, Anthony lost her chance to appeal. She was found guilty but refused to pay her fine.

Another suffragist did eventually make it to the Supreme Court. Virginia Minor, the president of the Missouri Woman Suffrage Association, had also attempted to vote in November 1872; unlike Anthony, she had been unsuccessful. Minor responded by suing the official who had refused to register her to vote. When the lower courts ruled against Minor, she appealed to the Supreme Court. In 1875, the Supreme Court justices handed down their unanimous decision, ruling that the Constitution did not automatically confer suffrage on all citizens. Women's suffrage, the justices declared, was a matter that fell under the jurisdiction of the individual states.

Retrenching and Reunion

The unfavorable Supreme Court decision in the Minor case effectively ended any further attempts to win suffrage in the courts by using the New Departure strategy. Instead, NWSA's members redoubled their efforts to pass a constitutional amendment that would specifically give women the right to vote. The first federal amendment for women's suffrage had been proposed in Congress in December 1868, but it did not progress very far. At NWSA's request, Senator A.A. Sargent introduced a differently worded amendment to Congress in January 1878; it was this version that would finally be ratified as the Nineteenth Amendment more than forty years later. Supporters of suffrage continued to reintroduce the measure at every session of Congress, and although it usually failed to make it past the initial committee hearings, the proceedings kept the issue of a national suffrage amendment alive.

Meanwhile, the members of AWSA channeled their energies into a long series of campaigns in various states and territories. Generally, they tried to convince the legislature of a state to hold a referendum on a women's suffrage measure; if successful, the suffragists would then canvass the state in an effort to persuade the male voters to support the bill on election day. Additionally, whenever a state held a constitutional convention, AWSA would lobby the convention's delegates to include suffrage for women in their revision of the state's constitution. This state-by-state process was intensive and exhausting. Frost and Cullen-DuPont write that during each campaign, "suffrage leaders left their homes and traveled to

The headquarters of an antisuffrage organization

the various states to work beside local suffragists. Countless numbers of women knocked on their neighbors' doors and asked for signatures in support of women's suffrage; speeches were made, tracts passed, legislators and male voters beseeched." Yet the results of this hard work were almost always discouraging: Between 1870 and 1910, only four states would grant women the right to vote.

One reason for the repeated defeats—both in the state campaigns and in the drive for a federal amendment—was the emergence of an organized opposition to women's suffrage. Although the suffragists had always had their critics, these antisuffragists did not feel the need to organize until after the foundation of the first two women's suffrage associations in 1869. The first antisuffrage organization was established in 1871, and others soon followed. The members of these groups employed many of the same tactics as the suffragists, such as petitioning Congress, distributing pamphlets, and publishing antisuffrage magazines. Whenever the suffragists lobbied Congress for a federal amendment or launched a campaign for a state referendum, the antisuffrage women also appeared to argue against the cause.

The liquor industry presented an even more powerful threat to the suffragists. The temperance movement and the women's rights movement had always been closely linked; they both pointed out the ways in which wives suffered when their husbands drank to excess. Not all temperance workers supported suffrage, but many believed that if women were given the franchise, they would overwhelmingly vote for prohibition. The liquor industry agreed with this assessment and therefore did everything in its power to prevent women from gaining the right to vote.

Eventually, many members of NWSA and AWSA came to the conclusion that the suffrage movement could better counter its opposition if it presented a united front. The two groups were already working in loose cooperation during the various state referendum campaigns, and over the years their ideological differences had lessened. The dissension that had split the movement in 1869 meant very little to the young suffragists who joined the movement in the 1880s.

And though hard feelings remained among the older leaders, they also yearned to mend the rift. Stone's daughter, suffragist Alice Stone Blackwell, played a major role in convincing her mother, Stanton, and Anthony to reconcile and to merge the two organizations. In 1890, the movement reunited as the National American Woman Suffrage Association (NAWSA).

The Doldrums

After the merger, NAWSA adopted the moderate policies and tactics that had been championed by AWSA. Over the previous two decades, Anthony had become single-mindedly fixed on the goal of suffrage—much to Stanton's dismay—and now tended to agree with Stone that the organization should not spread itself thin by addressing a wide range of feminist issues. Furthermore, while NAWSA's members did continue to lobby half-heartedly for a national suffrage amendment, they devoted the bulk of their time and effort to the strategy of winning suffrage in the individual states. Seventy years old at the time of the merger, Anthony spent most of the 1890s traversing the country in one state campaign after another. Her amazing fortitude and commitment endeared her to the younger suffragists, who dubbed her "Aunt Susan."

The period from the mid-1890s to 1910 has often been referred to as the doldrums; during these years, the movement expended considerable effort and yet seemed to remain at a standstill. As one state referendum after another failed, the suffragists understandably grew discouraged. Their attempts to build support in the South led them to employ racist arguments that alienated African-American suffragists but failed to sway many white Southerners. Furthermore, the original leadership was rapidly aging. Even the indomitable Anthony was slowing down, and in 1890 she resigned from the presidency of NAWSA. Two of Anthony's protégées, Carrie Chapman Catt and Anna Howard Shaw, hoped to succeed her. Anthony chose to back Catt's candidacy; Shaw was a gifted orator, Anthony reasoned, but Catt was more skilled as an organizer and had stronger leadership capabilities. With Anthony's support, Catt won the election, but she resigned in 1904 when her husband became fatally ill. Shaw then became NAWSA's president, a position she held for ten years. Unfortunately, she proved to be an ineffective leader, and morale fell significantly during her tenure.

The Militant Wing

At the same time that the American suffrage movement appeared to be at its lowest ebb, the English suffrage movement was bursting out in an astounding display of militant action. The English suffragettes, as they called themselves, had been trying for some years to convince Parliament to pass an act legalizing suffrage for women. At the turn of the century, frustrated with their lack of progress, they began to resort to radical and attention-grabbing tactics. The suffragettes disrupted government meetings, heckled legislators, staged demonstrations on the streets, held protests in front of Parliament, and handcuffed themselves to buildings. When jailed for disturbing the peace, they went on hunger strikes to protest their imprisonment.

The militancy of the suffragettes inspired the more radical members of the American movement. The first to import English tactics to the United States was Stanton's daughter, Harriot Stanton Blatch, who lived in England for many years. Blatch had grown up surrounded by her mother's revolutionary rhetoric, and in England she had moved in the same circles as the militant suffragettes. When she returned to America in 1902, she was stunned by the stagnancy and conservatism of what had once been a vital and radical suffrage movement. Determined to revitalize the movement, she arranged for the leading English militants to speak in New York, founded the Women's Political Union, and introduced some British tactics, such as suffrage parades.

Two younger American women, Alice Paul and Lucy Burns, actually took part in the British militant campaign for several years. Appropriately enough, Paul and Burns first met in London while being arrested for demonstrating for suffrage. When they returned to the United States, according to Wheeler, they "had no patience with the slow, state-by-state

In the early twentieth century, suffragists held a number of suffrage parades to publicize the cause.

plodding that had consumed much of the NAWSA's energy." Paul and Burns convinced Shaw to let them take over NAWSA's small Congressional Committee, which was the branch of the organization dedicated to lobbying for a federal suffrage amendment. Their first action was to organize a suffrage parade of several thousand women to be held in Washington, D.C., on the day before President Woodrow Wilson's inauguration. The parade was met by a mob of hostile men; the police stood by and did nothing while the crowd attempted to physically block the suffragists' path. Public outrage over the near-riots and the ineptitude of the police triggered a congressional investigation of the police department, which resulted in favorable press for the suffragists.

Shortly after the parade, NAWSA approved Paul and Burns' proposal to form an affiliated national group, the Congressional Union, that would concentrate on a federal suffrage amendment. Nevertheless, NAWSA's leaders, who had worked hard to cultivate a reputation for being staid and moderate, were not sure how to react to Paul, Burns, and their followers. As Flexner writes, they "were beginning to have an uneasy feeling that they had released a force they would have difficulty in controlling."

Meanwhile, NAWSA was starting to emerge from the doldrums. In November 1910, the suffragists finally won another state victory when Washington's voters approved a suffrage measure by almost two to one. Heartened by their success, the suffragists redoubled their efforts the following year and won in California. In 1912, an unprecedented total of three states granted women the right to vote. These successes were very welcome after fourteen years of failure, but all was not well within NAWSA itself. The national headquarters had contributed virtually nothing to the campaigns, which had been financed and won almost entirely by the members of local chapters. Furthermore, although three states did approve women's suffrage in 1912, this victory was tempered by the failure of referendums in three other states that same year. Discontent with Shaw's leadership grew throughout 1914, when only two of seven state campaigns ended in success, and reached its peak in 1915 as all four of the year's state referendums lost by embarrassingly large margins. At NAWSA's 1915 convention, Shaw was pressured to resign the presidency. Catt once again took the reins and began to repair the damage, shaping NAWSA into a tightly organized and disciplined force.

Another Split in the Movement

Just as NAWSA was making progress on the state front, the Congressional Union was reviving interest in the federal suffrage amendment. Congress had held annual hearings on the proposed amendment for decades, but since NAWSA had not lent the proposal strong support, each year a congressional committee on suffrage had dispatched the amendment with little fanfare. In 1913, however, the members of the Congressional Union concentrated on pushing the resolution through the committee. In June of that year, the committee sent a unanimously favorable report on the women's suffrage amendment to the Senate; in July, the Senate held discussions on the federal amendment for the first time since 1887. When the Senate voted on the amendment in 1914, the measure failed to win the necessary two-thirds majority, but the Congressional Union had still won an important victory by giving new life to the issue of a federal amendment. "From then on," Severn writes,

> the suffragists waged an incessant campaign both to persuade and compel Congress to act. They kept constant pressure on the President in the hope of making him come out for the amendment in his messages, lobbied without letup to win members of Congress to their views, and spread information to women throughout the country to inspire local mass meetings and demonstrations.

These were the same confrontational tactics that concerned NAWSA's leadership. Catt worried that Paul's theatrical demonstrations, relentless badgering of President Wilson, and militant stance would ultimately work against the suffrage movement. In a repeat of the earlier split between moderate and radical suffragists, in 1916 NAWSA and the Congressional Union finally reached the point where they could no longer work together and dissolved their organizational ties. The Congressional Union then transformed itself into a new organization, the National Woman's Party, headed by Paul and Burns.

Now that they were independent from NAWSA, the members of the National Woman's Party escalated their militant tactics. In January 1917, they began picketing the White House: Each day, regardless of the weather, a delegation of women would spend hours standing silently at the gates, holding banners that read "Mr. President, what will you do for woman suffrage?" and "How long must women wait for liberty?" The NAWSA leadership disapproved but could do nothing to stop the protestors. However, other suffragists supported the picketers, and their dedication to their cause elicited sympathy from much of the general populace.

When the United States entered World War I on April 6, 1917, the National Woman's Party steadfastly continued with its picketing. Blatch was now a member of the party, and she urged her colleagues not to let the war interfere with their work, reminding them of her mother's grievous error during the Civil War. As the war progressed, the tide of public opinion gradually turned against them; crowds gathered

A woman pickets for her right to vote amidst male hecklers.

to heckle the White House protestors, calling them traitors and trying to tear down their signs. In June, the police began to arrest the picketers for obstruction of traffic. During the next few months, more than two hundred women were arrested, and nearly one hundred were sentenced to prison. Led by Burns, some of the prisoners went on a hunger strike, demanding recognition as political prisoners. They smuggled out reports of forcible feedings and brutal treatment by their guards. The arrests did not discourage the steady stream of suffragists willing to walk the White House picket line, and in November Wilson ordered that the imprisoned suffragists be released unconditionally.

The Nineteenth Amendment

On January 9, 1918, President Wilson announced his support of the federal suffrage amendment. His decision to back the amendment was in part a response to the publicity generated by the White House protestors and the national outcry that arose over the harsh treatment of the suffrage prisoners. But it was also partly due to Catt, who had decided to increase NAWSA's efforts toward passing a federal amendment and had therefore been working quietly behind the scenes to establish good relations between the president and the organization. After Wilson pledged his support, NAWSA and the National Woman's Party lobbied Congress intensely throughout the year. In 1919, their efforts succeeded: Both houses of Congress approved the measure and forwarded it to the states for ratification.

Now NAWSA's years of grueling state-by-state campaigns paid off: NAWSA's extensive experience in state-based political activity and its network of state chapters enabled the suffragists to quickly mobilize to work for ratification. The suffragists needed to win ratification in thirty-six states in order to gain the necessary two-thirds majority. Some of the states ratified the amendment easily, while others presented more of a challenge. But the mood of the nation was largely pro-suffrage, and the suffragists achieved their goal within fifteen months—a stunningly short time compared to the long battle for suffrage that had preceded it.

On August 26, 1920, the Nineteenth Amendment was signed into law, enfranchising the women of the United States. Millions of women voted for the first time in the November elections that same year. Among them was an elderly woman in her nineties who despite her age and frailty was determined to proudly cast her ballot. She was Charlotte Woodward Pierce, the last remaining survivor of Seneca Falls.

Chapter 1

The Roots of the Women's Suffrage Movement

Turning | Points
IN WORLD HISTORY

Forerunners: The Struggles of Early American Women

Doris Weatherford

Although the women's suffrage movement did not begin until 1848, many of the ideas and goals that characterized the movement had already been expressed by American women as early as the mid-1600s. In this excerpt from *A History of the American Suffragist Movement*, Doris Weatherford describes the women of the colonial and Revolutionary era who defended their right to political power and equality. While these women often fell short of asking for the right to vote, Weatherford notes, their writings and actions still provided an important foundation for the movement that later arose. Weatherford is an adjunct professor of women's history at the University of South Florida in Tampa. Her books include *Foreign and Female: Immigrant Women in America*, *Milestones: A Chronology of American Women's History*, and *American Women's History: An A to Z of People, Organizations, Issues, and Events*.

Founded in England by George Fox [in the 1600s], the Society of Friends [more commonly called Quakers] quickly established itself in America. Women were important participants in the Quaker movement from the beginning: the group consistently committed itself to the idea of human equality. From the first, Quaker women were considered to have an inner light from God just as men did, and they were equally entitled to express moral and spiritual ideas. Nor were their views limited to the quiet of Quaker meeting houses; women were ordained and engaged in street preaching just as men did.

As Quaker culture evolved, especially in Pennsylvania, female leaders developed schools, hospitals, and other charitable organizations, and they controlled financial decisions on these enterprises. Older women also exercised strong powers over younger women, including resolving such personal issues as whether or not a young woman should accept a particular marriage proposal. Obviously, voting of a sort was inherent to such decision making, but because Quakers in general did not participate in secular government, their internal egalitarianism did not necessarily translate into a movement for political equality.

The Status of Indian Women

Quakers also were exceptional in seeing American Indians as full human beings—although even Quakers assumed their own religion to be the correct one. They sent missionaries to convert the natives, and, like virtually all other newcomers, took little heed of the political models offered by native societies. In some of these, especially the tribes of the northeastern Iroquois Confederacy, women were powerful. In many tribes that practiced farming, the culture was matrilineal. This was a crucial distinction from Europeans, for it meant that children took their mothers' names and traced their families through the maternal, not the paternal, lineage. . . .

Moreover, in many tribes women held genuine political and military power. Women in the Iroquois Confederation, for example, traditionally controlled the fate of captives: they decided if a prisoner of war was to be killed, tortured, held for ransom, or adopted into the tribe. . . .

Indian women held their own councils and participated in treaty-making with whites—much to the annoyance of a number of white writers. Indeed, in . . . 1848 . . . , the Seneca tribe of the Iroquois Confederation adopted a new constitution. Under its provisions, both men and women elected judges and legislators, and all major decisions had to be ratified by three-fourths of the voters and by three-fourths of the clan mothers. Despite this, historians deem this period to mark a decline in the status of Seneca women: after their men interacted with European men, Seneca and other native women would continually lose traditional rights as their cultures adopted the white example.

Colonial Leaders

Few Americans, however, were aware of these alternative societal structures, and almost none were willing to emulate the "savages"—or even the egalitarian ideas of their Quaker missionaries. Nevertheless, there were other female political leaders in mainstream colonial America, many of whom have been forgotten and remain unrecognized even by modern feminists. . . .

The least covert, most undeniable political power exercised by a colonial woman was that of Catholic Maryland's Margaret Brent. Although from a noble family, she emigrated when Lord Baltimore granted her a tract of land as an inducement. Presumably he saw her as more talented than two of her brothers, for she led them, a sister, and servants to Maryland in 1638. Remaining determinedly single, she owned thousands of acres of land. When the governor, Lord Baltimore's younger brother, lay dying, he granted his power-of-attorney to her, and she ran the colony after his death. After Lord Baltimore, comfortable back in England, complained about one of her decisions, Maryland's legislative assembly backed her judgment call, not his: without Mistress Brent, they averred, "All would have gone to ruin.". . .

The nation's first written feminist theory came from its original Puritan settlement, Salem. It was the work of a mental giant whose name should be well known, but again, few Americans are familiar with Judith Sargent Stevens Murray.

A childless sea captain's wife, Murray had time to think. In 1784—almost a decade before English Mary Wollstonecraft published the much more famous *Vindication of the Rights of Women*—she wrote on the need for improved female self-esteem, "Encouraging a Degree of Self-Complacency, Especially in Female Bosoms." The thoughts she expressed are still being rediscovered by women today:

> Will it be said that the judgment of a male of two years old is more sage than that of a female of the same age? I believe

the reverse is generally observed to be true. But from that period what partiality! How is the one exalted and the other depressed. . . . The one is taught to aspire, and the other is early confined and limited.

Murray eventually collected her essays into three books, the sales of which were promoted by George Washington, and at least one critic has compared her work with that of Noah Webster. Yet after her 1820 death in the wilderness of Mississippi, where she had gone to live with a daughter she bore by her second husband, Judith Sargent Murray's brilliant mind was soon forgotten.

A better-known writer of the same era is Mercy Otis Warren. Perhaps her work is remembered both because it was less feminist and because she was well-connected to male leadership. The wife and the sister of governmental officials, Warren had a political insider's view of the tumultuous days of the American Revolution; indeed, she played her own significant role in bringing on the rebellion by anonymously publishing satires of the British. While her chief purpose in writing was political in the usual sense of the word, Warren also included asides that made feminist points. "Hateall," for example, a character in one of her plays, not only represented British brutality toward colonists, but also was a blatant misogynist. In a tavern scene, he boasted that he married only to win his wife's dowry and then "broke her skirts." His recommendation for a "rebellious dame" was "the green Hick'ry or the willow twig."

Abigail Adams's Request

Although both Warren and Murray called for greater respect for women, they nevertheless published much of their work under pseudonyms, and neither ever suggested the vote for women or even demanded clearly defined rights to property, custody, or other legal empowerment. Abigail Adams, who never published, was more assertive about political inclusion of women in her voluminous correspondence with the era's important men.

Future president John Adams acknowledged that it was

his wife's property management ability that allowed him to spend his life in politics, and their records make it evident that she was the business executive of the family. And yet, although John had great respect for Abigail and their marriage was ideally companionate, he laughed off her most famous

Mary Wollstonecraft

Early feminist author Mary Wollstonecraft was extremely influential in both her own country of England and the United States. In the following paragraphs, retired social science professor Israel Kugler describes the impact of the first U.S. publication of Wollstonecraft's book.

The bombshell that exploded with the most impact on the American scene was Mary Wollstonecraft's *Vindication of the Rights of Women*, published in the United States in 1794. Throughout the entire history of the woman's rights movement this book remained a source of inspiration not only to the leaders of the agitation but also to many educated women in general. . . .

Mary Wollstonecraft denied the innate inferiority of women. She emphasized the importance of the environment and held that women's inferior state was a result of inequality of opportunity. She believed that if women had equal education, much of the behavior of subservient quiescence would disappear. Inequality of the sexes in marriage tended to distort the relationship into one of an unstable half-slave and half-free character. Women did not wish to lord it over men; they wanted fulfillment, respect, self-discipline, and control over their own person. Since men could not deny that women had reasoning power, why shouldn't it be exercised? . . .

Her book went into many editions and later was published serially in *Revolution*, the weekly newspaper put out by Susan B. Anthony and Elizabeth Cady Stanton. There is no question but that Mary Wollstonecraft's teachings have represented an important ideological base for the woman's rights movement to the present day.

Israel Kugler, *From Ladies to Women: The Organized Struggle for Woman's Rights in the Reconstruction Era*, 1987.

call for female freedom. When he met with the Continental Congress in Philadelphia, she wrote from their farm near Boston in March 1776—well before July's Declaration of Independence. "I long to hear you have declared an independency," she said, "and, by the way, in the new code of laws which I suppose it will be necessary for you to make,"

> I desire you would remember the ladies and be more favorable to them than your ancestors. Do not put such unlimited power into the hands of husbands. Remember all men would be tyrants if they could. If particular care and attention are not paid to the ladies, we are determined to foment a rebellion and will not hold ourselves bound to obey any laws in which we have no voice or representation. That your sex are naturally tyrannical is a truth so thoroughly established as to admit of no dispute, but such of you as wish to be happy willingly give up the harsh title of master for the more tender and endearing one of friend.

Her husband's reply was amused; rolling eyes and a quizzical grin seem to suffuse his words. Not only did he treat her demand for respect as cute, he could not even grant that these creative thoughts were her own:

> As to your extraordinary code of laws, I cannot but laugh. We have been told that our struggle has loosened the bands of government everywhere—that children and apprentices were disobedient, that schools and colleges were grown turbulent. . . . But your letter was the first intimation that another tribe, more numerous and powerful than all the rest, were grown discontented. . . . Depend on it, we know better than to repeal our masculine systems. . . . I begin to think the British as deep as they are wicked at stirring up Tories, Canadians, Indians, Negroes, Irish, Roman Catholics, and, at last, they have stimulated the women to demand new privileges and threaten to rebel.

Abigail Adams's and Mercy Otis Warren's feminist arguments were clearly subordinate to their mainstream political ideas, for it was the success of the new nation that motivated the majority of the words they wrote. Yet the rhetoric of freedom—as John Adams reluctantly acknowledged—inevitably encouraged rebellion among the less privileged. It was simply impossible to proclaim a Declaration of Independence that spoke of "life, liberty, and pursuit of happiness" and of "the consent of the governed" without inspiring hopes that those words might mean what they say.

Women Vote in New Jersey

Perhaps these women of the Revolutionary Age influenced the political climate more than is easily traced, for the same era did produce the first actual voting rights for women. In 1776, the first official year of the Revolution, New Jersey implicitly granted the vote to its women when it adopted a constitution that enfranchised "all free inhabitants." English-speaking women, however, had long experience with gender-neutral language that did not actually mean to include them. In Virginia, too, similar gender-neutral language implied an enfranchisement of which women remained unaware. When Hannah Lee Corbin wrote her brother, General Richard Henry Lee, in 1778 to protest the taxation of women without representation, he replied that Virginia "women were already possessed of that right"—something that seems to have been news to her.

Not surprisingly, such ambiguous and unpublicized enfranchisement meant that few women actually cast ballots. Surprisingly, almost a decade after the Revolution's end, its spirit still prevailed: in 1790 the New Jersey legislature confirmed that it indeed had meant what it said by adding the words "he or she" to its election codes. The amendment's sponsor was Joseph Cooper, a Quaker accustomed to voting women. More remarkable is the fact that only three of his male colleagues voted against this precedent-setting legislation.

The act was little publicized, though, and few women knew of this fundamental change in their status. Especially because many Quaker women refused to participate in secular government at all, the legalism made little difference for nearly a decade. In 1797, however, women in Elizabethtown marched together to vote against a legislative candidate who was backed by the male power structure. They nearly defeated him, and politicians began talking about repealing women's franchise. Newspaper editors backed the ruling cabal, ridiculing the female voters in print and intimidating them from casting ballots in the future. Like John Adams's view that the British had planted rebellious thoughts in his wife's mind, editorials portrayed the Elizabethtown women as the opposition's dupes—either ignorantly misled or forced to the polls by scheming, domineering husbands. That women were capable of both forming their own political views and organizing a coalition was a thought that these newspaper men simply could not entertain.

A decade later, in 1807, New Jersey women lost their vote, with the repeal sponsored by the Elizabethtown man they had nearly defeated. A recent campaign over whether a new courthouse would be located in Elizabethtown or Newark became his excuse for the repeal. The race was hotly contested, and there were newspaper allegations that women were so ignorant, corrupt, or obtuse that they "voted again and again." The guilty party, however, was likely to have been the "men and boys disguised as women" who cast multiple ballots. That women were disenfranchised for reasons of corruption and fraud is greatly ironic, because one of the strongest arguments against suffrage in the following decades was that women were naturally pure and should not engage in anything so dirty as politics.

The Limited Expansion of Suffrage

As the new republic developed, ideologies of individual liberty expanded. This was, after all, the first nation in the western world without a divine right personage at its head, the first in which citizens openly averred their intention to govern themselves, and the vote continually expanded as state governments grew from colonial ones. Disenfranchised males, including non-property holders, Catholics, Jews, and free blacks, were granted suffrage. Especially after frontiersman Andrew Jackson won the popular vote in the presidential elections of 1824 and 1828, the "common man" ideals of Jacksonian populism were assured.

This rise of democracy, however, would continue to ex-

clude the female half of the population. The only actual enfranchisement of women during the Jacksonian era was in
Kentucky in 1838, when widows were allowed to cast ballots
in school elections—but only if they had no children cur-
rently in school. The exclusionary provisions make it clear
that Kentucky's men did not believe that their wives, sisters,
mothers, and daughters were able to make informed judg-
ments: even when a woman was allowed to vote because
there was no man to cast a ballot in her stead, she apparently
could not be trusted to vote reasonably if an issue actually
might touch her personal life.

Yet it was, of course, for their own lives that women—like
men—wanted the vote. They wanted to improve educational
opportunities, especially for girls; they wanted to protect
property that they earned or inherited; they wanted custody
of their children when a man was abusive. And some of them
wanted grander, less personally necessary, political change;
many women did think of themselves as their brothers' keepers, as the most likely embodiment of purity and morality.

Women's Involvement in the Anti-Slavery Movement

Eleanor Flexner

The 1830s witnessed the rise of an organized movement to abolish slavery from the United States. The anti-slavery movement included women from the start, but these women quickly found that they were limited as to their role. Traditionally, women were not supposed to involve themselves with political causes, much less give public speeches to mixed audiences of both women and men. Frustrated over these restrictions, some abolitionist women began to defend their right to speak in public and to engage in political activities such as canvassing during petition drives. Author Eleanor Flexner writes that women's involvement in the anti-slavery movement made them more willing to protest their unequal status and provided them with organizational experience that they would later use to fight for their own rights. The following piece is excerpted from Flexner's book *Century of Struggle: The Woman's Rights Movement in the United States*, originally published in 1959 and considered to be the first professional history of the women's suffrage movement. Flexner's other writings include *Mary Wollstonecraft: A Biography*.

In 1831 the slave Nat Turner had led a slave revolt in Virginia, which had brought a wave of repressive measures throughout the South. That same year in Boston William Lloyd Garrison founded his abolitionist weekly, *The Liberator*, with its uncompromising opening salvo: "I will not equivocate, I will not excuse, I will not retreat a single inch—and I WILL BE

HEARD!" The first anti-slavery societies were formed, and the Underground Railway, that vast network of skilled "agents" and hidden "stations" which assisted runaway slaves to free territory, gained its name and began to pick up momentum.

Learning to Organize

Thousands of men and women were drawn into the work; among the latter were the first conscious feminists, who would go to school in the struggle to free the slaves and, in the process, launch their own fight for equality. It was in the abolition movement that women first learned to organize, to hold public meetings, to conduct petition campaigns. As abolitionists they first won the right to speak in public, and began to evolve a philosophy of their place in society and of their basic rights. For a quarter of a century the two movements, to free the slave and liberate the woman, nourished and strengthened one another.

The earliest rudimentary women's organizations had been church sewing circles, which were started to raise money for missionary or charitable work. Elizabeth Buffum Chace has recorded that the Smithfield (Rhode Island) Female Improvement Society met each week in the 1820's, to read "useful books" aloud, and hear original compositions by its members. Later, the women began to range farther afield; in 1840 Lucy Stone wrote her brother: "It was decided in our Literary Society the other day that ladies ought to mingle in politics, go to Congress, etc., etc. What do you think of that?"

Free Negro women in the North and West, while they ostensibly met for similar purposes, had other motives as well. There were Female Literary Societies of colored women in Philadelphia, New York, Boston, and other eastern cities in the 1830's; but the powerful incentive of getting an education for their children also brought about such organizations as the Ohio Ladies Education Society. . . .

The Beginnings of the Anti-Slavery Movement

When the leading abolitionists met in Philadelphia in 1833 to found the American Anti-Slavery Society, they permitted a few women to attend, and even to speak from the floor, but not to join the society or to sign the "Declaration of Senti-ments and Purposes." When the convention adjourned, some twenty women met to form the Philadelphia Female Anti-Slavery Society.

They were intrepid but still decorous; treading such an uncharted path, they asked a Negro freedman to preside at their first meeting. Within a few years other women were organizing for the same purpose in New York, Boston, and many other New England towns, and by 1837 the first Na-tional Female Anti-Slavery Society convention met in New York with eighty-one delegates from twelve states. Far from accepting the aid of a man as presiding officer, one of the delegates sent word to the abolitionist Theodore Weld: "Tell Mr. Weld . . . that when the women got together they found they had *minds* of their own, and could transact their busi-ness *without* his directions. The Boston and Philadelphia women were so well versed in business that they were quite mortified to have Mr. Weld quoted as an authority for doing or not doing so and so."

Women's Courage

From the beginning, the women showed great courage; be-cause they were overstepping time-honored bounds, they aroused the particular fury of adherents of slavery, of whom there were many in the North, and mob violence was not unusual. In Boston in 1835 a mob swarmed into the building where Garrison was to address the Boston Female Anti-Slavery Society and stormed up the stairs to the door of the very room in which the women were meeting. Garrison was whisked out a back door (he was later dragged through the streets at the end of a rope), and the Mayor himself came to beg the women to leave in order to avoid physical harm. At the direction of Maria Weston Chapman, each white lady present took a colored "sister" by the hand, and two by two, they walked calmly down the stairs and out the building, "their hands folded in their cotton gloves, their eyes busily identifying the genteel leaders of the mob," as author Hen-rietta Buckmaster writes.

Even small house gatherings were not immune. On one

such occasion, when the women heard that violence was planned, Mrs. Chapman personally went to warn every member of the Society of what might occur. The contemporary British writer Harriet Martineau recounted:

> Among those whom she visited was an artizan's wife, who was sweeping out one of her two rooms as Mrs. Chapman entered. On hearing that there was every probability of violence and that the warning was given in order that she might stay away if she thought proper, she leaned upon her broom and considered awhile. Her answer was: "I have often wished and asked that I might be able to do something for the slaves; and it seems to me that this is the very time and the very way. You will see me at the meeting and I will keep a prayerful mind as I am about my work until then."

After another such gathering Harriet Martineau wrote: "When I was putting on my shawl upstairs, Mrs. Chapman came to me, bonnet in hand, to say, 'You know, we are threatened with a mob today again, but I do not myself much apprehend it. It must not surprise us; but my hopes are stronger than my fears.'"

The women who took part in the operations of the Underground Railroad underwent the sharpest schooling of all. They were ready at all hours to welcome fugitives arriving at their homes, often in the middle of the night, feed and care for them, keep them in cellar or attic or secret chamber while the sheriff's posse hammered at the door or even searched the house; sometimes, in the absence of husband or father, when the danger was acute, they would mount the driver's seat and drive a wagon load of "freight" to a safer station up along the line toward freedom.

The Right to Speak in Public

It is therefore not surprising that so many women abolitionists became active on behalf of greater rights for women. The pioneers were the Grimké sisters, who first fought for—and won—woman's right to speak in public before any and every kind of audience, and who paved the way for the long roster of famous women orators in the anti-slavery cause: Lucy Stone, Lucretia Mott, Abby Kelley Foster, Frances Harper, Ernestine Rose, Sojourner Truth, Susan Anthony, and many more.

Since the colonial days, . . . women had remained silent in public. Alone among the larger religious denominations, the Quakers permitted them a voice in church affairs, allowed them to speak in "meeting," and ordained them as ministers. The other established Protestant churches followed the dicta of St. Paul . . . : "Let the women learn in silence with all subjection. . . . I suffer not a woman to teach, nor to usurp authority over the men, but to be in silence." And again: "Let your women keep silent in the churches, for it is not permitted unto them to speak." The churches merely expressed a dominant social pattern which dictated that the speaking of women in public was unseemly. Only the smaller sects permitted an active role to women, and they had to be of outstanding ability.

The first woman to pass through the curtain of silence had been Frances Wright, whose meteoric lecturing career in 1828–1829, while highly successful, had also been unpleasantly tinged with notoriety. She did not immediately pave the way for other women because—if only by a few years—she came upon the scene and left it, too soon.

Maria W. Stewart

Another short-lived attempt was that of a Negro woman, Mrs. Maria W. Stewart, who spoke several times in Boston between 1831 and 1833. Uneducated, impelled by strong religious beliefs, she was also an outspoken abolitionist and eager to see greater educational opportunities open to girls. Her attempts to lead her people to regeneration from the platform were not kindly received; in a "Farewell Address" to her friends in Boston she admitted failure: "I find it is no use for me, as an individual, to try to make myself useful among my color in this city. . . . I have made myself contemptible in the eyes of many."

In her addresses Mrs. Stewart not only summoned her listeners to live in greater righteousness; she pleaded for the slave, and stoutly defended her right as a woman to do so in

The Political Parallel

Helen Matthews Lewis is a sociologist, community educator, and Appalachian activist affiliated with the Highlander Research and Education Center in New Market, Tennessee. In the following, she delineates the similarities in legal status between early American women and African-American slaves.

When a legal status was necessary for the imported Negro servants in the 17th century, the nearest and most natural analogy was the status of women. At the beginning of the 19th century most of these similarities in the legal and political status of Negroes and women remained. It is small wonder that the women Abolitionists saw the similarities and declared with Emily Collins that:

> All through the Anti-Slavery struggle, every word of denunciation of the wrongs of the Southern slave was, I felt, equally applicable to the wrongs of my own sex. Every argument for the emancipation of the colored man, was equally one for that of woman; and I was surprised that all Abolitionists did not see the similarity in the condition of the two classes.

At law, [English jurist William] Blackstone's dictum that "the very being or legal existence of woman is suspended during marriage" was still authority. The legal discrimination which grew out of the feudal common-law theory that marriage destroyed a woman's separate identity still remained. . . . She had no standing before the law as a separate entity. The control of her real estate passed to her husband, and he could manage it and have the use of all income, rent and profits therefrom without her interference. . . . She could make no valid contract and had no right to her own children or any wages she might earn.

Politically women and slaves had no voice. Though none of the original thirteen state constitutions restricted suffrage, between 1790 and 1840 most of the states added "white, male" to the voting qualification.

Helen Matthews Lewis, *The Woman Movement and the Negro Movement— Parallel Struggles for Rights*, 1949.

words that heralded the arguments the Grimkés were to use a few years later:

> What if I am a woman; is not the God of ancient times the God of these modern days? Did he not raise up Deborah to be a mother and a judge in Israel? Did not Queen Esther save the lives of the Jews? And Mary Magdalen first declare the resurrection of Christ from the dead? . . . If such women as are here described once existed, be no longer astonished then, my brethren and friends, that God at this eventful period should raise up your own females to strive by their example, both in public and in private, to assist those who are endeavoring to stop the strong current of prejudice that flows so profusely, against us at present. . . . What if such women as are here described should rise among our sable race? And it is not impossible; for it is not the color of the skin that makes the man or the woman, but the principle formed in the soul.

Those who really opened the way to public speaking, and therefore enabled women to reach large numbers of people directly, were the Grimké sisters, Sarah and Angelina, whose achievement was the outcome of a now rapidly growing stream of social development. Where the Grimkés led, other women soon followed in growing numbers.

The Grimké Sisters

Sarah and Angelina Grimké were the daughters of a South Carolina slaveholding family; from earliest childhood they had loathed slavery and all its works. Nor could they close their eyes and live with it; first Sarah, the elder and plainer, and later the beautiful Angelina moved to Philadelphia, where they joined the Quakers. But they found that flight was no salve to conscience and for years they sought painfully for the way to strike a blow against the institution they abhorred.

In 1836 they made abolitionist friends, at whose suggestion Angelina began to write "An Appeal to the Christian Women of the South," urging them to speak out on behalf of the slave. About the same time, the American Anti-Slavery

Society invited the sisters to speak at small parlor gatherings of women in New York. The response was overwhelming. More than three hundred women appeared for the first meeting, which had to be transferred to the parlor of a small church. The sisters' eloquent description of slavery at first hand aroused so much interest that the next meeting was called in a church itself to accommodate all who wished to attend. A man slipped in, and was promptly ushered out. But others came, singly, then in twos and threes; before anyone really knew what was happening, the Grimkés were addressing large mixed public audiences. From New York they were invited to New England, where local anti-slavery societies, often of women, sponsored meetings in innumerable small towns and where tremendous gatherings were held in Boston.

Meanwhile a storm of controversy broke out. The main opposition came from the churches. The most powerful blast unleashed against the Grimkés, without mentioning them by name, was a Pastoral Letter from the Council of Congregationalist Ministers of Massachusetts, then the largest denomination in the state, denouncing their behavior as unwomanly and unchristian:

> We invite your attention to the dangers which at present seem to threaten the female character with widespread and permanent injury. The appropriate duties and influence of women are clearly stated in the New Testament. Those duties, and that influence, are unobtrusive and private, but the sources of mighty power. When the mild, dependent, softening influence upon the sterness of man's opinions is fully exercised, society feels the effect of it in a thousand forms. The power of woman is her dependence, flowing from the consciousness of that weakness which God has given her for her protection.
>
> We appreciate the unostentatious prayers of woman in advancing the cause of religion at home and abroad; in Sabbath-schools; in leading religious inquirers to the pastors for instruction; and in all such associated efforts as become the modesty of her sex. . . . But when she assumes the place and

tone of man as a public reformer . . . she yields the power
which God has given her for her protection, and her character becomes unnatural. If the vine, whose strength and
beauty is to lean on the trellis-work, and half conceal its clus-
ter, thinks to assume the independence and the overshadow-
ing nature of the elm, it will not only cease to bear fruit, but
fall in shame and dishonor into the dust.

Such attacks took a heavy toll of both women. At every
step of the path along which their consciences drove them,
they found themselves at odds with the traditions of decorum
in which nineteenth century women were bred. None who
overstepped those bounds in the quest for freedom and self-
realization suffered more from doubts and self-questioning
than the Grimkés. Angelina, who was the better speaker and
who bore the brunt of public utterance (she once spoke on
six successive evenings in the Boston Opera House, with
her voice reaching the topmost tier), actually broke down
under the strain in May 1838 and did not speak again for
many years.

Answering the Critics

But while they suffered deeply, they also gained insight from
the opposition they encountered. They began to answer
their critics, linking the two issues of slavery and the position
of women, Angelina in her speeches, Sarah in a series of articles in the *New England Spectator* on "The Province of
Women," which were issued as a pamphlet the following
year entitled *The Equality of the Sexes and the Condition of
Women* and widely circulated.

In these articles, Sarah Grimké met the assault of the Pastoral Letter head-on. She categorically denied any Biblical
justification for the inferior position of woman. An early ex-
ponent of the "Higher Criticism," she held that the Scrip-
tures were not divine in origin, and necessarily reflected the
agricultural, patriarchal society which produced them.

Accepting Eve's responsibility for Original Sin, she turned
it neatly on its advocates:

Adam's ready acquiescence with his wife's proposal does not

savor much of that superiority in *strength of mind* which is ar-
rogated by man. Even admitting that Eve was the greater
sinner, it seems to me that man might be satisfied with the
dominion he has claimed and exercised for nearly 6000 years,
and that more true nobility would be manifested by endeavoring to raise the fallen and invigorate the weak than by
keeping woman in subjection.

With some tartness, she added: "I ask no favors for my sex.
I surrender not our claim to equality. All I ask of our
brethren is that they will take their feet from off our necks,
and permit us to stand upright on the ground which God has
designed us to occupy."

Primarily Sarah Grimké saw the question of equality for
women, not as a matter of abstract justice, but of enabling
women to join in an urgent task:

In contemplating the great moral reformations of the day,
and the part which they [women] are bound to take in
them, instead of puzzling themselves with the harassing,
because unnecessary inquiry, how far they may go without
overstepping the bounds of propriety, which separate male
and female duties, they will only inquire, "Lord, what wilt
thou have me do?" They will be enabled to see the simple
truth, that God has made no distinction between men and
women as moral beings. . . . To me it is perfectly clear *that
whatsoever it is morally right for a man to do, it is morally right
for a woman to do.*

It is said, woman has a mighty weapon in secret prayer; she
has, I acknowledge, *in common with man:* but the woman who
prays in sincerity for the regeneration of this guilty world,
will accompany her prayers by her labors. A friend of mine
remarked: "I was sitting in my chamber, weeping over the
miseries of the slave, and putting up my prayers for his de-
liverance from bondage, when in the midst of my medita-
tions it occurred to me that my tears, unaided by effort,
could never melt the chain of the slave. I must be up and
doing." She is now an active abolitionist—her prayers and
her works go hand in hand.

The Reaction in the Anti-Slavery Movement

The Grimkés' advocacy of woman's rights evoked mixed reactions in the anti-slavery camp. Some of their staunchest friends, such as John Greenleaf Whittier and Theodore Weld (soon to marry Angelina), begged them to drop the woman's rights question, lest it impair their advocacy of abolition. But Angelina stood firm:

> *We* cannot push Abolitionism forward with all our might *until* we take up the stumbling block out of the road. . . . You may depend upon it, tho' to meet *this* question *may appear* to be turning out of our road, that *it is not.* IT IS NOT: we *must* meet it and meet it now. . . . Why, my dear brothers can you not see the deep laid scheme of the clergy against us as lecturers? . . . If we surrender the right to *speak* in public this year, we must surrender the right to petition next year, and the right to *write* the year after, and so on. What *then* can *woman* do for the slave, when she herself is under the feet of man and shamed into *silence?*

Among the women however their words fell upon eager ears. . . .

Angelina herself wrote to a Quaker friend, Jane Smith: "We find that many of our New England sisters are prepared to receive these strange doctrines, feeling as they do that our whole sex needs emancipation from the thraldom of public opinion. What dost thou think of some of them *walking* two, four, six and eight miles to attend our meetings?"

It was not mere restlessness or frustration that drove women into such wintry tramps; it was the knowledge, in Angelina's words, that "we abolitionist women are turning the world upside down." A dramatic instance was the series of hearings held on three separate days in February 1838 before a committee of the Massachusetts State Legislature, on anti-slavery petitions. Henry B. Stanton had suggested, half in jest, that Angelina Grimké speak for the abolitionists, and after the usual soul-searching, she agreed. When she rose to speak, the first woman ever to make such an appearance before a legislative body, she confessed:

> I was so near fainting under the tremendous pressure of feel-

ing, my heart almost died within me. The novelty of the scene, the weight of responsibility, the ceaseless exercise of mind thro' which I had passed for almost a week—all together sunk me to the earth. I well nigh despaired, but our Lord and Master gave me his arm to lean upon and in great weakness, my limbs trembling under me, I stood up and spoke for nearly two hours. . . . Many of our dear Abolition friends did indeed travail in spirit for me, wrestling in earnest prayer, and M. Chapman's "God strengthen you my Sister" just before I rose was a strength to my fainting spirit.

Among the abolitionist friends present was Lydia Maria Child, the successful writer who had sacrificed her career to the anti-slavery cause, and who wrote:

The Boston members of the legislature tried hard to prevent her [Angelina Grimké] having a hearing on the second day. Among other things, they said that such a crowd were attracted by curiosity the galleries were in danger of being broken down; though in fact they are constructed with remarkable strength. A member from Salem, perceiving their drift, wittily proposed that "a Committee be appointed to examine the foundations of the State House of Massachusetts to see whether it will bear another lecture from Miss Grimké!"

The Right to Collect Petitions

When Angelina Grimké wrote Theodore Weld that women would be jeopardizing their right to petition by retreating on other issues, she was not indulging in idle fantasies. Their right to petition was under fire at the time in Congress, for the same reason that she and her sister were being upbraided by the clergy for their public speaking; both were being energetically exercised on behalf of the slave.

In 1834 the American Anti-Slavery Society had initiated a petition campaign which had quickly snowballed to such proportions as to seriously perturb southern congressmen. In an attempt to stem the tide, the House of Representatives passed the Pinckney Gag Rule forbidding their presentation.

The first voice raised from the floor of the House against

this infraction of basic rights was that of John Quincy Adams, former president of the United States and now representative from Plymouth, Massachusetts. The seventy-year-old Adams, who earned the title of "Old Man Eloquent" during this last phase of his venerable career, at first defended merely the rights of his own constituents to petition Congress. But when his stand became known, anti-slavery petitions began flowing in to him from all over the North. A large proportion of these came from the Female Anti-Slavery Societies, which roused the particular ire of southern representatives, and Adams took up the right and propriety of women's signing petitions and collecting signatures. . . .

It seemed altogether appropriate for Abigail Adams' son to take up the cudgels for women in the controversy . . . , and he did so in a series of speeches from June 26 to 30, in which he spared the House nothing in the way of historical reflections on women's role during revolutionary struggles, or his own opinion that American women were moving into a broader sphere:

> Why does it follow that women are fitted for nothing but the cares of domestic life, for bearing children and cooking the food of a family, devoting all their time to the domestic circle—to promoting the immediate personal comfort of their husbands, brothers and sons? . . . The mere departure of women from the duties of the domestic circle, far from being a reproach to her, is a virtue of the highest order, when it is done from purity of motive, by appropriate means, and the purpose good.

In answer to [the] argument, that women had no right to petition because they lacked the vote, Adams went so far as to ask: "Is it so clear that they have no such right as this last?"

Engaging in Political Acts

Behind Adams' tenacity on this issue and the efforts of a small group of congressmen who gathered to support his battle for the right of free petition, there lay another saga—that of the campaign for signatures. The women who took part in it were taking a long stride ahead. Not only were they engaging in a *political act*, now on behalf of others, but they were also securing a right which they would use later in their own interests. They were the first detachment in the army of ordinary rank-and-file women who were to struggle for more than three quarters of a century for equality. It took the same kind of courage as that displayed by the Grimké sisters for the average housewife, mother, or daughter to overstep the limits of decorum, disregard the frowns, or jeers, or outright commands of her menfolk and go to her first public meeting, or take her first petition and walk down an unfamiliar street, knocking on doors and asking for signatures to an unpopular plea. Not only would she be going out unattended by husband or brother; but she usually encountered hostility, if not outright abuse for her unwomanly behavior. . . .

Today, countless file boxes in the National Archives in Washington bear witness to that anonymous and heartbreaking labor. The petitions are yellowed and frail, glued together, page on page, covered with ink blots, signed with scratchy pens, with an occasional erasure by one who fearfully thought better of so bold an act. Some are headed by printed texts, others are copied in careful, stilted script, or in a hasty scrawl. They petition Congress against the admission of more slave states into the Union—Florida, Arkansas, Texas; against slavery in the District of Columbia; against the interstate slave trade; for the total abolition of slavery. They bear the names of women's anti-slavery societies from New England to Ohio.

The World Anti-Slavery Convention: The Spark That Lit the Fire

Miriam Gurko

In June 1840, a World Anti-Slavery Convention was held in London, England. Among the American abolitionists selected to be official delegates to the convention were several women, including the renowned lecturer Lucretia Mott. However, when the women arrived at the convention, many British and American men objected to their serving as delegates. After a day of intense debate, the women were forbidden to take an active role in the convention, and all female delegates and attendees were required to sit in silence behind a curtained gallery. During the convention, Lucretia Mott befriended a young woman, Elizabeth Cady Stanton, who was outraged over the treatment of the female delegates. Mott and Stanton decided to organize their own convention to address the issue of women's rights. In the following excerpt from *The Ladies of Seneca Falls: The Birth of the Woman's Rights Movement*, author Miriam Gurko relates the story of how the humiliation of the women at the London convention led to the beginning of the women's suffrage movement.

The "woman question" agitated the whole reform movement. Even if the cause was righteous and pure, ran the argument, like antislavery or peace, was it morally acceptable for women to speak in public, work together with men on committees, become officers of organizations that included both men and women? Was it even permissible for women to belong to organizations that included men?

Divisions over Women's Proper Role

These questions tore the American Anti-Slavery Society apart. In May 1840 it split in two. One reason given for the break was the "insane innovation" of allowing women to serve as speakers and officers of the organization. Some of the anti-women abolitionists had been so busy trying to make women stop talking that they had scarcely any time left for the slaves.

Another reason for the division was the increasing dissension between the followers and the opponents of [radical abolitionist] William Lloyd Garrison. Since Garrison supported the women, the anti-Garrisonians became the anti-woman group. They broke off from the original organization and formed their own, which they called the American and Foreign Anti-Slavery Society. . . .

A month after the split, a World Anti-Slavery Convention met in London. American groups were invited to send delegates. Garrison's society selected five: four men and one woman, Lucretia Mott. Mrs. Mott was also chosen as one of the representatives of the Philadelphia Female Anti-Slavery Society. Other groups, like the Massachusetts Anti-Slavery Society and the Boston Female Society, also sent women.

When they arrived in London, however, they were told that women would not be accepted. Protests were made, and the first day of the convention was completely taken up with impassioned arguments for and against seating the female delegates. It was claimed that women were "constitutionally unfit for public or business meetings," and that their presence would injure the cause of emancipation. . . .

The women themselves were not permitted to take part in the discussion, but had to listen quietly, in what must have been an intensely frustrating silence. Among them were some of the most intelligent and educated women in the United States and Great Britain. To overcome the barriers of prejudice and custom and reach the position of delegate to a convention of this kind, a woman had to be at least twice as qualified as a man. The most mediocre male could take an active role in the reform movements of the period, and get himself appointed as an officer or delegate. For such men to presume the right to reject women like Lucretia Mott appeared both ludicrous and galling to the silent female listeners.

Despite the efforts of [the] supporters of the women, the final vote was against them, and they had to take seats in the curtained gallery. . . .

The issue of woman's rights remained the most absorbing one of the whole affair. Today the convention is remembered not at all for any help to the slaves, but as the initial spark of the organized woman's rights movement. . . .

Discussing Women's Rights

When Elizabeth Cady Stanton and Lucretia Mott met in London for the first time, at the World Anti-Slavery Convention in 1840, Mrs. Mott was forty-seven, Mrs. Stanton twenty-five. . . .

The two women spent hours in each other's company. Many of the delegates to the convention were staying at the same lodging house and took their meals together. After the women were denied their official seats and ignominiously relegated to the gallery, the subject of woman's rights and equality was energetically debated around the dinner table. . . .

These discussions and the women who took part in them were a revelation to Mrs. Stanton. "These were the first women I had ever met who believed in the equality of the sexes. . . . It was intensely gratifying to hear all that, through years of doubt, I had dimly thought, so freely discussed by other women."

She and Mrs. Mott took long walks together, on which the older woman opened to the younger "a new world of thought". . . .

They discussed the social theories and reform movements of the day. Most of all, they talked about women. The humiliating rejection of the female delegates by a convention called for the purpose of "liberation" had thrown the unliberated position of women into a new and sharper focus. Though not a delegate herself, Mrs. Stanton shared in the rebuff to someone of Mrs. Mott's caliber: here was an intelligent, experienced, capable adult who had as much to contribute to the convention as any man present, yet she had been dismissed as a childish incompetent. . . .

Discussing this unhappy and irritating state of affairs, Mrs. Mott and Mrs. Stanton agreed that women must not continue their meek passivity. Walking arm in arm through London, "we resolved to hold a convention as soon as we returned home, and form a society to advocate the rights of women."

Chapter 2

Forming the Movement

Turning|Points
IN WORLD HISTORY

The First Women's Rights Convention

Bill Severn

After women were barred from participating in the 1840 World Anti-Slavery Convention, Lucretia Mott and Elizabeth Cady Stanton vowed to hold a convention focused on women's rights. Mott and Stanton were not able to put this plan into action until 1848, but the convention that they and three other women organized in Seneca Falls, New York, created a firestorm of controversy. Most controversial of all was Stanton's speech demanding the right of suffrage for women. In the following reading, excerpted from his book *Free but Not Equal: How Women Won the Right to Vote*, Bill Severn explains that the Seneca Falls Convention gave birth to the women's suffrage movement. Despite the fact that most newspaper editorialists mocked the convention's participants and their goals, Severn writes, the news struck a chord with numerous American women, who quickly organized their own conventions and women's rights groups. A former news editor, Severn is the author of more than twenty-five books, including many biographies and popular social histories.

Five women got to talking things over around a tea table at the home of one of them in Waterloo, New York, in July 1848 and started something that stirred up almost as much of a sensation in the nation's newspapers as the discovery of gold in California. Two of them were Elizabeth Stanton and Lucretia Mott. Sharing tea with them at the home of Jane Hunt were Lucretia's sister, Martha Wright, and a neighbor, Mary McClintock. All but Elizabeth were Quakers.

Excerpted from *Free but Not Equal: How Women Won the Right to Vote*, by Bill Severn (New York: Julian Messner, 1967). Copyright ©1967 by Bill Severn.

Lucretia and her husband had come from Philadelphia to visit her sister and attend a Quaker meeting. Elizabeth had settled in nearby Seneca Falls. It was a chance to renew the friendship they had kept up by mail since those days in London when they had vowed to hold a convention to demand woman's rights. Both had been busy with their homes and families and in carrying on the battle against Negro slavery. Elizabeth's husband, Henry Stanton, had studied law and built up a successful practice, first in Boston and then in upstate New York, but the role of a small-town housewife filled her with restless discontent.

Her marriage was a happy one but Henry often was away from Seneca Falls on business and she was left in an isolated household with only the children for company and the boredom of routine housekeeping chores that were no challenge to her mind. "My experiences at the World Anti-Slavery Convention, all I had read of the legal status of women, and the oppression I saw everywhere, together swept across my soul," she later wrote, "intensified now by many personal experiences. I could not see what to do or where to begin—my only thought was a public meeting for protest and discussion."

Planning the Convention

The others at the tea party shared her feelings and the five of them decided something should be done then and there. They wrote out a public notice to be published in the next edition of the *Seneca County Courier*, announcing that a meeting would be held the following week in Seneca Falls "to discuss the social, civil and religious rights of woman." Ambitiously they advertised that it would be a two-day convention. "During the first day the meeting will be held exclusively for women, who are earnestly invited to attend," the notice said. "The public generally are invited to be present on the second day, when Lucretia Mott of Philadelphia and other ladies and gentlemen will address the convention."

Having made the public announcement, they began to wonder at their own courage. They had no experience in arranging conventions, no program planned, and only a short time to line up speakers and write resolutions. But, having gone that far, they couldn't back down so they met again at Mary McClintock's house. Gathering in her parlor, they drew chairs around Mary's antique mahogany center table and spent the whole day going through a stack of books and anti-slavery society pamphlets trying to find models for the resolutions they wanted to write. The table became one of the historic exhibits at the Smithsonian Institution in Washington years later because it was upon it that they wrote the first document to spell out woman's grievances.

The Declaration of Sentiments

It was Elizabeth Stanton's idea to change the Declaration of Independence into their own Declaration of Sentiments. She found a copy of it in Mary's bookcase and began reading it aloud, substituting words that declared woman's independence from man in the same stirring language of rebellion that had inspired the nation to fight for its freedom from King George. Because the declaration of 1776 had listed eighteen grievances against the King they were determined that women should list as many against men.

Holding that "all men and women are created equal" and that "the history of mankind is a history of repeated injuries and usurpations on the part of man toward woman," they declared that "in view of this entire disfranchisement of one-half the people in this country . . . and because women do feel themselves aggrieved, oppressed and fraudulently deprived of their most sacred rights, we insist they have immediate admission to all the rights and privileges which belong to them as Citizens of the United States."

Demanding Suffrage

Elizabeth took on the job of drafting the final document and the resolutions to go with it. Entirely on her own she worked out one demand she considered the key to winning all other rights for women. None of her friends knew about it until later. It read: "Resolved, That it is the duty of the women of this country to secure for themselves their sacred right to the elective franchise." Her final version of the declaration also made the extravagant promise that "we shall employ agents, circulate tracts, petition the State and National legislatures, and endeavor to enlist the pulpit and the press in our behalf. We hope this convention will be followed by a series of conventions embracing every part of the country."

When she showed her resolution on voting rights to her husband, he was strongly against it. Henry told her it was far too revolutionary and that she would turn the whole meeting into a farce if she offered it. He was willing to go along with the rest of her ideas but not that. When she wouldn't listen to his protests he threatened to leave her on her own and have nothing more to do with the affair. Elizabeth refused to give in and Henry packed a bag and left Seneca Falls until the convention was over.

Even Lucretia Mott was worried when Elizabeth showed her the voting resolution. "Oh, Lizzie! If thou demands that, thou will make us ridiculous," Lucretia said. "We must move slowly."

"We must have the vote," Elizabeth answered.

Nobody, not her husband and not Lucretia, could change her mind. None of the others would publicly support her in it even though most of them agreed suffrage was a goal to work toward in the years ahead. They argued, as Henry had, that it would get them a lot of bad publicity. The whole country would make fun of them for demanding such a thing.

When Frederick Douglass, the former Negro slave who had become editor of an abolitionist paper in Rochester, New York, arrived to take part in the meeting, Elizabeth took it up with him. She asked him what the Negroes needed more than anything else to win their rights.

"The ballot," Douglass said.

"And isn't that what women need?" she asked. "Will you speak for it? I cannot alone."

He agreed that he would. But she was troubled about it as the first day of the convention came. Perhaps she had gone too far. Maybe people who read the little notice in the paper were already laughing and nobody would turn up for the meeting that they had so grandly called a convention. They had been granted permission to hold it in the Wesleyan chapel. Because none of them knew how to conduct a public meeting and they didn't want to show their ignorance of parliamentary procedure they asked Lucretia's husband, James Mott, to preside.

The Seneca Falls Convention

July 19, 1848, was a sunny summer day and the small crowd began to grow from early in the morning. Neighbors came from fifty miles around by horse and buggy, in farm wagons, and some on foot. Despite the fact that it was the busy haying season almost as many men showed up as women. Most of the men were tolerantly curious to find out for themselves what it was all about. Although Elizabeth and the others had planned to keep men out on the first day, they decided they couldn't turn them away.

But when they reached the chapel to start the meeting they found the door locked against them. They had been promised the use of it but the minister had become convinced that he was inviting trouble. He wouldn't go back on his word and refuse them the hall but he hoped that when they found the door locked they would take the hint and realize they weren't welcome. Elizabeth called to a young nephew, got him to climb through a window and open the door from the inside, and the crowd moved in.

Lucretia, who was more accustomed to public speaking than the rest, started things off by explaining the aims of the convention. Her sister, Martha Wright, read some newspaper articles she had written, and Mary McClintock spoke about the resolutions that would be offered. A young law student, Samuel Tillman, read some of the laws that were on the books to deny women equal rights with men and Ansel Bascom, a member of the state constitutional convention, spoke about the recently passed law to protect the property of married women. Even when the usually fiery Frederick Douglass spoke, his tone was mild and reasonable.

A Calm Rebellion

There was none of the hysterical ranting of rebellious women bent upon destroying the established rule of men that the newspapers later described. It was a quiet, orderly, and even somewhat dull meeting, with one speaker after another going on at great length. The reading of the wordy resolutions and grievances seemed endless. But for all of that, it *was* a rebellion, and women across the country would be inspired by what was said and done.

After two days of debate and decision, sixty-eight women and thirty-two men signed their names to the Declaration of Sentiments and adopted the resolutions. The first convention for woman's rights approved nearly all the basic demands the suffrage movement would make during the next seventy-two years.

They demanded equal rights in the churches and universities, in trades and professions, the right to share in all political offices and honors, equality in marriage, freedom of person, property and wages, the right to speak in public and to take an equal part with men in deciding the great moral questions of the day, to make contracts, to sue and be sued, and to testify in courts of justice. All those resolutions were agreed upon unanimously. Then Elizabeth Stanton took to the floor and voiced the first formal demand for woman's right to vote that had ever been made in the United States.

"I should feel exceedingly diffident to appear before you at this time, having never before spoken in public," she said, "were I not nerved by a sense of right and duty, did I not feel that the time had come for the question of woman's wrongs to be laid before the public, did I not believe that woman herself must do this work; for woman alone can understand the height, the depth, the length and breadth of her degradation."

For a maiden speech what she went on to say was surprisingly eloquent. Clear, scholarly, delivered in a firm voice that took courage from her belief in what she said and that drew upon the study and the thoughts which had so long filled her mind, it captured her listeners with the spirit that was to become familiar to her audiences for the next fifty years. Her cheeks were burning before she finished, but her eyes were shining. The vote on her resolution was not unanimous, as it had been on the others, but by a narrow margin the convention did agree "that it is the duty of the women of this country to secure to themselves the sacred right of the elective franchise."

Ridicule and Criticism

Because of Elizabeth Stanton's determined boldness, the village meeting that called itself a convention did arouse the press. It wasn't important news to the nation's editors that some women had gotten together for a discussion with their neighbors in Seneca Falls. Such an event hardly rated notice by the city newspapers. But a local reporter wrote it up as a humorous item and before long it became a national joke. Readers chuckled over the wit and ridicule editors were able to poke at the notion of a woman's Declaration of Independence. The demand for the right to vote made news, even if only as something for men to laugh about.

"Insurrection Among Women," was one headline. Another newspaper warned in jest against "The Reign of Petticoats." Joking comments were captioned: "Women Out of Their Latitude," "Bolting Among the Ladies," and "Petticoats vs Boots." Papers almost everywhere began to take up the subject.

The *Rochester Daily Advertiser* said women wanted to change the sexes around so they would "wear the breeches" and hold public office while men put on petticoats "to nurse the babies, or preside at the wash tub, or boil a pot." Albany's *Mechanic's Advocate* said that if women took on men's jobs "males must change their position in society to the same extent in an opposite direction" and that "the order of things established at the creation of mankind would be completely broken up."

Philadelphia's women would have no part of any move to turn them into Amazons who would "mount the rostrum, do all the voting and, we suppose, all the fighting, too," declared the *Public Ledger and Daily Transcript*. "A woman is nobody. A wife is everything. A pretty girl is equal to ten thousand men and a mother is, next to God, all powerful. The ladies of Philadelphia are resolved to maintain their (present) rights as Wives, Belles, Virgins, and Mothers, and not as women."

James Gordon Bennett of the *New York Herald* thought the "little convention" at Seneca Falls was "amusing," but wondered if the ladies were really eager to "doff the apron and buckle on the sword." He jokingly suggested that perhaps Lucretia Mott wanted to become President herself and added that she might make a better one "than some of those who have lately tenanted the White House."

As Henry Stanton had warned, newspaper humorists turned the whole thing into a laughing matter. It wasn't easy for Elizabeth and her friends to take. But the enormous publicity, even in jest, drew great attention to the issue of woman's rights. Here and there papers such as Horace Greeley's *New York Tribune* discussed it seriously. Gradually others treated the question with some greater respect. As for the fun-making editorials, Elizabeth wrote Lucretia, "That is just what I wanted. Imagine the publicity given to our ideas. It will start women thinking, and men too; and when men and women think about a new question, the first step in progress is taken."

The Movement's Rapid Spread

While some men were laughing, and maybe because they were, women did begin to take up the battle started in Seneca Falls. There was another woman's rights convention in Rochester, New York, that same year. Reports about it were widely circulated in newspapers from Maine to Texas, again mostly in ridicule, but women started thinking. They talked about it at their church and literary clubs and in their own parlors. Without any direction from the outside and without knowledge at first of what others were doing, new woman's rights groups began to spring up in towns and cities. Before long there were state organizations in Ohio, Indiana, Pennsylvania, Massachusetts and Kansas.

A group in Salem, Ohio, decided to hold a convention for women from all parts of that state. They announced it would be run entirely by women, without the help of a single man. Women would preside as its officers and no man would be allowed to speak, vote or sit on the platform.

"Never did men so suffer," the women gleefully reported

afterwards. "They implored—just to say one word; but no; the president was inflexible—no man should be heard. If one meekly arose to make a suggestion he was at once ruled out of order. For the first time in the world's history, men learned how it felt to sit in silence when questions in which they were interested were under discussion."

Those planning the Ohio convention wrote to Elizabeth Stanton for advice about the rights and grievances they meant to include in a petition to the state. Her answer was firm:

"For what shall you first petition? For the exercise of your right to the elective franchise—nothing short of this. The grant to you of this right will secure all others; and the granting of every other right while this is denied is a mockery. It is our duty to assert and reassert this right, to agitate, discuss and petition, until our political equality be fully recognized. Depend upon it, this is the point to attack, the stronghold of the fortress—the *one* woman will find the most difficult to take; the *one* man will most reluctantly give up. . . . By her own efforts the change must come. She must carve out her future destiny with her own right hand."

Suffrage: The Cornerstone of the Movement

Ellen Carol DuBois

The women's rights movement that arose from the Seneca Falls Convention had many goals besides obtaining the vote for women, but the demand for suffrage soon became the central aspect of the movement. In the following essay, Ellen Carol DuBois explores the reasons why suffrage represented such an important part of the early feminists' agenda. When the United States was first formed, DuBois explains, the Revolutionary leaders believed that people who were economically and socially dependent on others—such as servants or wives—would be likely to vote as their masters or husbands dictated and therefore should not be allowed to vote. By the 1840s, however, white men had gained the right to vote regardless of their occupation, whereas women remained disfranchised, she writes. The leaders of the women's movement realized that suffrage would not only give them the political power that they lacked, DuBois contends, but that it would also signal their independence from and equality with men. DuBois is a professor of history and women's studies at the University of California at Los Angeles. She has written extensively on the women's rights movement, including *Feminism and Suffrage: The Emergence of an Independent Women's Movement in America, 1848–1869*, from which the following is excerpted.

From the beginning, gaining the franchise was part of the program of the women's rights movement. It was one of a series of reforms that looked toward the elimination of women's dependent and inferior position before the law. The women's rights movement demanded for married women control over their own wages, the right to contract for their own property, joint guardianship over their children, and improved inheritance rights when widowed. For all women, the movement demanded the elective franchise and the rights of citizenship. Compared to legal reforms in women's status articulated before 1848, for instance equal right to inherit real property, the women's rights program was very broadly based, and intentionally so. In particular, the right to control one's earnings and the right to vote were demands that affected large numbers of women—farm women, wives of urban artisans and laborers, millgirls and needlewomen.

Initial Reactions to Suffrage Demands

While part of this general reform in women's legal status, the demand for woman suffrage was always treated differently from other women's rights. In the first place, it initially met with greater opposition within the movement than other demands did. At the Seneca Falls Convention, Elizabeth Cady Stanton submitted a resolution on "the duty of the women of this country to secure to themselves the sacred right to the elective franchise." Lucretia Mott thought the resolution a mistake, and tried to dissuade her from presenting it. Mott's position may have been based on her objections to involvement in the world of electoral politics, but surely others recoiled from the woman suffrage demand because it seemed too radical. Although the convention passed all other motions unanimously, it was seriously divided over the suffrage. Frederick Douglass, who, himself disfranchised, appreciated the importance of membership in the political community, was Stanton's staunchest supporter at Seneca Falls. The woman suffrage resolution barely passed.

Soon, however, woman suffrage was distinguished from other reforms by being elevated to a preeminent position in the women's rights movement. After the Seneca Falls Convention, there is no further evidence of reluctance within the movement to demand the vote. On the contrary, it quickly became the cornerstone of the women's rights program. A resolution passed at the 1856 national convention may be taken as representative: "Resolved, that the main power of the woman's rights movement lies in this: that while always demanding for woman better education, better employment, and better laws, it has kept steadily in view the one cardinal demand for the right of suffrage: in a democracy, the symbol and guarantee of all other rights."

In keeping with the truth of this resolution, the demand for woman suffrage also generated much more opposition outside the movement. Public opinion and politicians were more sympathetic to feminists' economic demands than to their political ones. In the mid-1850's, state legislatures began to respond favorably to women's lobbying and petition efforts for reforms in property law. By 1860, fourteen states had passed some form of women's property rights legislation. Encouraged by these victories, the movement escalated its demands and shifted its emphasis from property rights to the suffrage. This was clearest in the case of New York. Initially, to gain maximum support for the less controversial demand, activists there circulated separate petitions for property rights and for the vote. As the movement gained strength, however, they included both economic and political demands on a single petition, and, in 1857, presented a unified program to the legislature. Three years later, the New York legislature passed the most comprehensive piece of women's rights legislation in the United States, the Married Women's Property Act. This law granted New York women all the economic rights they demanded, but still refused women the right to vote.

The Essential Nature of the Vote

To both opponents and advocates of women's rights, therefore, the demand for woman suffrage was significantly more controversial than other demands for equality with men. Why was this the case? Like the overwhelming majority of their contemporaries, nineteenth-century feminists believed that the vote was the ultimate repository of social and economic power in a democratic society. They wanted that power for women and relied on well-developed natural rights arguments and the rhetorical traditions of the American Revolution and the Declaration of Independence to make their demand. "In demanding the political rights of woman," the 1853 national convention resolved, "we simply assert the fundamental principle of democracy—that taxation and representation should go together, and that, if the principle is denied, all our institutions must fall with it."

The widespread belief in the importance of the ballot which feminists drew on to make their case for woman suffrage is a somewhat elusive aspect of the American political tradition because the extension of the franchise to the masses of white men had been such a gradual process. No organized political movement was required as Chartism had been in Britain. As a result, what the vote meant and promised to antebellum American men was not formalized into an explicit ideological statement, and is that much harder for us to assess in retrospect. However, American white working men seem to have attached considerable importance to their franchise. Even though they did not have to organize to win the vote, they did form working men's parties in every northern state to protect it and give it power. Believing that, in the words of [trade unionist] Frederick Robinson, the vote "put into our hands the power of perfecting our government and securing our happiness," they organized against obstacles to its use, such as indirect elections and caucus nominations. In addition, working men saw the democratic franchise, divested of property qualifications, as a victory against privilege. As a British Chartist put it in 1834, "With us Universal suffrage will begin in our lodges, extend to the general union, embrace the management of trade, and finally swallow up political power." To the degree that organized working men believed that universal white manhood suffrage established the necessary preconditions for social democracy, they looked to their own shortcomings for their failure to achieve such a society. "Our fathers have purchased for us political rights and an equality of privileges," Robinson chastised the trade unions of Boston in 1834, "which we have not yet had the intelligence to appreciate, nor the courage to protect, nor the wisdom to employ."

Yet these general ideas about the power and importance of the ballot are not sufficient to explain the special significance of the suffrage issue for women. The ideas of democratic political theory were not systematically applied to women until feminist leaders, anxious to challenge the subservient position of women, appropriated those ideas and demanded the vote. Like black men, women were excluded from the actual expansion of the suffrage in the late eighteenth and early nineteenth centuries, but the exclusion of women from political life went even further. Women were so far outside the boundaries of the antebellum political community that the fact of their disfranchisement, unlike that of black men, was barely noticed. The French and American Revolutions greatly intensified awareness of the educational, economic, and social inequality of the sexes, but few Revolutionary leaders considered the inclusion of women in the franchise, and even fewer . . . called for it. Further back in the democratic political tradition, the radical Levellers of seventeenth-century England made the same distinction between women's civil and moral rights, which they advocated, and women's political rights, which they never considered. In large part, the awareness that women were being excluded from the political community and the need to justify this disfranchisement came after women began to demand political equality. Prior to the women's rights movement, those who noticed and commented on the disfranchisement of women were not advocates of woman suffrage, but antidemocrats, who used this exception to disprove the natural right of people to self-government.

The Concept of Political Independence

On what basis were women excluded from any consideration in the distribution of political power, even when that power was organized on democratic principles? At least part of the answer seems to lie in the concept of "independence," which was the major criterion for enfranchisement in classical democratic political theory, and which acted to exclude women from the political community. Even the radical Tom Paine thought that servants should not have the vote because they were economically and socially dependent on their masters, and "freedom is destroyed by dependence." A contemporary political theorist, C.B. Macpherson, has defined the core of this concept of "independence" as self-ownership, the individual's right to possess his own person: "The essential humanity of the individual consisted in his freedom from the will of other persons, freedom to enjoy his own person and to develop his own capacities. One's person was property not metaphorically, but essentially; the property one had in it was the right to exclude others from its use and enjoyment." Women's traditional relationships to men within their families constituted the essence of dependence. When John Adams considered the question, "Whence arises the right of men to govern the women without their consent?" he found the answer in men's power to feed, clothe, and employ women and therefore to make political decisions on their behalf. Not only were eighteenth- and early nineteenth-century women prohibited from owning real property or controlling wealth; they could not be said even to hold property in themselves. Law and custom granted the husband ownership, not only of his wife's labor power and the wages she earned by it, but of her physical person as well, in the sexual rights of the marriage relation. No people, with the exception of chattel slaves, had less proprietary rights over themselves in eighteenth- and early nineteenth-century America than married women. Until the emergence of feminism, the dependent status that women held was considered natural, and if not right, then inescapable.

Thus, the demand that women be included in the electorate was not simply a stage in the expansion and democratization of the franchise. It was a particularly feminist demand, because it exposed and challenged the assumption of male authority over women. To women fighting to extend their sphere beyond its traditional domestic limitations, political rights involved a radical change in women's status, their emergence into public life. The right to vote raised the prospect of female autonomy in a way that other claims to equal rights could not. Petitions to state legislatures for equal rights to property and children were memorials for the redress of grievances, which could be tolerated within the traditional chivalrous framework that accorded women the "right" to protection. In 1859 the *New York Times* supported the passage of the New York Married Women's Property Act by distinguishing the "legal protection and fair play to which women are justly entitled" from "the claims to a share of political power which the extreme advocates of Women's Rights are fond of advancing." By contrast, the suffrage demand challenged the idea that women's interests were identical or even compatible with men's. As such, it embodied a vision of female self-determination that placed it at the center of the feminist movement. "While we would not undervalue other methods," the 1851 national women's rights convention resolved, "the Right of Suffrage for Women is, in our opinion, the corner-stone of this enterprise, since we do not seek to protect woman, but rather to place her in a position to protect herself."

A Challenge to Male Power

The feminist implications of the suffrage demand are further evident in the reverberations it sent through the ideology of sexual spheres, the nineteenth-century formulation of the sexual division of labor. Most obviously, woman suffrage constituted a serious challenge to the masculine monopoly of the public sphere. Although the growing numbers of women in schools, trades, professions, and wage-labor were weakening the sexual barriers around life outside the family, most adult women remained at home, defined politically, economically, and socially by their family position. In this context, the prospect of enfranchisement was uniquely able to touch all women, offering them a public role and a relation to the community unmediated by husband or children. While the suffrage demand did not address the domestic side of the nineteenth-century sexual order directly, the connections between public and private spheres carried its implications into the family as well. In particular, the public honor of citizenship promised to elevate women's status in the home and raised the specter of sexual equality there. Women's rights leaders were relatively modest about the implications of the franchise for women's position in the family, anticipating reform of family law and improvement in the quality of domestic relations. Their opponents, however, predicted that woman suffrage would have a revolutionary impact on the family. "It is well known that the object of these unsexed women is to overthrow the most sacred of our institutions . . . ," a New York legislator responded to women's rights petitions. "Are we to put the stamp of truth upon the libel here set forth, that men and women, in the matrimonial relation, are to be equal?" In the introduction to the *History of Woman Suffrage*, Elizabeth Cady Stanton penetrated to the core of this antisuffrage response. "Political rights, involving in their last results equality everywhere," she wrote, "roused all the antagonism of a dominant power, against the self-assertion of a class hitherto subservient."

The Working Relationship of Elizabeth Cady Stanton and Susan B. Anthony

Alice S. Rossi

Of all the early feminists, Elizabeth Cady Stanton and Susan B. Anthony were the best known and played the largest role in developing the fledgling women's rights movement. As one of the organizers of the Seneca Falls Convention in 1848, Stanton was part of the movement from the very beginning. Anthony, a teacher and temperance activist, did not become involved in the suffrage cause until the early 1850s, but it rapidly became her life's work. Stanton and Anthony developed a unique working relationship that served as the backbone of the movement for decades. In the following essay, Alice S. Rossi examines the way in which Stanton and Anthony merged their contrasting but complementary skills to create a "sum that was greater than its parts." Rossi is a retired professor of sociology from the University of Massachusetts at Amherst and a founding member of the original governing board of the National Organization for Women. She has written several books, including *The Feminist Papers: From Adams to de Beauvoir*, from which the following essay is taken.

The two women most closely associated with the emergence of the woman's-rights movement in the nineteenth century are Elizabeth Cady Stanton and Susan B. Anthony. From the spring of 1851, when they first met, until Elizabeth's death in 1902 they were the most intimate of friends and the closest collaborators in the battle for women's rights in the United States. Together they were Lyceum lecturers in the

1850s, founders of equal-rights and suffrage associations, organizers of annual conventions, hardy suffrage campaigners in the western states, and coeditors of the massive first three volumes of the *History of Woman Suffrage*; the contributions of these two pioneers are so intertwined that it is nearly impossible to speak of one without the other. They were in and out of each other's personal lives and households for more than fifty years. Their friendship and shared commitment to the cause of women's rights were the solid, central anchor in both their lives. As Elizabeth wrote to Susan in 1869, "no power in heaven, hell or earth can separate us, for our hearts are eternally wedded together."

Complementary Skills

It is fitting, therefore, to introduce these two remarkable women in one essay and to focus on their friendship and the nature of their collaboration. The key to their effectiveness lies in the complementary nature of their skills. It can truly be said in this instance that the sum was greater than its parts, for either woman by herself would have had far less impact on the history of women's rights than they had in combination. Elizabeth had the intellect and ability to organize thought and evidence in a pungent, punchy prose. Susan was a master strategist, the "Napoleon" of the movement, as [Unitarian minister] William Channing described her, superb at managing large-scale campaigns, quick and nimble in handling the give-and-take of convention meetings, and an effective public speaker. Elizabeth had only average stage presence and delivery as a speaker, and Susan's ability to conceptualize and develop her ideas was poor. Between them, Elizabeth's effective prose found its perfect outlet in Susan's public speaking. Elizabeth summed up their complementarity very well:

> In writing we did better work together than either could alone. While she is slow and analytical in composition, I am rapid and synthetic. I am the better writer, she the better critic. She supplied the facts and statistics, I the philosophy and rhetoric, and together we have made arguments that have stood unshaken by the storms of thirty long years.

Down through the years Susan turned to Elizabeth for help in drafting speeches, testimony, and letters for presentation to conventions on education, temperance, and women's rights. A good example of this pressure on Elizabeth is in a letter appealing for her help in preparing a speech for a convention of school teachers which Susan was invited to give in 1856:

There is so much to say and I am so without constructive power to put in symmetrical order. So, for the love of me and for the saving of the reputation of womanhood, I beg you, with one baby on your knee and another at your feet, and four boys whistling, buzzing, hallooing "Ma, Ma," set yourself about the work. . . . Now will you load my gun, leaving me to pull the trigger and let fly the powder and ball? Don't delay one mail to tell me what you will do, for I must not and will not allow these school masters to say: "See, these women can't or won't do anything when we give them a chance." No, they sha'n't say that, even if I have to get a man to write it. But no man can write from my standpoint, nor no woman but you; for all, all would base their strongest argument on the unlikeness of the sexes. . . . And yet, in the schoolroom more than any other place, does the difference of sex, if there is any, need to be forgotten. . . . Do get all on fire and be as cross as you please.

The letter captures several of Susan's qualities: blunt speech, a badgering of her associates to give her the help she needs (always in a hurry), a fighting spirit, and an ability to point to a central theme she wishes stressed. Elizabeth's response to this particular call for help came just five days later. She says in part:

Your servant is not dead but liveth. Imagine me, day in and day out, watching, bathing, dressing, nursing, and promenading the precious contents of a little crib in the corner of the room. I pace up and down these two chambers of mine, like a caged lioness longing to bring to a close nursing and housekeeping cares. . . . Is your speech to be exclusively on the point of educating the sexes together, or as to the best manner of educating women? I will do what I can to help you with your lecture.

The "baby" referred to is five-month-old Harriot, Elizabeth's sixth child, and the speech, entitled "Co-education," was written by Elizabeth and delivered by Susan less than two months later.

Collaboration and Support

This particular collaborative effort differed from most of their team work only in that it involved no face-to-face working out of the ideas to be developed in the speech. In most of their joint efforts they worked together more closely; Susan often visited the Stanton home in Seneca Falls, New York, for this purpose. Elizabeth described these occasions:

> whenever I saw that stately Quaker girl coming across my lawn, I knew that some happy convocation of the sons of Adam were to be set by the ears, by one of our appeals or resolutions. The little portmanteau stuffed with facts was opened. . . . Then we would get out our pens and write articles for papers, or a petition to the Legislature, letters to the faithful . . . call on *The Una*, *The Liberator*, and *The Standard*, to remember our wrongs as well as those of the slave. We never met without issuing a pronunciamento on some question.

Thirty years later, when Elizabeth was no longer burdened with housekeeping and child-rearing responsibilities, she commented that in the 1850s, had it not been for Susan, who provided her with enough evidence of injustice to "turn any woman's thoughts from stockings and puddings," she might in time, "like too many women, have become wholly absorbed in a narrow family selfishness."

But a supportive friend who applied continual pressure to produce speeches and resolutions and articles for the press would hardly suffice to carry Elizabeth through the arduous years of child-rearing, from 1842 to the Civil War. During these years she not only bore seven children, but did a good deal of entertaining, produced reams of written material, served in temperance and abolition societies, lectured widely with the Lyceum circuit, and ran the household in Seneca Falls for long stretches of time without a man in the house.

An Important Asset to the Movement

The following passage is taken from Eleanor Flexner's pioneering history, Century of Struggle: The Woman's Rights Movement in the United States. *According to Flexner, the working relationship formed by Elizabeth Cady Stanton and Susan B. Anthony was one of the main assets of the early movement for women's suffrage.*

If the women lacked many weapons for achieving their goals easily, they had some very real assets. Perhaps one of the greatest was the working partnership between Mrs. Stanton and Miss Anthony. Few associations have been more fruitful. Their talents and the circumstances of their lives complemented each other. Miss Anthony was an organizer, Mrs. Stanton a thinker, writer, and speaker. Mrs. Stanton was tied down by a large family for twenty years of their association; Miss Anthony was more mobile, and could either travel, or rush in answer to a distress call from the Stanton home, to care for children and household, while Mrs. Stanton shut herself up to prepare a needed brief or speech. When Mrs. Stanton on occasion wandered afield, Miss Anthony was usually able to bring her back into line. (Their co-workers frequently complained that Mrs. Stanton was forever bringing up new and controversial issues—divorce, the Bible, the "educated vote," which would "rock the boat.") Although Susan Anthony and Elizabeth Cady Stanton had their differences, the deep bond between them never frayed.

Eleanor Flexner, *Century of Struggle: The Woman's Rights Movement in the United States*, 1975.

Elizabeth was clearly a woman of enormous physical energy coupled with a very strong will; these were needed to cope with such a regimen and to thrive on it. She was not a woman easily threatened by new experiences. . . . Among Elizabeth's prescriptions for a healthy womanhood was one she clearly followed herself, but which it would take many decades for medicine and psychiatry to learn: she insightfully put her finger on an important cause of hysteria and illness among the women of her day, in a 1859 letter to a Boston friend:

> I think if women would indulge more freely in vituperation, they would enjoy ten times the health they do. It seems to me they are suffering from repression.

Elizabeth was not a woman to suffer from such repression herself. She showed none of the modern ambivalence about complaining when her responsibilities became onerous. One feels sure that in the intimacy of a friendly visit she let off steam in much the way she did in her letters during the 1850s, either by frankly admitting that she longed to be "free from housekeeping and children, so as to have some time to read and think and write" or by chafing at some affront to women and writing to Susan: "I am at a boiling point! If I do not find some day the use of my tongue on this question I shall die of an intellectual repression, a woman's rights convulsion."

Rebels for a Cause

There was probably not another woman in the nineteenth century who put her tongue and pen to better use than Elizabeth Stanton. She and Susan clearly viewed themselves as rebels in a good fight for justice and equality for women. They wrote each other in martial terms full of "triggers," "powder and balls," "Thunderbolts." Locust Hill, Elizabeth's home in Seneca Falls, was dubbed the "center of the rebellion" and from here Elizabeth "forged the thunderbolts" and Susan "fired them."

Early African-American Suffragists

Rosalyn Terborg-Penn

Rosalyn Terborg-Penn is a history professor and the co-ordinator of graduate programs in history at Morgan State University in Baltimore, Maryland. She is a founder of the Association of Black Women Historians and coeditor of *Black Women in America: An Historical Encyclopedia*, *The Afro-American Woman: Struggles and Images*, and *Women in Africa and the African Diaspora: A Reader*. In the following excerpt from her book *African American Women in the Struggle for the Vote, 1850–1920*, Terborg-Penn discusses the involvement of African Americans in the beginning stages of the suffrage movement. She points out that the very first man to defend women's right to vote was Frederick Douglass, a former slave and famous abolitionist who backed the suffrage resolution proposed at the Seneca Falls Convention. During the 1850s, numerous African-American women who worked for the anti-slavery cause also became involved in the suffrage movement, the author notes. The white suffrage leaders who chronicled the history of the movement often left these black women out of their records, Terborg-Penn maintains, or recorded their names without identifying their race. Nevertheless, she writes, well-known activists such as Sojourner Truth and many lesser-known black suffragists all played an important role in the early days of the women's rights movement.

The official birth of the woman suffrage movement occurred at the women's rights convention held at Seneca Falls, New

York, in July 1848. In the formative years of this movement—its first generation—the number of suffragists grew slowly from a small group of reformers within the confines of abolitionist circles in the northeast to a more diversified, but still limited number of individuals and groups nationwide. Diversification occurred as individuals, both Blacks and whites, joined the movement from regions throughout the nation. During these formative years the majority of the participants came from the more affluent and educated white abolitionists, who can be classified among the mainstream reformers coming out of the antebellum era. Yet a handful of African American men and women added their color to the proceedings.

The Beginning of Black Participation

The early feminists who emerged from abolitionist circles held periodic conventions, wrote letters to editors, and sent petitions to government officials. Aside from their demand for woman suffrage, their activities were conventional compared to subsequent woman suffrage actions. Yet the political consciousness of the white women involved, and their ability to act upon their convictions, were much higher than for the majority of Black women, whether free or enslaved. Elite and middle-class white women did not normally work outside of the home. They did not have to contend with the realities of poverty, illiteracy, or menial employment, as did most Black women. Even the more fortunate Black women who were living in a quasi-free status outside of slavery, often had to work for wages or services.

Despite the disparity of lifestyles, African American participation in this movement began with the initiation of the struggle. Frederick Douglass, a former slave and Black abolitionist living in Rochester, New York, was at the Seneca Falls meeting. He became the first male of any color to advocate publicly for woman suffrage. Black participation continued from that point forward. . . .

Throughout the 1850s, a growing number of Black female abolitionists joined the small circle of suffragists. Identifying their names was tedious, but less difficult than recovering their ideas and activities as woman suffragists.

A Glaring Absence

Aside from Sojourner Truth, the former New York slave and itinerant abolitionist preacher whose words were often quoted, the mainstream woman suffrage chroniclers did not identify most other women in the circle as African American. Early chroniclers were the women who edited the first three volumes of the *History of Woman Suffrage*: Elizabeth Cady Stanton, Susan B. Anthony, and Matilda J. Gage. The history writing began in 1876, when the women agreed to compile the data they had collected through the years. The data included personal reminiscences, biographical sketches, photographs, state reports, speeches, resolutions, excerpts from the *Congressional Record*, newspaper clippings, and items from the editors' personal files. The first volume was published in 1881, bringing the movement history from 1848 to 1860. Not one Black woman's photograph appeared in the volume, not even the celebrated Sojourner Truth. Aside from excerpts from Truth's speeches, the words of other Black female suffragists were all but absent. A function of the present study is to recover the Black women known to the contemporaries of the movement, but who became lost to later generations of woman suffragists and those who wrote about the movement.

Sojourner Truth

In 1850 the first Massachusetts women's rights convention met at Worcester, and Sojourner Truth attended. Throughout the formative years of the movement, Truth attended women's rights conventions held in the North, earning her keep by doing domestic work, selling her narrative, performing the songs she composed, and making speeches. Unlike the other suffragists who made the women's rights circuit, staying with friends who in turn stayed with them on other occasions, Truth was homeless and had to provide for her own survival with little ability to reciprocate short of providing services. Perhaps her overwhelming presence and unique oratorical style prompted chroniclers of the movement to record her works, for the opinions of other Black women were rarely recorded. . . .

It appears that Sojourner Truth captivated even unwilling audiences, winning skeptics to the women's rights cause. In 1851 she attended the convention at Akron, Ohio, where she spoke on behalf of all women, despite attempts by white women to prevent her from taking the podium. Frances D. Gage presided over the meeting. She reported how fearful her colleagues were that allowing a former slave and an abolitionist to speak before the hostile audience would ruin the cause. Truth prevailed and delivered a heart-rending speech that resulted in "long and loud" cheers.

In 1853 Truth attended the Broadway Tabernacle meeting in New York City, where she reportedly spoke about the legal disabilities that kept women downtrodden. Despite their low status, she believed all women would someday overcome the discrimination against them. An example of how the white women who remembered Truth's "classic style" reported it reads as follows:

> I've been look'n round and watchin' things and I know a little mite 'bout Woman's Rights too. I know that it feels a kind O'hissin' and ticklin' like to see a colored woman geet up and tell you 'bout things, and Woman's Rights. We have all been thrown down so low that nobody thought we'd ever get up again; but we have been long enough trodden now; we will come up again, and now I am here.

> Now women do not ask half of a kingdom, but their rights, and they don't get 'em. When she comes to demand 'em, don't you hear our sons hiss their mothers like snakes, because they ask for their rights; and can they ask for anything else? . . . But we'll have our rights; see if we don't and you can't stop us from them; see if you can. You may hiss as much as you like, but it is comin'. . . .

Whether she spoke in the southern dialect reported is debatable, since Truth was born and raised and lived much of her life in what historian Margaret Washington has described as a Dutch-speaking region of the North. Nonetheless, Truth used what scholars of the Black Church call a classic African American preaching style, which has components of poetry, wit, and symbolism that stir congregations.

Silencing Black Women

In the following excerpt from his book Women's Movements in the United States: Woman Suffrage, Equal Rights, and Beyond, *Steven M. Buechler describes the general resistance of white women to African-American women's involvement in the suffrage movement. Buechler is a professor of sociology at Mankato State University in Mankato, Minnesota.*

Virtually all scholars have described the woman suffrage movement as a white, middle-class movement. Although this truism is accurate as far as it goes, it has obscured variations and complexities of class and race relations within the movement. At various points in its history, the woman suffrage movement ignored black women, actively rejected black women, spoke eloquently against slavery, and engaged in explicit and virulent racism. . . .

The women's movement inherited a particular view of racial differences from abolitionism. Blending abolitionist goals with varying forms of paternalism, this view sought the eradication of slavery but not full and unlimited equality between the races. This tension was evident when black women tried to join female antislavery societies to work for the abolition of slavery. Discrimination against black women in such female abolitionist societies was a frequent occurrence and often prompted black women to form their own separate antislavery societies—just as white women had been forced to form their own female antislavery societies when male abolitionists rejected any meaningful role for white women in abolitionist work. In fact, as Rosalyn Terborg-Penn notes, the best-known black supporters of the early women's rights campaign were men, among whom Frederick Douglass is the most widely known example. The fact that white women mobilizing an equal rights campaign in the context of the abolitionist movement were more likely to accept support from black men than from black women is an interesting testimony to the intersecting hierarchies of race and gender, which provided at least a partial voice for white women and black men while effectively silencing black women.

Steven M. Buechler, *Women's Movements in the United States: Woman Suffrage, Equal Rights, and Beyond*, 1990.

Plausibly, she utilized that style effectively, and for the first years of the movement, her voice appeared to be a solitary one among Black females.

The African American Elite

However, by 1854, African American women's participation in the women's movement became more evident. Harriet Forten Purvis and her sister, educator and abolitionist Margaretta Forten, became two of the "chief actors" responsible for organizing the Fifth National Woman's Rights Convention, the first such gathering to be held in their home city of Philadelphia. The sisters were the daughters of the wealthy Philadelphia sail maker and Black abolitionist, James Forten, and his wife, Charlotte Forten, Sr. Students of the Black abolitionist movement recognize the Forten and Purvis families as prime movers among the African Americans in the movement. However, the Pennsylvania state suffrage records, which contained the names of the Forten sisters, did not indicate that they were Black. At the suffrage meeting, Harriet's husband, Robert Purvis, was chosen vice president for Pennsylvania, an indication of the movement's preference for Black male leadership. Consequently, it is not surprising that the Forten sisters would take an active, but behind-the-scenes, role in this event. They and their mother Charlotte were members of the interracial Philadelphia Female Anti-Slavery Society, many of whose members became active in the early women's rights movement. Like their white counterparts, the Forten sisters were educated and affluent. Unlike Sojourner Truth, who was illiterate, they had never been enslaved. . . .

Feminist sentiments characterized other free Blacks of the times. Charlotte Forten, Jr., a niece of Harriet Purvis and Margaretta Forten's, was a high school student in Salem, Massachusetts, at the time. In 1855, while living with the Charles Remond family, she was introduced to the women's rights movement, which she supported enthusiastically. Charlotte had been sent to school in Salem by her father, Robert Forten, because Black students were refused admission to the public schools in Philadelphia. The Remonds were noted abolitionists, who traveled within the network of

Black antislavery circles. In 1858 Sarah Remond and her brother Charles spoke for the first time at a national women's rights convention. They attended the meeting held at Mozart Hall in New York City, where both were honored for their remarks in favor of woman suffrage. By the mid-1850s, in addition to the Remonds, Mary Ann Shadd Cary joined these other Black women in the movement. Her activities started when she returned to the United States from Canada to raise money for her antislavery newspaper, *The Provincial Freeman*. For at least twenty-five years thereafter, she attended woman suffrage conventions and campaigned for women's rights. . . .

Fighting Both Slavery and Sexism

By the 1850s, white women undertook political action outside the traditional sphere of women reformers by becoming abolitionists in mainstream organizations. As a result, their tactics and ideology, though not as radical as the Black organizations that directly confronted the slaveholding authorities, rejected the early nineteenth-century notion of women's sphere and women's moral superiority over men. Women's sphere was an ideal developed by middle-class notions about placing females in the privacy of their homes, where they were believed to belong. The early woman suffragists who grew out of this abolitionist movement were radical in their attempts to oppose gender conventions by moving outside of the so-called women's sphere and acting independently in calling for their rights. Like Black women abolitionists, they had learned about political organizing, public speaking, and the use of tactics such as moral suasion to make political demands.

However, some African American women learned the skills and tactics, used radical steps to oppose racism, and then took even more risky tactics to oppose sexism. In so doing, they fought both types of oppression, simultaneously. Mary Ann Shadd Cary . . . exemplified such African American feminists. Although the *History of Woman Suffrage* editors made reference to Cary's and Sarah Remond's participation in the suffrage movement, they neglected to record these two noted abolitionists' views about women's rights.

Cary's position on women's rights can be gleaned from the pages of her newspaper *The Provincial Freeman*. On numerous occasions she and her sister, Amelia Shadd, printed news items and editorials about women's struggle against slavery and against gender discrimination. According to the editors, "woman's work was anything she put her mind or her hand to do." They encouraged women to write letters to the editors of newspapers and to share their views as well as their accomplishments.

Cary's affiliation with feminist leaders was evidenced by her words of excitement noting suffragist Lucy Stone's visit to Toronto in 1854. Cary published *The Freeman* from this Canadian city at the time when Stone arrived to lecture on women's rights. Cary reported that a crowd of Stone's supporters attended her lecture on "Woman's Rights." Lamenting that the number of Blacks in attendance was few, Cary commented that even in Toronto, "with the strong attachment to antiquated notions respecting woman and her sphere so prevalent, Stone was listened to patiently and applauded abundantly.". . .

Changes in the Larger Community

By 1859 the women's rights perspective was spreading among Blacks in the United States, as advocates made their philosophies known. At the New England Convention of Colored Citizens, held in Boston that year, Charles Remond declined a nomination to the business committee and said that it was time to elect women to leadership positions in the organization. As a result, several Black women accepted the challenge. Ruth Remond of Newport, Rhode Island, and another Black New Englander, a Mrs. Lawton, were elected to the business committee. One of the major demands that ultimately developed as a result of the convention was the call for universal suffrage, a position among African Americans that predated the woman suffragists' move in this direction a decade later.

Chapter 3

Tactics and Disagreements

The Division of the Movement

Anne Firor Scott and Andrew MacKay Scott

Prior to the Civil War, the women's rights movement consisted of a loosely organized group of like-minded reformers. When the war began, leaders in the movement argued that women might be able to "earn" suffrage by actively supporting the war effort. Their hopes were dashed, however, with the proposal and subsequent passage of the Fourteenth and Fifteenth Amendments, which secured voting rights for black men but specifically excluded women. Members of the movement disagreed over the best approach to take: to support the amendments in solidarity with the newly freed slaves or to oppose the amendments because they withheld suffrage from women. Two different factions formed, and these groups increasingly found themselves at odds over other questions of tactics and ideology. In 1869, the movement officially split into the National Woman Suffrage Association and the American Woman Suffrage Association—a division that would last for more than twenty years.

The following selection, which examines the events and issues that led to the division of the women's rights movement, is taken from *One Half the People: The Fight for Woman Suffrage* by the husband-and-wife team of Anne Firor Scott and Andrew MacKay Scott. Andrew MacKay Scott is a retired professor of political science from the University of North Carolina at Chapel Hill and the author of several books on politics and government. Anne Firor Scott is a retired history professor from Duke University in Durham, North Carolina. She has written and edited numerous books on women's history, including *The Southern Lady: From Pedestal to Politics, 1830–1930* and *Natural Allies: Women's Associations in American History*.

Excerpted from *One Half the People*, by Anne Firor Scott and Andrew MacKay Scott. Copyright ©1982 by Anne Firor Scott and Andrew MacKay Scott. Reprinted with the permission of the University of Illinois Press.

By 1860 a social and political movement was taking shape around the demand for women's rights. It was a small, somewhat beleaguered movement, whose principal accomplishments had been some changes in state laws governing married women's property rights and a considerable broadening of women's educational opportunities. Enfranchisement was only one of the broad spectrum of rights for which women contended, but woman suffrage was emerging as a clear, easily understood goal around which support could be mobilized and which could tap the strain of natural rights doctrine in American thought. But to gain suffrage from male voters women needed a broad constituency and an effective political strategy.

The movement's natural supporters—women—had proved hard to mobilize. Male values shaped the culture, and anything which alienated men was apt to cost women dearly. The "true woman" was supposed to be pious, submissive and domestic, and many women were frightened when their more adventurous sisters began to challenge the taboos of this male-dominated society. Even women who privately applauded such challenges were often afraid to do so openly. The challengers therefore faced the twofold task of emboldening or persuading their potential constituency and then forcing male politicians to take that constituency seriously.

The Civil War

The legal and educational changes accomplished in the first twelve years after Seneca Falls were encouraging. Then came the Civil War, and new complications. Persuaded, over Susan Anthony's objections, to forego agitation in favor of war work, women contributed in many ways to the conduct of the war itself. Elizabeth Cady Stanton and Anthony organized the Women's National Loyal League to press for quick passage of the Thirteenth Amendment in its 1865 version. Striking an indirect blow for suffrage, they launched a massive petition campaign with the words: "Women, you cannot vote or fight for your country. Your only way to be a power in the government is through the exercise of this one, sacred, constitutional 'right of petition,' and we ask you now to use it to the utmost. . . ." Antislavery senators assured the women that the 400,000 signatures to their petitions contributed significantly to the adoption of the amendment abolishing slavery.

With the ratification of the Thirteenth Amendment the antislavery goal which had brought so many women into public life was achieved. It was not immediately clear where this left women's rights. In May 1865 the Anti-Slavery Society met to hear William Lloyd Garrison argue that the organization could now dissolve. Wendell Phillips disagreed on the grounds that until the freedmen had the right to vote, the society still had hard work to do.

Black Suffrage vs. Woman Suffrage

Most women in the society stood with Phillips, partly for reasons of their own. It was clear that black suffrage held out the promise of a Republican South; Mrs. Stanton, for one, understood that woman suffrage could offer no such clear payoff for the party in power. She believed women's best hope, therefore, was to link their cause with that of the freedmen. This, as it turned out, was not quite what Wendell Phillips and the antislavery leadership had in mind. They wanted women's support in their drive for black enfranchisement, but not at the price of supporting woman suffrage. Phillips felt it would be difficult enough to persuade moderate Republicans and Democrats, many of whose states did not permit blacks to vote, without the complication of inducing them also to support the unpopular issue of woman suffrage. Only four antislavery men stood with the increasingly indignant women. Thus began what would become a bitter division among prewar reformers, one which would separate men from women and, in a short time, would split the ranks of women themselves.

Despite Phillips's opposition, Elizabeth Cady Stanton stood her ground and told the first postwar Women's Rights Convention, meeting in New York in May 1866, that women should avail themselves of "the strong arm and blue uniform of the black soldier to walk in by his side, and thus make the gap so wide that no privileged class could ever again close it against the humblest citizen of the republic."

Women, she argued, should close ranks with the blacks and antislavery men and appeal for universal suffrage on the basis of natural rights. Members of the convention accepted her reasoning, and constituted themselves the American Equal Rights Association open to men and women, blacks and whites.

The Equal Rights Association was hardly in being when Congress passed and sent to the states for ratification the Fourteenth Amendment, which did not enfranchise the blacks, but instead guaranteed them equal protection of their state's laws, and provided for a reduction in representation if a state denied the vote to male citizens. Not yet alert to any possibilities for themselves in the equal protection clause, suffragists in the Equal Rights Association were incensed by the proposal to add the word "male" to the constitution, and therefore the members undertook to oppose ratification of this amendment. The Republicans campaigned on a platform of ratification of the Fourteenth Amendment in the 1866 congressional elections, and won. They then moved to a firmer position on black suffrage, and began to formulate the Fifteenth Amendment.

That amendment represented a fundamental change in American government. The 1789 Constitution had left the determination of the qualifications of voters entirely to the states. The Fifteenth Amendment limited state options for qualifying voters, forbidding states to deny the right to vote to citizens of the United States on account of race, color or previous condition of servitude. Women's rights advocates saw hope for their cause in this shift, since a single federal amendment would surely be easier to obtain than amendments in all the states. They proposed that the Fifteenth Amendment be drawn to include sex as well as race. Few Republican leaders in Congress, however, were in favor of woman suffrage, and even those who were thought its inclusion at such a critical time might jeopardize their effort to enfranchise black men.

The introduction of the word "male" into the Constitution for the first time in the Fourteenth Amendment and the ratification of the Fifteenth Amendment without mention of sex were the most serious of a series of disappointments. In 1867 the New Jersey legislature, despite Lucy Stone's best efforts, had rejected a suffrage proposal thirty-two to twenty-three. Also in 1867 the New York constitutional convention had proved resistant to the women's arguments. And in the same year a dramatic campaign in Kansas for black and woman suffrage saw the defeat of both propositions, though the women drew nine thousand votes, which represented one-third of the total vote.

Divisions in the Movement

In the midst of these defeats a conflict arose between old friends in the women's movement. Stanton and Anthony on the one hand and Lucy Stone and her husband Henry Blackwell on the other—each surrounded by like-minded friends—began to diverge. Differences centered on a number of issues: how the funds of the Equal Rights Association were to be used; whether men should be welcomed as allies after their apostasy in the case of the reconstruction amendments; and, most important, whether the amendments themselves should be supported despite their failure to include women. In 1869 Stanton and Anthony quietly gathered their supporters into a new organization, the National Woman Suffrage Association. A few months later Stone and Blackwell called a general meeting of women's rights advocates in Cleveland which proceeded to organize the American Woman Suffrage Association, on what they described as a more representative basis. Soon the two groups were vying with each other for the loyalty of state and local suffrage organizations, as well as that of particular individuals. In Massachusetts, the still-powerful Radical Republicans supported the American Association and helped with its funding, apparently fearing the Stanton-Anthony group as a possible center for an independent radical movement.

Though there were a number of abortive efforts to bring the divergent groups together, it soon became clear that their differences were not trivial. One recurrent issue centered on the question of strategy: whether the central focus should be on a national suffrage amendment or whether

Three Important Changes

In the following passage, Suzanne M. Marilley, a professor of history and political science at Capital University in Columbus, Ohio, describes the changes that affected feminists after the Civil War. Following the split of the women's rights movement, she writes, the politics of the Reconstruction era forced the two groups to focus on women's suffrage, to cultivate male allies for their cause, and to devise a variety of strategies, including some that required them to sacrifice certain principles for the sake of their primary goal.

Through a series of unanticipated but unavoidable collisions between competing conceptions of citizenship and political goals, the reconstruction process following the Civil War transformed the woman's rights movement into a woman suffrage movement. Before the Civil War, woman's rights reformers promoted the political integration of women without interference from major political parties because the parties were not interested in issues of citizenship, especially abolition. . . . The war and Reconstruction irrevocably removed the insulation that had fostered collective action for woman's rights as voluntarist and legislatively situated in the states.

The politics of Reconstruction brought three changes for woman's rights reformers. First, the woman's rights nongovernmental social movement became a single-issue political movement for woman suffrage led by two competing organizations. Second, women reformers learned that when men agreed as *men* about what issues belonged on the government agenda, women could not stop them. Women required male allies to support and promote their cause; they also needed to exploit conflicts between men. Third, majority rule and many points of access into the power centers of the American political system encouraged woman suffragists to design multiple strategies, occasionally to eschew principle for expediency's sake, and to discover favorable entry points onto the legislative reform agenda.

Suzanne M. Marilley, *Woman Suffrage and the Origins of Liberal Feminism in the United States, 1820–1920,* 1996.

state-by-state enfranchisement was to be preferred. Both factions accepted the principle of moving forward on both fronts, but in practice Lucy Stone and her associates were inclined to concentrate on the states, while Stanton and Anthony experimented with a number of approaches to national enfranchisement. "We have puttered with State rights for thirty years," Anthony would argue in 1877, "without a foothold except in the territories."

In hindsight it seems clear that underlying conflicts on particular issues were two different philosophies concerning the way a reform movement should operate. The drive for women's rights was taking place in a conservative cultural milieu which historians have characterized as Victorian. In the context of extraordinarily rapid demographic and economic change and accompanying political and ideological conflict, many people were fearful of changes in middle-class social arrangements, especially those having to do with the family. While actual changes in women's life experience were being brought about by economic growth, by new educational opportunities, openings in business and the professions, new laws and the like, the ideology of "woman's place" was adamant about the sacredness of home and motherhood and the perceived threat of suffrage to both.

In the simplest terms, Stanton and Anthony were willing to attack this ideology head-on; Stone and Blackwell were more deeply attached to it, and did not want to arouse anxiety among potential supporters. "It is a settled maxim with me," Elizabeth Stanton wrote, "that the existing public sentiment on any subject is wrong. . . ." Her behavior demonstrated this conviction. She travelled about the country lecturing, earned money to educate her children, gave private talks to women in which she urged them to limit the size of their families and demand absolute control over their sexual relationships, ran for Congress to test woman's right to do so, and wrote on a variety of highly controversial subjects. Anthony, for her part, was willing to form alliances with all sorts of people—Democrats, Republicans, third-party adherents, the American section of the First International, the National Labor Union, and even, briefly, Victoria Woodhull, if there seemed to be profit to the cause of suffrage. Stanton was a consistent theoretical radical; Anthony was a radical on the level of tactics. Both came to seem shocking to Lucy Stone. In her youth she, too, had boldly challenged social convention, but by the late sixties she and Henry Blackwell found it more profitable to work within the framework of gentility, cooperating politically with their friends among the Radical Republicans in Massachusetts.

The Revolution

In the 1867 Kansas campaign Stanton and Anthony had met a wealthy, eccentric Democrat named George Train, and with his money began, in 1868, *The Revolution*, a paper which in addition to supporting suffrage and equal pay for equal work, discussed practical education for girls, workers' demands, and the movement for an eight-hour day. Mrs. Stanton wrote vigorous editorials on marriage, divorce, prostitution, infanticide, the inequality of wealth, and conditions in the slums. In the same year Susan Anthony, rebuffed by the Republicans, took a woman's rights document to the Democratic Convention where at least it was read, though to the accompaniment of jeers and shouts, and died in the Resolutions Committee. Declaring a plague on both Democrats and Republicans, Anthony turned to organizing working women and exploring the possibilities of a third party.

When *The Revolution* responded to "many letters" asking if the editors opposed marriage by saying that the editors only opposed the *present system* of marriage, in which "nearly every man feels that his wife is his property, whose first duty, under all circumstances, is to gratify his passions, without the least reference to her own health . . . or to the welfare of their offspring," or when Susan Anthony associated with labor unions, Lucy Stone's anxiety mounted. Their once warm friendship began to cool.

Victoria Woodhull

The differences between the two groups were dramatically illuminated in the early 1870s when Stanton and Anthony briefly associated themselves with the beautiful, clever and unprincipled Victoria Woodhull who had burst upon the suffrage scene with a memorial presented in person to a fascinated congressional committee, in which she argued that the Fourteenth and Fifteenth Amendments had already enfranchised women.

This argument, initially developed by Francis Minor, a St. Louis attorney, was that the Constitution gave the states the right to regulate suffrage but not the power to prohibit it. The Fourteenth Amendment confirmed this, he argued, since it provided that "no State shall make or enforce any law which shall abridge the privileges or immunities of citizens of the United States." From this it followed, he believed, that since women were citizens, no state could deny them the vote. Therefore women possessed the right to vote and all state laws providing otherwise were unconstitutional. Needless to say, this was a very appealing idea to women who were realistic about the effort which would be required to attain an additional constitutional amendment, and they welcomed Woodhull to their ranks.

The "Free Love" Scandal

From Mary Wollstonecraft's time antifeminists had argued that sexual license was the inevitable concomitant of women's rights. Frances Wright had been vigorously attacked for her views on marriage. When Woodhull and [Tennie C.] Claflin's *Weekly* began publishing such statements as: "The time is approaching when public sentiment will accord to women the complete protectorship of their own persons, with the right to choose the fathers of their own children, and hold their relations with whom their hearts may be inclined . . ." [August 27, 1870], as well as revelations about a presumed illicit sexual relationship between Rev. Henry Ward Beecher and one of his parishioners, what one historian called "the free love storm" broke over the suffrage movement. Timid local groups retreated in panic, while Mrs. Stanton's stouthearted reminders that members of Congress were not discredited in the political arena for their private sexual behavior, only added to the furor. In time Susan Anthony detached herself and Mrs. Stanton from the Woodhull influence, but not before much damage had been done. The American Woman Suffrage Association (whose president Beecher had once been) maintained a discreet silence, and no doubt the Blackwells were duly thankful they had earlier separated themselves from firebrands who had no more sense than to make such friends.

In any case, the two organizations were destined for twenty more years to go their separate ways. While the American Association worked to persuade state legislatures that they should vote for suffrage amendments and published its excellent and well-financed *Woman's Journal*, Susan Anthony and the National Association gradually became the chief representatives of the movement in the public eye, partly because of the imagination with which she seized every opportunity to dramatize the suffrage demand.

Protest at the Polls

Ellen Carol DuBois

Ellen Carol DuBois is a professor of history and women's studies at the University of California at Los Angeles and the author of numerous articles and books about women's suffrage. In the following essay, DuBois describes the militant action taken by some suffragists in the face of women's exclusion from the Fourteenth and Fifteenth Amendments. Once the amendments had been passed, she explains, these suffragists shifted from opposing them to arguing that the wording of the amendments actually gave women the right to vote. Moreover, a number of activists put their interpretation of the amendments to the test by attempting to vote, DuBois writes. She provides an illuminating account of the court cases that resulted, including Susan B. Anthony's infamous 1873 conviction for voting illegally.

Most histories of women's rights—my own included—have emphasized the initial rage of women's rights leaders at the Radical Republican authors of the Fourteenth and Fifteenth Amendments. In 1865 Elizabeth Cady Stanton was horrified to discover what she called "the word male" in proposals for a Fourteenth Amendment. The second section of the amendment defines the basis of congressional representation as "male persons over the age of twenty-one" and in doing so makes the first reference to sex anywhere in the Constitution. The passage of the Fifteenth Amendment in 1869, a much more powerful constitutional defense of political equality, only deepened the anger of women's rights advocates because it did not include sex among its prohibited disfranchisements.

Excerpted from "Taking the Law into Our Own Hands," by Ellen Carol DuBois, in *Visible Women*, edited by Nancy Hewitt and Suzanne Lebsock. Copyright © by Board of Trustees of the University of Illinois. Reprinted with the permission of the University of Illinois Press.

In 1869 the crisis split suffragists into two camps—the National Woman Suffrage Association, which protested the omission of women from the Reconstruction amendments, and the American Woman Suffrage Association, which accepted the deferral of their claims. This part of the story is well known to students of woman suffrage, as is the National Association's concentration, through most of its twenty-one-year life (in 1890 it amalgamated with the American Association), on securing a separate amendment enfranchising women. Inasmuch as the form that federal woman suffrage ultimately took was precisely a separate constitutional amendment—the Nineteenth, ratified in 1920—this strategy is taken as the entirety of woman suffragists' constitutional claims. Yet, in the first few years after the passage of the Fourteenth and Fifteenth Amendments, suffragists in the National Association camp energetically pursued another constitutional approach. They proposed a broad and inclusive construction of the Fourteenth and Fifteenth Amendments, under which, they claimed, women were already enfranchised. This constitutional strategy, known at the time as the New Departure, laid the basis for the subsequent focus on a separate woman suffrage amendment, even as it embodied a radical democratic vision that the latter approach did not have.

A Question of Wording

While the Fourteenth Amendment was in the process of being ratified, woman suffragists concentrated on its second clause, because of the offensive reference to "male persons." This phrase was included by the amendment's framers because in 1867 there was an active movement demanding the franchise for women, and it would no longer do to use such gender neutral terms as "person" to mean only men. Yet such explicit exclusions of particular groups from the universal blessings of American democracy were not at all in the egalitarian spirit of the age. Perhaps it was for this reason that in writing the first section of the Fourteenth Amendment, which defines federal citizenship, the framers could not bring themselves to speak of races or sexes but instead relied on the abstractions of "persons" and "citizens." In other words, the universalities of the first section of the Fourteenth Amendment, where federal citizenship is established, run headlong into the sex-based restrictions of the second section, where voting rights are limited. Those Reconstruction Era feminists angered at the restrictive clause quickly recognized these contradictions and became determined to get women's rights demands included in the broadest possible construction of the terms "persons" and "citizens" in the first section, to use, in other words, the first section to defeat the second.

After the Fifteenth Amendment was finally ratified, the suffragists of the National Association therefore shifted from the claim that the Reconstruction amendments excluded women and began to argue instead that they were broad enough to include women's rights along with those of the freedmen. This strategic turn, known within woman suffrage circles as the New Departure, was first outlined in October 1869 by a husband and wife team of Missouri suffragists, Francis and Virginia Minor. They offered an elaborate and elegant interpretation of the Constitution to demonstrate that women already had the right to vote. Their construction rested on a consistent perspective on the whole Constitution, but especially on a broad interpretation of the Fourteenth Amendment.

The Minors' Constitutional Argument

The Minors' first premise was that popular sovereignty preceded and underlay constitutional authority. In exchange for creating government, the people expected protection of their preeminent and natural rights. This is a familiar element of revolutionary ideology. Their second premise was to equate the power of the *federal* government with the defense of individual rights, to regard federal power as positive. Historically, the federal government had been regarded as the enemy of rights; the Bill of Rights protects individual rights by enjoining the federal government from infringing on them. In the wake of the devastating experience of secession, the Fourteenth Amendment reversed the order, relying on federal power to protect its citizens against the tyrannical action of the states. The Minors thus argued in good Radical Reconstruction fashion that national citizenship had finally been established as supreme by the first section of the Fourteenth Amendment: "the immunities and privileges of American citizenship, however defined, are national in character and paramount to all state authority."

A third element in the Minors' case was that the benefits of national citizenship were equally the rights of all. This too bore the mark of the Reconstruction Era. In the words of the amendment, "all persons born or naturalized in the United States" were equally entitled to the privileges and protections of national citizenship; there were no additional qualifications. . . .

Finally, the Minors argued that the right to vote was one of the basic privileges and immunities of national citizenship. This was both the most controversial and the most important part of the New Departure constitutional construction. Popular sovereignty had always included an implicit theory of political power. The Minors' New Departure argument took this article of popular faith, reinterpreted it in light of Reconstruction Era egalitarianism, and gave it constitutional expression to produce a theory of universal rights to the suffrage. The New Departure case for universal suffrage brought together the Fourteenth Amendment, which nationalized citizenship and linked it to federal power, and the Fifteenth Amendment, which shifted the responsibility for the suffrage from the state to the national government. This theory of the suffrage underlay much of the case for black suffrage as well, but because the drive for black suffrage was so intertwined with Republican partisan interest, it was woman suffrage, which had no such political thrust behind it, that generated the most formal constitutional expression of this Reconstruction Era faith in political equality.

The New Departure was not simply a lawyer's exercise in constitutional exegesis. Reconstruction was an age of popular constitutionalism. Although presented in formal, constitutional terms, what the Minors had to say had much support among the rank and file of the women's rights movement.

The underlying spirit of the Minors' constitutional arguments was militant and activist. The basic message was that the vote was already women's right; they merely had to take it. The New Departure took on meaning precisely because of this direct action element. Many women took the argument to heart and went to the polls, determined to vote. By 1871 hundreds of women were trying to register and vote in dozens of towns all over the country. In 1871 in Philadelphia, to take one of many examples, Carrie Burnham, an unmarried tax-paying woman, got as far as having her name registered on the voting rolls. When her vote was refused, she formed the Citizens Suffrage Association of Philadelphia, dedicated not only to the defense of women's political rights but also to the greater truth that the right to vote was inherent, not bestowed. . . .

Women's Attempts to Vote

That the first examples of women's direct action voting occurred in 1868 and 1869, before the Minors made their formal constitutional argument, suggests that the New Departure grew out of a genuinely popular political faith. In 1868 in the radical, spiritualist town of Vineland, New Jersey, almost two hundred women cast their votes into a separate ballot box and then tried to get them counted along with the men's. "The platform was crowded with earnest refined intellectual women, who feel it was good for them to be there," *The Revolution* reported. "One beautiful girl said 'I feel so much stronger for having voted.'" The Vineland women repeated the effort for several years, and the ballot box eventually became an icon, which the local historical society still owns. From Vineland, the idea of women's voting spread to nearby towns, including Roseville, where, despite the American Association's official disinterest in the New Departure, Lucy Stone and her mother tried—but failed— to register their votes. . . .

News of the efforts of women to register and vote spread through formal and informal means. Women's rights and mainstream journals reported on them, but information also might have been passed by word of mouth through networks of activists. Many sisters and friends, often in different states, turn up in the stories of New Departure voting women. . . .

The voting women of the 1870s often went to the polls in groups. They believed in the suffrage as an individual right, but an individual right that would be achieved and experienced collectively. The most famous of these voting groups was the nearly fifty local activists, friends, and relatives who joined Susan B. Anthony in attempting to vote in Rochester, New York, in 1872. Virginia Minor herself was swept up in this collective activism. When she and some of her friends, all suffrage activists and Republican partisans, tried to register in St. Louis and were refused, she sued.

The Enforcement Act

The congressional passage of the Enforcement Act in May 1870 to strengthen the Fifteenth Amendment greatly accelerated women's direct action voting. The Enforcement Act was meant to enforce the freedmen's political rights by providing recourse to the federal courts and penalties against local election officials who refused the lawful votes of citizens. Women who wanted to vote saw the act as a way to use the power of the federal government for their own benefit. Benjamin Quarles reports that freedwomen in South Carolina were encouraged by Freedmen's Bureau officials to attempt to vote by appealing to the Enforcement Act. Some election officials responded to the Enforcement Act by accepting women's votes. When Nanette Gardner went to vote in Detroit in 1871, the ward official in her district was sympathetic to her protest and accepted her vote. The same man accepted Gardner's vote again in 1872, and she presented him with "a beautiful banner of white satin, trimmed with gold fringe on which was inscribed . . . 'To Peter Hill, Alderman of the Ninth Ward, Detroit. . . . By recognizing civil liberty and equality for woman, he has placed the last and brightest jewel on the brow of Michigan.'"

Most local officials, however, refused to accept women's votes. While Nanette Gardner voted successfully in Detroit, her friend Catherine Stebbins (the daughter of one of the Rochester voters) was turned away in the next ward. . . . In

Santa Cruz, California, when Ellen Van Valkenberg was similarly turned back at the polls, she became the first woman to sue an election official under the Enforcement Act for refusing her vote. By 1871 numerous New Departure woman suffrage cases were making their way through the federal courts.

Going to Congress and to the Courts

Meanwhile, the New Departure gained an advocate who moved it from the local level into national politics: Victoria Woodhull. In January of 1871 Woodhull appeared before the House Judiciary Committee to make the constitutional case for women's right to vote. No woman had ever before been invited to address a committee of the U.S. Congress. Her appearance was sponsored by Massachusetts Republican Benjamin Butler, who may have helped her outline her constitutional case. The deeply felt conviction about women's rights underlying her argument was undoubtedly her own, however. Her memorial asked Congress to pass legislation clarifying the right of all women to vote under the new Reconstruction amendments. The major difference between Woodhull and the Minors was tactical; she urged women to turn to Congress to resolve the question, while they relied on the courts. . . .

In late 1871, . . . the first New Departure cases began to reach the dockets of the federal courts. One was the case of Sara Spencer and seventy other women from the District of Columbia, who sued election officials under the Enforcement Act for refusing to permit them to vote. The District of Columbia was a deliberate choice for testing the New Departure argument. There, as advocates of black suffrage had first realized in 1867, the power of the federal government over the suffrage was not complicated by questions of dual sovereignty and states rights.

In October Judge Cartter of the Supreme Court of the District of Columbia ruled against Spencer. . . .

Susan B. Anthony's Arrest

The election of 1872 was a crisis for the Republicans. In June 1872 an important group of reformers split off from regular Republicans to run an independent presidential campaign. These political rebels, the Liberal Republicans, based their revolt on the old opposition between central government and individual rights. From the perspective of feminists, who were also looking for a political alternative to the regular Republicans, the terms of the bolt were particularly disappointing. Feminists had learned from freedmen to see the federal government not as a threat to their rights but as the agency for winning them.

To add insult to injury, the Liberal Republicans picked as their candidate Horace Greeley, a man who had made his opposition to woman suffrage clear many years before. Infuriated by the nomination of Greeley, many New Departure suffragists campaigned actively for Ulysses Grant in 1872. The regular Republicans cultivated their support, sending them about the country on official speaking tours and inserting a timid little reference to "additional rights" for women in their platform, a plank so insignificant that suffragists called it a "splinter." . . . Anthony expected that if Republicans won, they would reward women with the suffrage by recognizing the New Departure claims. She was so sure that when she came home from her last speaking tour on election day, she gathered together friends and relatives and went down to her local polling place to submit her vote for Grant. Although the local Republican official accepted the votes of fifteen of the demonstrators, including Anthony, a few weeks later a U.S. marshal came to her house and arrested her for violation of federal law—the Enforcement Act.

Anthony's arrest was a signal that the Republicans were ready to dispose of the New Departure. Because she was the most famous woman suffragist in the nation, there is good reason to suspect her arrest had been authorized at the highest level of government. The conduct of her trial several months later reinforces this suspicion. The trial was moved from her home county, where she had lectured extensively to educate potential jurors, to another venue. The judge was no small-town jurist but a recent appointee to the U.S. Supreme Court. He refused to submit the case to the jury, instead directing a guilty verdict from the bench, a practice that was later found unconstitutional. Years later, Anthony's lawyer observed, "There never was a trial in the country with one half the importance of Miss Anthony's. . . . If Anthony had won her case on the merit it would have revolutionized the suffrage of the country. . . . There was a prearranged determination to convict her. A jury trial was dangerous and so the Constitution was deliberately and openly violated." Anthony was not even permitted to appeal. . . .

The Supreme Court ruled conclusively against the New Departure two years later, in 1875. The case in which it did so was *Minor v. Happersett*, brought, appropriately enough, by Virginia Minor, the woman who had first argued that as a citizen of the United States, she was constitutionally protected in her right to vote. Like Anthony, Minor had tried to vote in the 1872 election, but when her vote was refused, she brought suit under the Enforcement Act. The Missouri courts ruled against her, and she appealed to the U.S. Supreme Court on the grounds that constitutional protections of the citizen's right to vote invalidated any state regulations to the contrary. The Court ruled unanimously against her. . . . The Court ruled starkly that "the Constitution of the United States does not confer the right of suffrage upon any one."

Effects on Black Suffrage

Here, too, there was an intimate link between the fate of woman suffragists' constitutional claims and that of the Reconstruction amendments in general. The day after the Court delivered its opinion in *Minor*, it heard arguments in *United States v. Cruikshank*. In this case and in *United States v. Reese*, black men for the first time brought suit under the Enforcement Act for protection of their political rights under the Fourteenth and Fifteenth Amendments, and the Court ruled against them. In the process of ruling against the plaintiffs, the Court found the Enforcement Act, under which both feminists and freedmen had sought protection, unconstitutional. Citing the recent decision in *Minor*, the Court ruled that inasmuch as the Constitution did not bestow the suffrage on anyone, the federal courts were outside their jurisdiction in protecting the freedmen's political rights.

The rejection of woman suffrage arguments on the grounds that the Fifteenth Amendment was only intended to forbid disfranchisement by race paved the way for a reading of the Fifteenth Amendment that was so narrow it did not even protect the freedmen themselves. In its decision in *United States v. Reese*, the Court argued that the plaintiff, although a black man, had not proved that his vote was denied on the grounds of race and so was not covered by constitutional protections. Eventually, of course, the freedmen were effectively disfranchised on grounds of income, residence, and education, all surrogates for race. Anthony had anticipated this connection. At her own trial, she predicted that the general narrowing of the Reconstruction amendments would follow on the heels of the repudiation of women's claims of equal rights under them. "If we once establish the false principle, that United States citizenship does not carry with it the right to vote in every state in this Union," she said, "there is no end to the petty freaks and cunning devices that will be resorted to to exclude one and another class of citizens from the right of suffrage."

Pursuing a New Tactic

Three years after the *Minor* defeat, suffragists began their pursuit of a separate constitutional amendment to prohibit disfranchisement on account of sex. At many levels, this was a less radical strategy. With the defeat of the New Departure, winning the vote for women was no longer tied to an overall democratic interpretation of the Constitution. To the degree that the struggle for women's votes was not strategically linked to the general defense of political democracy, that its goal was "woman suffrage" not "universal suffrage," elitist and racist tendencies faced fewer barriers, had freer reign, and imparted a more conservative character to suffragism over the next half-century.

Yet, despite this very important strategic shift, the New Departure period left a deep mark on the history of feminism. From time to time, some suffragist would see possibilities in the existing propositions of the Constitution and propose some clever legal mechanism for exploiting them. Even direct action voting never completely died away. Twenty years after the *Minor* decision, Elizabeth Grannis of New York City made her eighth attempt to register to vote. Certainly the larger spirit of militant direct action resurfaced in a spectacular way in the last decade of the American suffrage movement. The deepest mark of the New Departure, however, was to make women's rights and political equality indelibly constitutional issues. As Susan B. Anthony wrote, she "had learned . . . through the passage of the Fourteenth and Fifteenth Amendments that it had been possible to amend [the Constitution] in such a way as to enfranchise an entire new class of voters." The *Minor* case, the historian Norma Basch has observed, "drew the inferiority of women's status out of the grooves of common law assumptions and state provisions and thrust it into the maelstrom of constitutional conflict. The demand for woman suffrage . . . acquired a contentious national life."

The Adoption of Racism as a Deliberate Strategy

Barbara Hilkert Andolsen

After the women's suffrage movement was torn apart over the Reconstruction amendments that granted black men the right to vote, many white suffragists started to employ racist arguments. Ironically, women who had once been deeply involved in the abolitionist movement began to contend that they, as educated middle-class whites, were far more capable of voting intelligently than were uneducated former slaves. In the following excerpt from her book *"Daughters of Jefferson, Daughters of Bootblacks": Racism and American Feminism*, Barbara Hilkert Andolsen explores the adoption of racist rhetoric by the majority of the white suffragists. By the 1890s, Andolsen writes, the suffragist leaders realized that a federal amendment was their best hope for obtaining the franchise, which meant they would need to sway the southern states. They therefore employed racist arguments and rhetoric designed to assure southern politicians that women's suffrage would not threaten the white supremacy policy of the South, she maintains. If the suffragists had not resorted to racist tactics, the passage of the Nineteenth Amendment undoubtedly would have been delayed, according to the author, but this fact in no way excuses their betrayal of black women's right to vote. Andolsen is the Helen Bennett Mc-Murray Professor of Social Ethics at Monmouth University in West Long Branch, New Jersey.

Appeals to Anglo-Saxon superiority undercut the moral foundation for white women's suffrage. Suffragists claimed that all Americans shared a fundamental right as persons to participate in the political decisions that shaped their personal and corporate lives. Racist appeals and tactics are absolutely inconsistent with this belief. . . . Appeals to female superiority as well as racist appeals eviscerated the moral fiber of a movement that offered at its best a fresh vision of American society as a society in which all men *and women* are created equal and endowed with equal political rights. In order to evaluate suffragists' tactics and arguments fairly, it is necessary to place them within the specific political context in which they were used. White suffragists resorted to tacit cooperation with segregation practices and to racist and nativist claims in part because Southern support was essential for ratification of a woman suffrage amendment to the federal constitution.

The Necessity of Southern Support

Feminists tried several tactics to gain the vote for women. First, they attempted to convince Republicans to draft the Fourteenth and Fifteenth Amendments in universal terms. Thus, early in the Reconstruction period, some supporters of woman suffrage tried to secure the suffrage for black men and all women at the same time. But the Republicans refused to draft such a universal suffrage amendment, insisting that there was no general public support for woman suffrage. They feared that black male suffrage would be threatened by coupling it with the more controversial woman suffrage.

Republicans supported black male suffrage not only because it was morally right, but also because black men, grateful to the party of Abraham Lincoln for emancipation, were likely to vote Republican. White women, who constituted the bulk of women to benefit from woman suffrage, found it hard to persuade either political party to support their cause, because women were not likely to vote for a single party. Woman suffrage did not benefit Republicans in the same direct way that Negro suffrage did.

Second, suffrage leaders attempted to secure a Supreme Court decision declaring that women as citizens had a constitutionally guaranteed right to vote. This hope was dashed by the 1874 Supreme Court decision in the case of Minor vs. Happersett. In that case the justices declared unanimously that the United States Constitution does not guarantee suffrage to *any* citizen. Therefore, state laws restricting suffrage to men were not unconstitutional.

A Different Voice

History professor Rosalyn Terborg-Penn is the author of African American Women in the Struggle for the Vote, 1850–1920. *In the following excerpt, Terborg-Penn explains that African-American women continued to work for suffrage after the Civil War, but their arguments and strategies began to significantly converge from those of white suffragists.*

In the period following the collapse of the American Equal Rights Association, African American women's voices became more evident as their views about woman suffrage began to differ from those of white women. Even the watersheds in the movement differed for the two groups. For white women, the schism that had resulted with the birth of two rival national woman suffrage associations ended in 1890, when the two organizations reunited to achieve votes for women. For Black women the turning point began in the 1870s and 1880s, as their suffrage arguments took on new meaning, more closely identified with their unique status as women of color. They never abandoned the universal suffrage cause, as did many mainstream suffragists. As a result, African American woman suffrage strategies combined demands for Black women's right to vote and civil rights for all Black people. Even when African American women adopted the strategies of the larger woman suffrage movement—demanding suffrage based on the citizenship clause of the Fourteenth Amendment, or calling for a federal amendment to enfranchise women—they included caveats specifically designed for the needs of Black women.

Rosalyn Terborg-Penn, *African American Women in the Struggle for the Vote, 1850–1920*, 1998.

The Failure of the State Suffrage Approach

Third, woman suffrage leaders attempted to obtain the suffrage on a state by state basis. They tried to get state legislators to enfranchise women through legislative action. In a few states such as Wyoming, this was a successful tactic. But in some states the legislators refused to take direct action. In other states, where they were prohibited from enacting woman suffrage through legislation alone, voter referenda were held on the issue. According to Carrie Chapman Catt, suffragists engaged in 56 state woman suffrage campaigns, made 480 attempts to get state legislatures to pass state woman suffrage amendments, and petitioned 47 state constitutional conventions to enfranchise women. Most of these attempts were unsuccessful. By the turn of the century, after more than twenty-five years of effort, women had full suffrage in only four states—Wyoming, Utah, Colorado, and Idaho.

Since state by state suffrage campaigns were so slow and so unproductive, astute suffrage leaders finally realized that a federal constitutional amendment was the only realistic means to secure the franchise for American women. Once women like Catt committed themselves to a federal constitutional amendment, they needed the support of some Southern states in order to ensure ratification. If thirteen states failed to ratify a proposed amendment, women would not be able to vote. Suffrage leaders considered Maryland, Mississippi, Louisiana, Florida, Kentucky, Tennessee, Virginia, North Carolina, South Carolina, Georgia, Alabama, and Delaware as Southern states. If these twelve held against woman suffrage, the loss of even one other state would defeat the amendment. Since a margin of one state was too slender, suffragists sought to crack the solid South. This refusal to write off the Southern states was vindicated when Tennessee became the final state to ratify the Nineteenth Amendment.

White Dominance in the South

White suffragists began serious organizational work throughout the South about 1890. In the 1890s white Southerners were struggling to reestablish absolute dominance over blacks. Black men were being disfranchised in state after state, and stringent Jim Crow codes were being enacted. The race question was the paramount social issue in the minds of Southerners during this period. Therefore, the most expedient way to gain white, Southern support was to insist that woman suffrage in no way affected the social arrangements of the region. . . .

The race question bedeviled white woman suffrage leaders from their first serious efforts to organize Southern white women until the last state, Tennessee, ratified the suffrage amendment. . . . White Southern men constantly claimed that black women would vote in large numbers while white "ladies" would remain modestly at home. Thus these men concluded that woman suffrage would bring more blacks than whites to the polls.

Black women voters posed a special threat to Southern political arrangements. Whites prevented black *men* from voting through the use of terrorist tactics, including arson, beating, maiming, castration, and lynching. But "chivalrous" white men sometimes drew the line at employing similar violence against black women. One Mississippi senator told Catt bluntly, "We are not afraid to maul a black man . . . if he dares to vote, but we can't treat women, even black women, that way. No, we'll allow no woman suffrage. It may be right, but we won't have it." W.E.B. DuBois also judged that widespread press attention would prevent Southerners from using violence to keep enfranchised black women from the polls, although he had few illusions about Southern chivalry where black women were concerned. "Even Southern 'gentlemen,' as used as they are to the mistreatment of colored women, cannot in the blaze of present publicity physically beat them away from the polls."

At least one powerful Southern politician, Senator Benjamin R. Tillman, believed that black women were more dangerous foes than black men were. He told the editor of a suffrage newspaper, "Experience has taught us that negro women are much more aggressive in asserting the 'rights of that race' than the negro men are." He had no wish to see such implacable opponents of white supremacy gain the added weapon of the ballot.

Finally, white Southern political leaders feared that agitation for woman suffrage in the South would draw unwanted attention to Southern polling practices in general. By the 1890s the federal government had pulled back completely from enforcement of the Fifteenth Amendment guarantee of black male suffrage. Federal officials looked the other way while Southern legislators systematically stripped black men of their right to vote. White Southerners feared that a successful campaign for woman suffrage would reopen the question of suffrage in general. The federal authorities might challenge such Southern state constitutional provisions as the grandfather clause and the poll tax. Southerners feared that discussion of woman suffrage would ultimately open up subjects better left closed.

The Southern Strategy

If white suffragists had spoken out consistently for the civil rights of blacks and/or if they had enforced a policy of racial equality in all National American Woman Suffrage Association (NAWSA) activities, they would have aroused strong white, Southern antipathy toward woman suffrage. If white suffragists had analyzed how racism as well as sexism barred black women from the polls and if white suffragists had explicitly stated that woman suffrage must include federally enforced access to the polls for black women, they would have played right into the hands of antisuffragists who had a Southern strategy for preventing ratification of woman suffrage. Carrie Chapman Catt informed a colleague,

> The plan of the antis is to find thirteen states which they can hold out against ratification. They have been good enough to give us the list of the states. They are the solid south states. . . . I do not think they would have very much trouble in holding all of these out. Now they will get their thirteenth state in New Jersey, Connecticut, Vermont, or New Hampshire. They tell us so.

If suffragists lost all the Southern states they stood to lose the ratification campaign itself.

Times had changed since the 1860s, when many American reformers supported universal human rights, struggling to advance the cause of women and blacks at the same time. By the last quarter of the nineteenth century the moral fervor that had fueled the antislavery movement and the Civil War was exhausted. The nation sought reconciliation between North and South. If that reconciliation was purchased at the expense of black civil rights, there were few to protest. In the words of [historian] Vernon Parrington, "the New England leadership subsided and the tired New England conscience went on vacation."

The tired New England conscience was sorely pressed to deal with immigration and industrialization at home. Carrie Chapman Catt described the late nineteenth century as a period characterized by "inertia in the growth of democracy which has come as a reaction following the aggressive movements that with possibly ill-advised haste enfranchised the foreigner, the negro, and the Indian. Perilous conditions, seeming to follow from the introduction into the body politic of vast numbers of irresponsible citizens, have made the nation timid." Universal suffrage was not a self-evident good. White, native-born suffragists either had to stand for universal suffrage out of season or deemphasize their universal claims, while stressing the numbers of able Anglo-Saxon women whose enfranchisement would benefit society. They chose the latter course.

Elizabeth Cady Stanton's Racist Rhetoric

White suffragists had a right to concentrate their energies on obtaining political justice for women. They acted on the basis of legitimate group interest when they opposed the Fourteenth and Fifteenth Amendments to the Constitution as hindrances to woman suffrage. Elizabeth Cady Stanton's position was convincing: "If you are a slave, it is your business to break the yoke that galls your own neck; you are to accept slavery and degradation at no price, from no mistaken notions of white men's rights or black men's wrongs." Disturbingly, however, Stanton used hyperbole to describe the plight of white women, who never experienced slavery. She also seemed to deny or to trivialize "black men's wrongs" by connecting them with "mistaken notions."

In fact, Stanton's Reconstruction-era position was fraught with moral ambiguity. On the one hand, Stanton's ideal policy was the immediate enfranchisement of black men and all women. She genuinely thought that now that the "constitutional door" was open, women should "avail ourselves of the strong arm and blue uniform of the black soldier to walk in by his side, and thus make the gap so wide that no privileged class could ever close it against the humblest citizen of the republic." On the other hand, Stanton was an elitist. She clearly viewed herself and other educated women as superior citizens. Her class elitism combined with racist and nativist prejudice. Stanton stereotyped blacks and immigrants as an ignorant, degraded, and dangerous political element that needed to be outweighed by refined Anglo-Saxon women. In Reconstruction-era debates about suffrage, Stanton used demeaning racial nicknames and appealed to racist and nativist prejudice in her attempt to rouse women and men who shared her race and class privilege to support woman suffrage.

Moreover, Stanton's commitment to *black women's rights* was ambivalent at best. She criticized those reformers who made black male suffrage their highest priority. She accused them of ignoring the needs of one half of the black race. She alleged that her opponents were leaving two million black women "with but a change of masters, still in a condition of slavery." Stanton's own energies were increasingly focused on gaining the ballot for educated, cultured women. Her grudging admission that she would prefer to see Bridget and Dinah enfranchised rather than Patrick and Sambo showed that she did not accept most immigrant and black women as equals. Stanton's appeals to race and class sentiments cannot be condoned. . . .

The Failed Vision

The moral irony of the American woman suffrage movement is that the suffragists committed the very sin for which they called others to task. They themselves lost sight of the vision of a society in which *all* adults have a voice in government. They insisted on the universality of human rights principles when they were the beneficiaries of a thorough-going application of the principles; but, in their concern to defend their own rights, they gradually turned away from situations in which they were called upon to demand unequivocally those same rights for black women and men. . . .

Anna Howard Shaw recognized the moral loss white suffragists inflicted upon the movement when they made overtly racist appeals. In private correspondence Shaw argued that the NAWSA should repudiate claims that woman suffrage would safeguard white supremacy throughout the South lest it appear that "we really don't believe in the justice of suffrage, but simply that certain classes or races should dominate the government." Shaw also argued for the primacy of universal human rights as a moral position in her first address as president of the NAWSA. Shaw reminded her audience that any social movement must have both an ideal and an organization to promote that ideal. However, as a social movement begins to experience some success, there is a temptation to compromise the ideal in order to build a more effective social organization. Shaw understood the seductive lure of policies that would enhance the numerical strength and/or public influence of a social movement at the expense of a clear advocacy of its original principles. So she cautioned that the suffrage movement must not grow silent concerning its own highest principles, but ever more clearly articulate them in its public discourse.

> We must guard against the reactionary spirit which marks our time, and stand unfalteringly for the principle of perfect equality of rights and opportunities for all. *We must refuse to restrict our demand for justice or bound it by any line or race, sex, creed, or any other condition which does not apply equally to every citizen of the republic.*

A Black Suffragist's Opinion

Black suffragist Anna Julia Cooper also urged suffragists to be loyal to the movement's broadest vision. She judged that the women's movement was of great moral significance because it was "an embodiment, if its pioneers could only realize it, of the universal good." Cooper was convinced that when race, color, sex, and condition no longer nullified a person's inalienable right to life, liberty, and the pursuit of happiness, "then woman's lesson is taught and woman's cause is won—not the white woman nor the black woman nor the red woman, but the cause of every man or woman who has writhed silently under a mighty wrong." Cooper believed that white women's rights were inextricably linked to the rights of all other human beings. Any tactic that obscured that link diminished the moral force of the woman suffrage movement.

Cooper understood the pressure white Southerners were exerting on the women's movement. She appreciated the firm commitment to principle that was required to refrain from advancing only the narrow interests of privileged white women. It was very tempting to promote the rights of such women at the expense of blacks, immigrants, and Native Americans. "But, may it not be that, as women, the very lessons which seem hardest to master now, are possibly the ones most essential for our promotion to a higher grade of work?"

Unfortunately, Shaw and Cooper were never able to persuade their fellow suffragists that compromising their call for universal human rights would be fatal to the moral significance of the suffrage movement. So women won the vote, but lost the soul of a movement that originally had advocated full political rights for all citizens of the republic—female as well as male, black as well as white, foreign-born as well as native-born. . . .

The Price of Integrity

If the suffragists had continued to state clearly that they favored the vote for women as an aspect of the universal human right to a voice in government, the passage of the Nineteenth Amendment could have been seriously delayed. If they had frankly acknowledged that the logic of their position encompassed genuine access to the polls for blacks and immigrants, the chance to get the vote in 1920 would have been jeopardized. . . .

Once it became clear that a federal constitutional amendment would be necessary in order to ensure woman suffrage, suffragists needed the support of at least some white Southern politicians. However, most white Southerners opposed any public policy that threatened white supremacy. Woman suffragists faced a hard choice: they could pander to white supremacists in order to gain the ballot, or they could stand for woman suffrage as one aspect of universal suffrage—white and black, male and female—and lose crucial political support.

White suffragists were entitled to press for woman suffrage as a priority, but they were wrong to use racist means to obtain their goal. They eviscerated the moral power of the woman suffrage movement when they denigrated black, Native American, and immigrant men. . . . White suffragists should have refrained from using racist and nativist arguments even at the cost of delaying passage of a woman suffrage amendment. When these white suffragists squandered the moral capital of the natural rights tradition in order to ensure prompt ratification of the Nineteenth Amendment, they impoverished their moral legacy for twentieth-century women and men.

Chapter 4

The Antisuffragists

Turning|Points
IN WORLD HISTORY

The Various Factions of Antisuffragists

Anastatia Sims

In the following article, Anastatia Sims lists some of the key players in the opposition to women's suffrage and examines their motivations. For example, she writes, liquor manufacturers worked against the passage of suffrage because they feared that women voters would favor measures to prohibit alcohol. Although antisuffragists were active throughout the United States, Sims notes that people in the South—who tended to be more conservative and traditional—were extremely opposed to women's suffrage, and the suffrage movement had difficulty making inroads in that region. Sims particularly focuses on the women who formed such antisuffragist organizations as the National Association Opposed to Woman Suffrage. In many respects, according to the author, these women understood better than the suffragists did that the right to vote would introduce radical changes into the lives of American women. Sims is a professor of history at Georgia Southern University in Statesboro and the author of *The Power of Femininity in the New South: Women and Politics in North Carolina, 1883–1920.*

"Victorious movements record their history," wrote Carrie Chapman Catt and Nettie Rogers Shuler in 1923; "vanquished ones rarely do." Thus Catt and Shuler, along with other veterans of the seventy-two-year campaign to win votes for women, produced numerous books and articles detailing their struggle, while most antisuffragists remained silent. Since the antis (as they were called) refused to speak

Excerpted from "Beyond the Ballot: The Radical Vision of the Antisuffragists," by Anastatia Sims, in *Votes for Women! The Woman Suffrage Movement in Tennessee, the South, and the Nation,* edited by Marjorie Spruill Wheeler. Copyright ©1995 by the University of Tennessee Press. Reprinted with permission from the University of Tennessee Press.

for themselves in the aftermath of their defeat, historians have had to rely heavily on the unflattering portraits the victors painted of their opponents—accounts that emphasize adjectives like "sinister" and "unscrupulous" and "vile."

The "Antis"

The antis were the villains in the suffrage drama, and they played their part well. Their alliances with liquor manufacturers, railroad companies, and cotton mill owners linked them to political corruption, dishonest business practices, and exploitative labor policies. Their dire predictions that woman suffrage would destroy the home and family and, in the words of one opponent, "ring the death-knell of modern civilization," made them easy to ridicule at the time and sound downright absurd to modern ears. Their devotion to states' rights and white supremacy places them in the category of losers who, by current standards, deserved to lose. While acknowledging their significance, then, it is also tempting to treat them as narrow-minded reactionaries who were unable to envision a role for women that reached beyond the traditional boundaries of domesticity.

But the antis cannot be dismissed so easily. An analysis of the arguments against suffrage in general, and against the federal amendment in particular, suggests an alternative interpretation. By 1920, opponents of the Nineteenth (or Susan B. Anthony) Amendment had a wider vision of its implications than some of its advocates. Unlike many white suffragists, who had come to regard the vote as the capstone of the women's rights movement, white antisuffragists, especially those in the South, saw it as the harbinger of more radical reforms. The Nineteenth Amendment, they believed, raised questions that extended far beyond the immediate issue of enfranchising women. They predicted that if it passed, it would unleash forces that would rip apart the fabric of racial and gender relations. The antis looked beyond the ballot to the potentially revolutionary consequences of votes for women.

Opposition to woman suffrage was born along with the suffrage movement itself. To many nineteenth-century

Americans, the idea of women voting seemed ludicrous, and most people refused to take the early suffragists seriously. Opponents attempted to organize for the first time in Washington, D.C., in the early 1870s. As the suffrage movement gained momentum, the antis stepped up their activities. In 1911, female antis in the Northeast formed the National Association Opposed to Woman Suffrage (NAOWS). By 1916, it had branches in twenty-five states and claimed three hundred and fifty thousand members. Ad hoc committees, leagues, and associations for both men and women appeared in states where suffrage legislation was being considered. The antisuffrage organizations were never as large or as structured as the National American Woman Suffrage Association. Antisuffrage was less a cohesive movement than a loose coalition of forces with a common goal. But the antis succeeded in keeping their ideas in the public mind, and in setting the terms of the debate over votes for women.

The antis assumed that the battle over woman suffrage was the opening round in a full-scale revolution in relations between the sexes. They recognized that the demand for the ballot challenged the distinction between public (masculine) and private (feminine) spheres that was the foundation of white, middle-class gender relations. As antisuffrage pamphleteer Emily Bissell explained, "The vote is part of man's work. Ballot-box, cartridge box, jury box, sentry box all go together in his part of life. Woman cannot step in and take the responsibilities and duties of voting without assuming his place very largely." If women were accepted as the equals of men in politics, they might also expect economic and social equality. They might reject domesticity and seek to enter "male" professions (as, in fact, some women were already doing). If they refused to accept male dominance in the public realm, women might question men's authority at home as well. The Reverend Albert Taylor Bledsoe, writing in the *Southern Review* in 1871, cited the example of ancient Rome to demonstrate the consequences of women's rights. Quoting from the work of historian Edward Hartpole Lecky, Bledsoe argued that when Roman women won legal independence, "the principles of co-equal partnership" replaced "autocracy" in marriage. Later anti literature echoed the same theme. "Woman suffrage," wrote [antisuffragist] Isaac Lockhart Peebles in 1920, "wants the wife to be as much the ruler as the husband, if not the chief ruler."

The antis opposed woman suffrage because they saw it as one plank in a wide-ranging feminist platform. Suffragists repelled the anti attack by retreating from feminism, at least in public. They called the anti charges that women would use public power to restructure private relationships absurd. Increasingly, the moderate suffragists who came to dominate the movement in the twentieth century insisted that they were content with their jobs as wives and mothers and wanted the ballot in order to fulfill their domestic duties more effectively. They hoped, as well, to impose "feminine" standards of purity, morality, and cooperation on a corrupt, competitive political system. Many suffragists believed the vote would enable women to apply their home-making skills to "public housekeeping" in ways that would benefit women themselves and society as a whole. However, they did not expect enfranchisement to lead to a radical redefinition of gender roles. They argued, as Professor Jean Elshtain wrote in an essay published in 1982, that "Women would use the vote to change society, but the vote would not change women."

While the antis predicted that political equality might enhance woman's power in the private sphere, they also feared (ironically) that it would diminish her status in public. Anticipating the arguments some former suffragists would use against the Equal Rights Amendment in the 1920s, the antis warned that legal and political equality would eradicate laws designed to protect women. Women would have to pay alimony and serve on juries. Legislation regulating the wages and hours of working women would be struck down. "To treat women exactly as men," wrote NAOWS president Josephine Jewell Dodge, "is to deny all the progress through evolution which has been made by an increasing specialization in function. Woman suffrage in its last analysis is a retrogressive movement.". . .

Antisuffragism in the South

The South was a stronghold of antisuffrage sentiment, and southern opponents made their own contributions to antisuffrage ideology. White southerners never forgot that the women's rights movement was an offspring of the abolitionist crusade. Long after the Civil War, some continued to regard the effort to enfranchise women as part of a Yankee plot to overthrow southern civilization. White southerners continued to cherish the ideal of the lady. They were slower than other Americans to accept *any* alteration in women's roles, and they were particularly distressed by women's increasing involvement in politics. Furthermore, woman suffrage was part of a package of Progressive reforms—including prohibition, regulation of child labor, and expanded social welfare programs—that many of the South's political and economic elite opposed. In a region that historically resisted change—particularly change imposed from the outside—antisuffrage propaganda found a receptive audience.

In the South, more than in any other section of the nation, any change in women's status brought with it portents of social upheaval, for in the South ideas about gender were inextricably intertwined with ideas about race. The exaltation of white women went hand in hand with the degradation of African-American men. At one end of the South's racial spectrum was the lady, her unblemished white skin a visible sign of her purity. White men worshiped her as the symbol of all that was good in their civilization. At the opposite end of the scale was the lustful and strong African-American male. Whites saw him as a savage brute who must be controlled because he could not be tamed. White southern men, self-appointed guardians of the lady and all she represented, used the need to "protect" white women to justify slavery, lynching, disfranchisement, and segregation. The survival of the South's social hierarchy—and the white male dominance that went along with it—depended on everyone—male, female, white, black—accepting the place assigned by race, class, and gender. Any rebellion from any quarter could topple the entire structure. Many white southerners (male and female) feared that an expansion of power for white women would necessarily expand the power of African Americans. . . .

The Liquor Industry

Long before they got the vote, southern women of both races in clubs, temperance societies, and civic leagues committed themselves to stamping out political corruption, exploitative labor practices, and immorality. They won some important victories. The Woman's Christian Temperance Union, for example, played a key role in prohibition campaigns throughout the South. Industrialists feared that women voters would be formidable adversaries. As the president of the Wholesale Brewers' Association declared in 1912: "We need not fear the churches; the men are voting the old tickets; we need not fear the ministers, for the most part they follow the men of the churches; we need not fear the YMCA; it does not do any aggressive work; but gentlemen, we need to fear the Woman's Christian Temperance Union and the ballot in the hands of women, therefore, gentlemen, fight woman suffrage." And fight they did. "We now know," Ella Stewart reported in the *Annals of the American Academy of Political and Social Science* in 1914, "that the center and strength of the antisuffrage army are the liquor traffic and its vicious allies." Distillers, mill owners, and railroad executives, armed with plenty of money and reinforced by powerful political friends, waged a covert war against woman suffrage. . . .

Across the nation, distillers, brewers, and factory owners (particularly those who employed large numbers of women and children) subsidized campaigns against state suffrage referenda and against the Susan B. Anthony Amendment, although they worked, for the most part, in secrecy. A Senate investigation of the United States Brewers' Association in 1918 revealed that the organization had actively tried to defeat woman suffrage in several states. In some states textile manufacturers joined with liquor interests. Walter Clark, chief justice of the North Carolina Supreme Court, believed that "the Whiskey Interests and the Cotton Mill owners of New England and the South" underwrote antisuffrage campaigns. . . .

Women's Power and Influence

One of the underlying themes of the antisuffrage campaign [was that] antisuffragists never underestimated the power of women. Male antisuffragists might talk of feminine frailty, irrationality, and emotionalism. Female antis might insist that women needed male protection or that they were above politics. But antisuffragists—male and female alike—agreed that women were a powerful force. As Ella Stewart explained, the strength of the opposition was "a high tribute to womanhood."

Antis disagreed among themselves, however, over how suffrage would affect feminine power. Men feared that enfranchised women would use the vote to undermine existing political and economic structures and to challenge masculine authority throughout society. The prospect of a united bloc of female voters voting *against* child labor and *for* prohibition, *against* political corruption and *for* honest government, had wealthy, influential men running scared, willing to resort to extreme tactics to keep the ballot out of women's hands. Female antis, on the other hand, believed that the vote might actually *reduce* women's power and influence in the public arena. The vision of women using the vote as a stepping stone to step off the pedestal and compete with men repelled many intelligent, capable women who realized that votes alone would not ensure political equality.

Both men and women in the anti ranks acknowledged the symbolic potential of suffrage. They recognized that, for better or for worse, if women took on one "masculine" role they might also attempt to assume—or be forced to accept—rights, responsibilities, and privileges reserved to men in other areas as well. The antis knew—to return to Jean Elshtain's observation about the suffragists—that women could change society with the vote and that the vote *could* change women. Antis saw the power inherent in woman suffrage, and they fought long and hard to keep that power from being unleashed. Far from misunderstanding the implications of votes for women, the antis understood them all too well.

Antisuffragist Arguments

Aileen S. Kraditor

Aileen S. Kraditor is a retired professor of history from Boston University in Massachusetts and the author of *The Ideas of the Woman Suffrage Movement, 1890–1920*, from which the following essay is excerpted. In it, Kraditor describes the major arguments against women's suffrage as presented in the antisuffrage movement's propaganda. These arguments were typically based on theological, biological, or sociological premises, the author notes, and tended to contradict each other. According to Kraditor, a close examination of these arguments reveals the fear that motivated the antisuffrage movement's objection to votes for women. She writes that both male and female antisuffragists believed that giving women the franchise would destroy the cohesiveness of the home by placing husbands and wives in political opposition. Since the antisuffragists considered the family to be the main unit of society, they feared that society itself would be irrevocably harmed by the family instability that women's suffrage would create, Kraditor explains.

The movement of women to secure the vote was a conscious assault on ideas and institutions long accepted by most middle-class Americans. In response to the suffragist challenge, the antisuffragists made those ideas explicit and rationalized those institutions. That antisuffragism was essentially defensive is evidenced by the pattern of its organizational activity, which waxed or waned as the suffragist campaigns intensified or stagnated. Unlike the suffragist movement, antisuffragism was not characterized by mass activity. The antis published several periodicals and organized many societies, but their activity was sporadic. It was their ideology that was significant. The antis defined the context within which suffragist ideas developed, posed the problems the suffragists had to solve, and asked the questions they had to answer. They even inadvertently pointed out which parts of the fortress could be taken with ease and which parts could not be captured without ingenious new weapons. Their propaganda will be examined to discover what the world, real and ideal, looked like through the antisuffragists' eyes, and what they considered woman's place in it to be.

Theological Arguments

Close to the heart of all antisuffragist orators, particularly congressmen, was a sentimental vision of Home and Mother, equal in sanctity to God and the Constitution. Although all four entities regularly appeared in various combinations in antisuffragist propaganda, it was the link of woman to the home that underlay the entire ideology. The antis regarded each woman's vocation as determined not by her individual capacities or wishes but by her sex. Men were expected to have a variety of ambitions and capabilities, but all women were destined from birth to be full-time wives and mothers. To dispute this eternal truth was to challenge theology, biology, or sociology.

The commonest form of the theological argument was no argument at all, but the mere announcement that God had ordained man and woman to perform different functions in the state as well as in the home, or that he had intended woman for the home and man for the world. . . .

St. Paul was the other religious authority for antisuffragism; the relevant passages were those in the Epistles to the Corinthians and to the Galatians, in which the apostle enjoined women to silence in the church and obedience to their husbands. One scholarly essayist [Robert Afton Holland] declared that "The first principle of religion is obedience. The woman who does not rightly obey her husband will not obey the God who enjoins her submission. Her rights-ism is simply sex-atheism, and can only generate atheistic minds." But since the religious argument against woman suffrage was intended to persuade women and must also appeal to men who approved of higher education and other nineteenth-century advances in women's status, the antis had to demonstrate that the divinely ordained division of labor and male headship in the family did not imply male superiority. How well the attempt to reconcile the antis' interpretation of the Bible with their own conception of the equality of the sexes succeeded may be judged from the following analysis [published by the Man-Suffrage Association in 1915]:

> In the origin of civilization there is every evidence *(see Genesis)* that woman was given by the Creator a position that is inseparable from and is the complement of man. She was made man's helper, was given a servient place (not necessarily inferior) and man the dominant place (not necessarily superior) in the division of labor.

In fact, the antis maintained that this division, far from implying woman's inferiority, actually insured her supremacy as long as she remained in the sphere to which she had been assigned. The division of labor required men to work, govern, and protect and women to bear and raise children and create for their men a refuge from the cares of the world.

Biological Theories

The biological argument, designed to appeal to people who needed a scientific sanction for their beliefs, rested on two assumptions: that souls as well as bodies had sexual attributes, and that women were physically incapable of undertaking the various duties concomitant with voting. The first assumption underlay those antisuffragist arguments which identified femininity with inherent emotionalism and illogicality, traits inconsistent with the proper exercise of the suffrage. [Minister] Octavius B. Frothingham explained the difference between masculine and feminine characteristics:

> The masculine represents *judgment*, the practicable, the expedient, the possible, while the feminine represents *emotion*, what ought to be, the dream of excellence, the vision of complete beauty. . . . The predominance of sentiment in woman renders her essentially an idealist. She jumps at con-

clusions. . . . She can make no allowance for slowness, for tentative or compromising measures. Her reforms are sweeping. She would close all the bars and liquor saloons, and make it a crime to sell intoxicating drink.

Antis who resorted to this argument frequently took care to disclaim any implication of contempt for illogical woman. On the contrary, woman had a higher faculty than logic, "woman's intuition," which yielded a perception of truth beyond that possible to man, provided the intuition was employed in its proper sphere. Just as women were superior to men in the feminine sphere, so their own method of arriving at truths was also superior to men's, but was useless in the political realm. Since feminine illogic was believed to be an attribute of sex, the antis felt that the possession of it made women especially attractive to men. A minister [Charles H. Parkhurst] spoke of that "logical infirmity of mind which constitutes one of the weaknesses, and I might also say, one of the charms of the feminine constitution." Thus the innate emotional differences made it imperative for women to use their "feminine intuition" and visions of abstract justice to instill the proper ideals in their young sons who would then grow up into fine citizens, employing their masculine logic and reasonableness to govern wisely, tempering idealism with practicality.

The second variety of the biological argument described woman's physical constitution as too delicate to withstand the turbulence of political life. Her alleged weakness, nervousness, and proneness to fainting would certainly be out of place in polling booths and party conventions. The following pronouncement [by Max G. Schlapp] combined both types of biological argument in charming fashion and bore the endorsement of both a scientist and a priest:

A woman's brain evolves emotion rather than intellect; and whilst this feature fits her admirably as a creature burdened with the preservation and happiness of the human species, it painfully disqualifies her for the sterner duties to be performed by the intellectual faculties. The best wife and mother and sister would make the worst legislator, judge and police.

The excessive development of the emotional in her nervous system, ingrafts on the female organization, a neurotic or hysterical condition, which is the source of much of the female charm when it is kept within due restraints. In . . . moments of excitement . . . it is liable to explode in violent paroxysms. . . . Every woman, therefore, carries this power of irregular, illogical and incongruous action; and no one can foretell when the explosion will come.

A different sort of biological argument purported to deduce antisuffragism from the theory of evolution which was then rapidly becoming respectable. Darwinism was cited to demonstrate that the highest forms of life were the most specialized. Therefore, the proposal that woman invade man's sphere must be retrogressive rather than progressive.

Inconsistencies

Suffragists often expressed amused perplexity at the antis' inconsistency. The latter insisted that the eternal differences between the sexes were so great that women *could* not participate in government, and in the next breath assumed that those differences were so fragile that to preserve them women *must* not participate in government. Perhaps the antis were manifesting something more than inconsistency. They were living in a period in which the traditional roles of men and women, hitherto clearly defined and separated, were changing. Men were performing women's tasks, as chefs, tailors, and laundry operators. Women were entering the male sphere as voters, scholars, and breadwinners. The literature of antisuffragism understandably contains few explicit statements of the widespread confusion that existed in that period as to the social implications of sex differences. But perhaps that confusion may help to explain both the antis' inconsistency and their fierce determination to maintain the traditional distinctions, whatever the source of those distinctions might be.

This "separate but equal" doctrine of the respective spheres of man and woman was a central part of the sociological argument against woman suffrage, which declared that social peace and the welfare of the human race depended upon woman's staying home, having children, and keeping out of politics. Voting implied much more than simply dropping a ballot in a box once a year. It meant on the part of woman an entire intellectual reorientation. Having the right to vote imposed the duty of exercising that right competently, which required doing whatever was necessary to become politically intelligent. At the very least it meant that women must become informed on political issues, and the inevitable discussions on such subjects between spouses would cause disagreements which in turn would raise the divorce rate. Woman suffrage would lead to neglect of children by politically active mothers and, thereby, to increased juvenile delinquency, because the franchise would inexorably draw women into political organization and even into office. And, of course, women's political activity would inject sex into politics. To illustrate this danger, the Massachusetts Anti-Suffrage Committee warned that woman suffrage meant "pretty girls buttonholing strange men on the streets on Election Day in behalf of the 'Handsome' candidate" and that it meant women on juries listening to shocking testimony which they would then have to discuss with strange men behind locked doors through the night; such things, the committee concluded, were of course "unthinkable." The rewards of office, which interfered with maternal duties, would put a premium on singleness and childlessness. Women who thus invaded the masculine sphere would forfeit their right to chivalry, that mode of male behavior which ennobled society. Such activity would also encourage that specious independence of woman slyly advocated by supporters of free love and socialism.

The Family and Social Stability

To comprehend the horror with which the antis contemplated these possibilities, it is necessary to understand their belief that the unit of society was not the individual but the family. A man voted not for himself alone but for all the members of his family, as their political representative. Social stability depended upon the existence of many tightly knit families, each of which was, in the antisuffragist view, a state in miniature, relatively isolated from outside influences and interests. . . .

The head of each family was its sole link to the outside world and its spokesman in the state. The family's leader within each home was the wife and mother. To endow that wife and mother with the franchise, therefore, would dissolve society

No Visible Effects

One of the suffragists' primary arguments was that women voters would introduce many beneficial reforms. After a number of western states gave women the vote, antisuffragists quickly pointed out that these promised reforms were not taking place, as William O'Neill writes in the following excerpt from his book Feminism in America: A History. *O'Neill is a history professor at Rutgers University in New Brunswick, New Jersey.*

The most valuable weapon in the anti-suffragist arsenal was not rhetorical. It was the evidence accumulated in those states and territories where women did vote. Few of the early examples proved much one way or another. They were all in underpopulated Western areas with atypical problems. . . . Colorado, on the other hand, was a reasonably good demonstration of what woman suffrage would mean in practice. It had at least one real urban center, and was more highly developed than the other mountain states. Although antis had naturally opposed woman suffrage in Colorado . . . it proved in many ways a blessing to them. Almost immediately they began pointing out that Colorado did nothing to advance the case for woman suffrage. As antisuffragist Priscella Leonard wrote, "Equal Suffrage has not raised the pay of women workers in Colorado, during its three years of trial there, nor in Wyoming where it has been in force for a quarter of a century; a fact which its advocates agree to ignore, but which is convincing to any intelligent mind." Federal Judge Moses Hallett summed up the feelings of most Colorado citizens when he remarked that "the presence of women at the polls has only augmented the total votes; it has worked no radical changes. It has produced no special reforms, and it has had no particularly purifying effect upon politics."

William O'Neill, *Feminism in America: A History*, 1989.

into a heterogeneous mass of separate persons, whose individual rather than family interests would thenceforth receive political representation. For this reason, the vote would not be merely a quantitative addition to all the other rights women had acquired in the preceding two generations. The franchise was not just another new right to add to higher education, equal guardianship of children, and ownership of one's own earnings in the march of women toward full equality with men. Suffrage meant a qualitative change in the social and familial role of women, antis believed, and the demand for it consequently met with more determined resistance than did women's struggles for other rights. . . .

What Women Want

Antisuffragist women who subscribed to this picture of society provided antisuffragist propaganda with the additional argument that "women do not want to vote." The suffragists, declared the antis, were a small minority of women, and humanity was fortunate that they were, for if they were to achieve their goal, women would become large-handed, big-footed, flat-chested, and thin-lipped. The qualities of emotionalism and sensitivity which disqualified most women for the political life became, when thrown into the political arena, the unlovely traits of the shrew. History proved that when women participated in government, their nations suffered: consider Cleopatra, Marie Antoinette, and Catherine de Médicis. Even Queen Elizabeth I's reputation was beginning to crumble under the weight of new historical discoveries. The *womanly* woman who knew her true vocation did not want to vote. She would not insult her men by implying that they had failed to protect her interests. She insisted that the American colonists' arguments against the theory of virtual representation were misapplied to this question, for woman was not a class apart but a part of every class. Since she was adequately represented by her menfolk, why should two do what one could do at least as well? The colonists' argument against "taxation without representation" was likewise irrelevant, since minors, corporations, and aliens paid taxes, but did not vote. Moreover, for every taxpaying woman who would vote, there would be many nontaxpaying women whose votes would more than cancel hers. For all these reasons, contended the antis, the majority of women did not want the ballot; to force it upon them would be undemocratic. . . .

Race and Class

When the antis spoke of the majority of women who did not want the suffrage, they meant the majority of middle-class, white, native-born women. That is the only interpretation which reconciles their appeal to majority will with their demand that immigrant, poor, and Negro women be prevented from voting. They were saying, in effect, that the majority of that class of women who alone could use the suffrage wisely did not want it, not only because their time was already fully occupied with home and charity but also because it was unfortunately no longer possible to give *them* the vote and deny it to the others. Further, the woman whose time was taken up by home and philanthropy was obviously not the beneficiary of that philanthropy. The woman who was too weak to survive the emotional and physical stresses of political campaigns could not be the woman who had to stand ten hours a day before a machine-loom. The woman who shrank from entering a polling-place filled with inelegant workers was certainly not the wife of one of them. The frequency with which *ignorant* and *poor* and *immoral* were used as equivalent terms shows that the combination fit naturally into the thinking of antisuffragist propagandists and formed an integral part of their ideology.

The Dilemma of the Antisuffrage Movement

Susan E. Marshall

The women of the antisuffrage movement were faced with a difficult balancing act. On the one hand, they advocated the idea that women's proper place was in the home, uninvolved in the world of politics. On the other hand, the antisuffragists found that to fight effectively for their cause, they had to involve themselves in the political arena. Susan E. Marshall explores this conundrum in the following selection from her book *Splintered Sisterhood: Gender and Class in the Campaign Against Woman Suffrage*. Opponents of suffrage, Marshall writes, were particularly skillful at maintaining an image of traditional womanhood while taking part in untraditional activities. She points out that the antisuffrage movement underwent an impressive organizational evolution during the struggle over the right to vote. However, she concludes, the antisuffragists' reluctance to adopt openly political tactics hindered their ability to counteract the more flexible suffragists. Marshall is a professor of sociology at the University of Texas at Austin.

> If we fail to vote, we are moral shirkers.
> —Women Voters' Anti-Suffrage Party

Antisuffragists' rhetoric convinced many voters, suffragists, politicians, and pundits that they were traditional homebound women who eschewed politics. Public statements and literature articulated for public consumption their tactics as well as beliefs. Antisuffragists effectively distinguished themselves from their female opponents, whose behavior they denounced as a violation of gender norms, by recasting their own political activities in traditional terms. Their retiring image, largely undisturbed to the present day, is testimony to their political skills. But it also suggests a limitation of studies of the antisuffrage movement, which too often represent only this public side.

Like all social movements, antisuffragism had a backstage, where leaders planned various responses to the suffrage threat and devised skillful rationales to legitimate and obfuscate deviations from traditional gender arrangements. . . . Women's opposition campaign strategies were not simply a reaction to the suffrage movement. They constituted a more complex response that involved competition with suffragists, organizational exigencies such as membership retention and leadership composition, and emergent political demands. While the ideology of true womanhood continued to shape the tactics of the antisuffrage movement until the end, it was only one factor among many and its influence waned over time. . . .

Political Evolution

The tactical evolution of the antisuffrage movement is striking. From a genteel group meeting in residential parlors for self-study and public education, they increasingly adopted more visible means of promoting the cause. These changes were partly a consequence of pressure from male advisers, competition with suffragists, and demands from political candidates. The establishment of a national coalition [the National Association Opposed to Woman Suffrage] in 1911 incited innovation by improving the flow of information and other resources among state antisuffrage associations, but also by multiplying their financial burdens. Suffrage opponents publicly legitimated deviations from traditional gender norms in numerous ways; they blamed suffragists for forcing them into public battle, emphasized distinctions between themselves and their adversaries, or simply denied the obvious political dimensions of their work. Traditional rhetoric extolling motherhood and the sanctity of the home functioned partly to shield the true extent of women's activism from public notice and potential criticism. Women remonstrants commonly appealed to male lawmakers and voters for protection, invoking norms of chivalry that underscored women's dependency and their position as political outsiders.

Both sides adopted a nonpartisan stance, but the suffrage establishment benefited from the existence of a radical flank in the form of the National Woman's Party that absorbed controversy while putting pressure on both parties. There was no parallel organization within the antisuffrage movement; the men's associations, dominated by elite lawyers, largely eschewed electoral politics and sought redress in the courts. Women's antisuffrage organizations repeatedly beseeched politicians for protection, but the policy of nonpartisanship prevented them from bestowing quid pro quo political rewards in the form of candidate endorsements. The perceived political leverage of newly enfranchised women voters prodded many elected officials to endorse suffrage, siphoning off politically moderate antisuffragists for leadership positions in Republican women's associations. The loss of this segment of the antisuffrage movement to party participation illuminates the extent to which the fight against woman suffrage, at least for the privileged leadership, centered less on protecting the home than on preserving group power.

This conclusion is supported by antisuffrage strategies during the declining phase of the movement, when the remaining opposition activists were drawn into political battle. Having lost informal channels of influence stemming from their positions of privilege, antisuffragists had no choice but to compete in the public sphere. They now mounted an overt defense of class interests; the Women Voters' Anti-Suffrage Party focused on fighting radicalism—a code word for anti-labor and anti-immigrant sentiments—and so did the official organ of the National Association, renamed the *Woman Patriot*. The home, motherhood, and children's welfare took a backseat to issues of patriotism and socialism; in the southern mobilization against ratification, the defense of southern civilization was paramount. After the passage of the Nineteenth Amendment, their gendered appeals addressed primarily the question of masculinity, excoriating presidents and their policies for being too "soft" on domestic reform or national security. The remaining true believers persisted in the view that women were bad for politics, but this had more to do with differences in political ideology—particularly the successes of female reformers in getting social welfare legislation through Congress—than with the deleterious consequences of enfranchisement for home-loving women and their families. The right-wing associations of the 1920s formed from the ashes of the antisuffrage movement protested their own loss of influence, brought on by the mass empowerment of women as well as the rise of trained female professionals who threatened to displace the society volunteer.

The Antisuffragists' Difficulties

This examination of antisuffrage tactics over time not only challenges the notion of a lockstep reaction by countermovements to the initial movement, but also suggests that the tactical responses of countermovements vary according to the phase in which they occur. For example, suffrage victories when antisuffragists were less mobilized seemed to spur further activation efforts, whereas a referendum defeat coming after a host of significant antisuffrage victories led to organizational conflict and demobilization. The difficulties of holding together suffrage opponents derived not merely from social position or domestic responsibilities, but from the problems confronting all movements of maintaining consensus and dedication over the course of a protracted contest. In this task, the repertoire available to suffragists was less constrained by ideology. Antisuffrage organizations, while more flexible than their rhetoric implied, viewed open political engagement as certain defeat, given their strong moral pronouncements against women's political participation. While we will never know if their assessment was accurate, the exhortation to vote by the Women Voters' Anti-Suffrage Party that began this essay encapsulates the movement's dilemma as much as its desperation. Antisuffragists' hesitancy to cross that line until so late in the struggle gave suffragists a major tactical advantage and contributed to the successful outcome of women's campaign for political equality.

Chapter 5

The Final Push for Women's Suffrage

Turning | Points
IN WORLD HISTORY

The New Suffragists

Christine A. Lunardini

With the healing of the rift in the suffrage movement, the National Woman Suffrage Association (NWSA) and the American Woman Suffrage Association (AWSA) merged in 1890 as the National American Woman Suffrage Association (NAWSA). Although NAWSA paid lip service to the idea of a federal suffrage amendment, the leadership favored the old AWSA strategy of working to pass suffrage laws in each state. They also abandoned the more radical ideas and arguments of NWSA. By the early 1910s, many young suffragists were becoming dissatisfied with NAWSA's approach, and the movement again began heading toward a split between the moderates and the radicals. According to women's historian Christine A. Lunardini, these young women, having benefitted from opportunities that the women who began the movement could only dream of, represented a new breed of suffragist. The "New Suffragists" also drew much inspiration from the militant campaign undertaken by the British women's suffrage movement, she writes. In fact, Lunardini points out, a number of American suffragists—most notably Alice Paul and Lucy Burns—first became involved in the militant British movement and then transferred their experiences to the U.S. cause. A former history professor, Lunardini is the author of several books concerning women's history, including *From Equal Suffrage to Equal Rights: Alice Paul and the National Woman's Party, 1910–1928*, from which the following selection is excerpted.

By 1913, a new generation of women—the *New Suffragists*—were ready to take their place in the ranks of the American

Excerpted from *From Equal Suffrage to Equal Rights: Alice Paul and the National Woman's Party, 1910–1928*, by Christine A. Lunardini (New York: New York University Press, 1986). Reprinted with permission from the author.

women's movement. They were among the first and second generations of women to enjoy the opportunities for higher education that had opened up with the initiation of co-education in colleges and universities like Oberlin and Berkeley, and with the founding of the prestigious women's colleges, from Mount Holyoke to Barnard. They were also the beneficiaries of the decades of voluntary, organized club affiliation which had helped to sharpen their political skills and administrative talents. In a broader vein, industrialization, advances in technology, unprecedented immigration, and rapid urbanization combined to alter significantly women's perceptions of society as well as their status in that society. New attitudes and perceptions led women to question old assumptions on issues such as marriage, family, work, and career. The *New Suffragists* were the products of the combined social, political, and economic changes of the preceding half century.

The more involved women became, either in their own careers or jobs, or in the problems they perceived in society, the more apparent became the multiple disadvantages that they faced simply because they were women. For many women, the suffrage movement was the political focus of their new awareness, critical to their aspirations for active participation in the affairs of society. And, perhaps predictably, the changes in society that created a new landscape for women also worked to change the way in which some of them perceived the strategy that the suffrage movement should adopt.

Shifts in Rationale

The arguments used by suffragists in their efforts to secure the vote had shifted in the 1890s. When the vote became a goal of the women's movement in the mid-nineteenth century, women had claimed it as a natural right, nothing more and nothing less. In the latter decades of the century, the rationale changed. Women, long the recognized keepers of the flame, would use their votes to help create a better society by acting as a moral balance of power. Temperance, protective legislation for women and children, better city and state government—all of these would be acted upon in a positive fashion by women voters. As an additional incentive, participation in the rights of citizenship would make women better wives and mothers.

Strategically, this shift in the rationale for suffrage proved to be beneficial. On principle, it was ultimately counterproductive to real equality. Once women gave up their claim to suffrage as their natural right as full and equal citizens, it was difficult to maintain that men and women were in fact equal. For most women, however, this was not a problem since it squared with their own beliefs in any case. They forged ahead secure in the belief that they would indeed create a better world.

Dissatisfaction in the Movement

Just after the turn of the twentieth century, new fissures began to appear in the suffrage movement. A growing sense of dissatisfaction developed among some women over the way in which the National American Woman Suffrage Association (NAWSA) conducted its suffrage campaign. NAWSA's strategy of individual state campaigns seemed to grow increasingly more cumbersome and tired, and increasingly less realistic with each defeat. NAWSA conducted well over 400 state campaigns intended to induce state legislators to submit constitutional amendments to their electorates. An additional 300 campaigns were waged to persuade state party leaders to include suffrage planks in their party platforms. The overwhelming majority of these costly and dispiriting campaigns ended in failure. Following Wyoming's entry into the Union as a suffrage state in 1890, three more states enfranchised women during that decade: Colorado in 1893, and Idaho and Utah in 1896. But between 1896 and 1910, they remained the only four suffrage states—testimony that state-by-state methods were both cumbersome and slow to produce results. In November 1910, Washington state voters extended the franchise to women, and California followed suit in October 1911.

While NAWSA leaders and most of its membership were in a celebratory mood following the California victory, others were far less sanguine. In their view the at best incremental gains achieved by NAWSA provided little cause to pursue the same strategy, and they were wary of remaining enmeshed in state work. In Massachusetts, Maud Wood Park, a NAWSA officer, suggested not only a move toward greater emphasis on federal work, but also toward less tried and tired tactics as well. New York's Harriot Stanton Blatch, the daughter of women's rights pioneer Elizabeth Cady Stanton, organized the first American suffrage parade as she, too, expressed willingness to adopt less genteel methods and to shift the focus to federal work. Dora Lewis, of main-line Philadelphia society, and Caroline Katzenstein, both members of the Philadelphia Equal Franchise Society, were similarly chafing under NAWSA's tight rein. And in California, Alice Park Lock agreed wholeheartedly with Lydia Kingsmill Commander of New York, that the time was ripe to "appeal to the women voters in the West" to use their political power in helping to secure a federal suffrage amendment. For these and many other women, their impulse to seek new tactics reflected a common disaffection with the moribund NAWSA campaign.

An Emphasis on State Suffrage Work

Despite the grass-roots sentiment for federal suffragism exhibited by many of its members, NAWSA was not prepared to undertake a major shift in emphasis away from state work. NAWSA had affiliations in every state, almost all major cities, and many smaller cities and towns. It could boast of a vast machinery to work on behalf of suffrage. The campaign run by each state affiliate was generally aimed at the state's political party machines, or at the state legislature. The campaigns were, as a rule, run independently of any other state campaign, and frequently lacked thorough organization or planning. NAWSA's national office provided some guidelines, but it had no real overall strategy beyond encouraging the continuation of such campaigns, supplying speakers, and raising money. In those instances when a state did enfranchise women, NAWSA and the successful affiliate considered the work finished in that state. It did not occur to NAWSA to reap the benefit of the new political power held by the female voters in the state. . . .

To be sure, NAWSA paid lip service to the idea of a federal amendment. They even took advantage of opportunities as they arose to make a case for federal action. Carrie Chapman Catt, for example, testified before the Senate Committee on Woman Suffrage in 1910: "Ordinary fair play should compel every believer, no matter what are his views on woman suffrage, to grant to women the easiest process of enfranchisement and that is the submission of a federal amendment." But this was more in deference to Susan B. Anthony than it was a serious indication of a change of direction. Even the establishment of a congressional liaison committee in 1910, called the Congressional Committee, did not signal change. . . .

The concession to federalism made by NAWSA in establishing the Congressional Committee created a misconception that the organization was vigorously pursuing an amendment on all fronts. In truth, its leaders were reluctant—partially out of inertia, partially out of sporadically incremental gains—to reorient the machinery already in place in the states. The winning over of five suffrage states between 1910 and 1912 produced two reactions. On the one hand the victories provided a much-needed boost to NAWSA members whose morale had been badly waning. At the same time, the victories sparked a vigorous interest in a federal amendment, particularly among younger women. Buoyed by the potential that they saw for their own lives and confident that victory could be obtained in the short run, the *New Suffragists*, in concert with some of the older generation of suffragists, became the core of the militant suffrage movement in the United States. Surprisingly, the source of inspiration for the *New Suffragists* came not from the conservative American suffrage tradition, but from the much more aggressive British woman suffrage movement.

The Impact of British Militancy

The British suffragettes, under the leadership of the Pankhursts—Emmeline, and her two daughters, Christabel and Sylvia—began their militant campaign in 1905. Christabel, a young lawyer, originated the militant strategy. Beginning with the mild action of "questioning" Members of Parliament and the Cabinet when they appeared in public, the suffragettes gradually escalated their activity to the point of minor violence, such as window smashing and rock throwing. The Women's Social and Political Union (WSPU) and the Pankhursts, who founded the organization, soon made suffrage a national issue in England. . . .

The model for militancy provided by the Pankhursts included all of the elements subsequently adapted to the American situation, as well as some that were not incorporated, notably violence and zealous martyrdom. Even at the height of their militant campaign in 1917, American suffragists never advocated a policy of violent militance, though violence was often directed at them. . . . The three main tactics employed by the Americans were drawn directly from the British movement: first, holding the political party in power responsible for failure to enact a suffrage amendment; second, publicity; and third, protest suitable to focus attention on the demand for a federal amendment.

The independence, courage, and audacity of the British women captured the imagination of the *New Suffragists* in America. Inez Haynes Irwin reported her own reaction to the English movement: "When in England, the first militant of Mrs. Pankhurst's forces threw her first stone, my heart went with it. . . . At last the traditions of female patience . . . had gone by the board. Women were using the tactics that, through all the ages men had used; the only tactics that were sure to bring results; rebellion and violence." Mrs. Pankhurst had a similar effect on many who heard her speak. When she first spoke in Hartford, Connecticut, Mrs. Pankhurst galvanized Katharine Houghton Hepburn. Hepburn later recalled the seminal event "as one of the most remarkable speeches I have ever heard." She pointed to it as the catalyst of her involvement in the suffrage movement. "I remember so well [it was] the first time I even thought of [suffrage] as something I must work for myself.". . .

But even before the word had reached American shores, there were Americans in England and on the Continent who witnessed first-hand the actions of the suffragettes, and in some cases worked with them. Their views, unhampered by the critical filter of the British government and a frequently unsympathetic press, had a profound influence on the *New Suffragists*.

Harriot Stanton Blatch, perhaps the first American to be influenced by the Pankhursts, married English businessman William Henry Blatch, in 1882. For the next twenty years, the Blatch's lived in Basingstoke, England, a small town west of London. Every bit her mother's daughter, Harriot threw herself into a variety of social and political movements, including the Women's Local Government Society. . . . She was most impressed, however, with the work of the Women's Franchise League, the suffrage group organized by Emmeline Pankhurst in 1889. During her stay in England, Blatch's home was open to a stream of feminists, socialists, and other assorted radicals. By the time she returned to the United States in 1902, both Blatch and her daughter, Nora, had forged strong international ties with many of England's soon-to-be-militant feminists, including the Pankhursts. . . . Both Blatches were quick to defend militant feminism at home and were instrumental in bringing Emmeline Pankhurst to the United States some years later for her first speaking tour. . . .

Lucy Burns and Alice Paul

Lucy Burns, who worked closest with Alice Paul during the final years of the American suffrage campaign, gave up a promising academic career in favor of political activism after working with the Pankhursts in 1909. Burns was in Germany to attend graduate school. Traveling to England for a brief holiday, she met Emmeline, Christabel, and Sylvia, and was so inspired by both their cause and their charismatic appeal that she gradually abandoned her graduate work entirely in order to organize for the WSPU. The chief organizer for the Congressional Union and later the National Woman's Party, Burns spent more time in prison—both in America and in England—than any other American suffragist.

The woman most directly responsible for transferring

militant tactics to the American campaign was, of course, Alice Paul. The founder of the National Woman's Party, Paul became the dynamic that propelled American suffragism to its successful end. . . .

After graduating from Swarthmore in 1905, Paul spent several years pursuing her studies, and in social work. She . . . enrolled at the University of Pennsylvania where in 1907 she earned a master's degree in sociology with minor fields in economics and political science. Her academic interest in the problems faced by women because of their legal status began to take shape while she was at the University of Pennsylvania. Research that ultimately became her doctoral dissertation entitled "Towards Equality," begun at this time, was an examination of the legal status of women in Pennsylvania.

Paul interrupted work on her doctorate in order to accept a fellowship to study social work at Woodbridge, England, the central training school for Quakers. . . .

While she was in England, Paul found the cause that integrated and brought into focus her . . . service-oriented Quaker education and interests in economics, political science, and the status of women. Christabel Pankhurst spoke at the University of Birmingham where Paul was fulfilling the academic requirements of her fellowship. Suffrage, then even less popular than it was respectable, incited the mostly male student audience to rowdy behavior. Christabel was shouted down, and embarrassed Birmingham officials were forced to cancel her speech. The reaction to Christabel's attempt to speak both angered and surprised Paul. . . .

When Paul finished her work at Woodbridge, a representative of the Charity Organization Society of London invited her to become a case worker in the working-class district of Dalston. There, in the fall of 1908, Paul took part in her first suffrage parade and began an association with the WSPU which lasted for two years. During that time she became thoroughly versed in the strategy and tactics of militant suffragism. She participated in demonstrations which led to her arrest and imprisonment. Along with her English comrades, she took part in hunger strikes to protest the British government's treatment of suffrage prisoners. It was a profoundly formative period in her political education. Prior to this, Paul exhibited little interest in political activism and belonged to no American suffrage organization.

It was in Europe that Paul first met Lucy Burns, the red-headed Irish American from Brooklyn who was to become her alter ego in the American suffrage campaign. Burns had graduated from Vassar, attended Yale's graduate school briefly, then returned to Brooklyn to teach English at Erasmus High School. Lucy resigned her teaching position in 1906 in order to study languages in Europe. . . . During a vacation break from her studies, Lucy traveled to England where she met the Pankhursts, developed an intense interest in their suffrage activities, and decided to continue her studies at Oxford. In 1909, she enrolled at Oxford, ostensibly to begin work on her doctorate. In fact, she spent little time in study, preferring instead to throw herself into the thick of the suffrage campaign. For the next three years, until her return to the United States in 1912, Lucy worked with the WSPU as an organizer, primarily in Edinburgh. There, she gained invaluable experience that served the American cause well in later years.

Two Prisoners Meet

Alice Paul first met Lucy Burns in a London police station. Both had been arrested for demonstrating. As they stood about the station, waiting for the police to process their cases, Alice noticed the tiny American flag pinned to Lucy's lapel. She introduced herself and the two young women, seating themselves on a tabletop, quietly compared suffrage experiences, ignoring the stationhouse bedlam around them as though the entire situation was perfectly ordinary. As they discussed the American movement, it became clear to both that they shared many of the same hopes for the situation at home. It was a propitious meeting and the beginning of a mutually rewarding alliance. . . .

After her imprisonment in Halloway Prison in England, in 1910, Paul returned to the United States and resumed graduate study at the University of Pennsylvania. She left England with a prison record and ill-health. Lucy, on the other hand, remained in Europe to continue organizing for the WSPU. The two were not re-united until 1912, when they joined forces to work on the American scene.

"The New Woman"

Other American women associated with the Pankhursts included nursing pioneer, Lavinia Dock; labor organizer, Josephine Casey; historian and United States Senate candidate, Anne Martin; socialite Eleanor Doddridge Brannon and her mother, Elizabeth Brannon; and patron of the arts and heiress, Louisine Havemeyer. All were active in the militant suffrage movement. Collectively, they conformed in background to the description of the modern American woman—the New Woman—then emerging. . . .

As a group, these women were singularly independent and aggressive. They confronted society on its own terms, found those terms unacceptable, and determined to follow the path that they perceived led most directly to their emancipation, regardless of the barriers encountered. It is hardly surprising that, given the opportunity to work with or observe the English suffragettes, the Americans would applaud and imitate the directness and aggressiveness of their English sisters.

These were the *New Suffragists*: women who were better educated, more career-oriented, younger, less apt to be married, and more cosmopolitan than their counterparts of the previous generation. Still, these differences between the Old Suffragists and the *New Suffragists* should not be overdrawn. The critical factor that distinguished Old from New was their brand of feminism. For both groups, suffrage was the issue around which they rallied. However, for the younger generation the fight for suffrage was one means to challenge a social system that attempted to refute their feminist ideology and deny them their identities. Among the *New Suffragists*, militancy was the chief weapon. In this respect, they were united with Alice Paul. No longer would they beg for their rights. They would, henceforth, demand them.

Militant Suffragism

Edith Mayo

Edith Mayo is the executive advisor of the National First Ladies' Library in Canton, Ohio, and the editor of *The Smithsonian Book of the First Ladies: Their Lives, Times, and Issues.* She is also Curator Emerita in political history at the Smithsonian Institution's National Museum of American History. In the following essay, Mayo provides an overview of the militant tactics employed by Alice Paul and other radical suffragists during the 1910s. These activists staged numerous nonviolent demonstrations and pioneered the technique of picketing the White House, the author writes. In addition, she explains, militant suffragists who were arrested and sentenced to prison insisted on being treated as political prisoners and engaged in hunger strikes that won them much sympathy from the general public. Although the militants' adoption of increasingly controversial tactics provoked a split in the movement between the moderate and militant wings, it also spectacularly revitalized the moribund movement, Mayo concludes.

The pioneering work of Lucy Stone, combined with the intellectual and organizational partnership of Elizabeth Cady Stanton and Susan B. Anthony, dominated the drive for woman suffrage from the mid-nineteenth century until their deaths in 1893, 1902, and 1906, respectively. Despite their unflagging efforts and Anthony's rallying cry, "failure is impossible!" uttered at her last public appearance shortly before her death, success did not come in their lifetimes. At the turn of the century, only four Western states, Wyoming, Utah, Idaho, and Colorado, allowed women the right to vote. As the

Excerpted from the Introduction, by Edith Mayo, to *Jailed for Freedom: American Women Win the Vote,* by Doris Stevens, edited by Carol O'Hare (Troutdale, OR: NewSage Press, 1995). Reprinted with permission from NewSage Press.

twentieth century began, the fifty-year-old suffrage movement, now represented by the National American Woman Suffrage Association (NAWSA), was thoroughly mired in what its own leaders termed "the doldrums." Congressional hearings on a constitutional amendment for suffrage had not been held since 1887. Success was nowhere in sight.

Yet, the NAWSA and its predecessor organizations had sown the educational seeds of enfranchisement, ensuring abundant recruits for the new period of activism. By 1900, the movement's focus broadened and shifted from education to agitation, employing dramatic publicity, dynamic nonviolent confrontation, and civil disobedience to promote the cause.

A convergence of events also helped reinvigorate the movement. The Progressive Era (1890–1925) gave an impetus to all reform. Millions of women from all ethnic, class, and racial backgrounds entered public life to address severe social problems through innovative reform movements. As women's roles expanded in society, so did the political activism that politicized women and brought them into mainstream politics. Soon realizing that virtually every reform they sought was regulated by law, and that the legislators who passed these laws responded to voters, suffragists and women reformers alike believed that the social policy they supported could be achieved only if women had the vote. The question of woman suffrage had become mainstream politics.

New Suffrage Leaders

New leaders emerged whose brilliant organizational abilities and innovative tactical and political approaches revitalized the suffrage drive. One of these was Harriot Stanton Blatch, daughter of Elizabeth Cady Stanton. In 1902, she returned to New York after many years of living in England where she had witnessed the radical and innovative tactics and publicity generated by the militant British suffrage movement led by the Pankhurst women, Emmeline, Christabel, and Sylvia. Blatch was convinced that working women needed the vote to better their economic status, and that the suffrage movement needed working-class support. . . . She pioneered political alliances between middle-class and working-class suffrage supporters. Blatch set up a separate New York suffrage organization, the Equality League of Self-Supporting Women (later known as the Women's Political Union), introducing outdoor rallies, suffrage parades, and automobile tours that gained wide publicity for the cause and infused the American suffrage campaign with new life.

After Anthony's retirement in 1900, longtime organizer Carrie Chapman Catt assumed the leadership of the NAWSA. But only four years after emerging as the NAWSA's new leader, Catt was forced to leave office to care for her dying husband. Anna Howard Shaw, a close personal friend of Anthony's, became the NAWSA's leader. Although a veteran suffragist, a medical doctor, an ordained Methodist minister, and a powerful orator, Shaw was neither a strong leader nor an effective organizer. The NAWSA drifted.

Carrie Chapman Catt continued to pursue her commitment to suffrage once again after the death of her husband. With Shaw at the helm of NAWSA, Catt continued her suffrage work through other routes—as a founder and president of the International Woman Suffrage Alliance, and as the leader of the New York State suffrage campaign. She swiftly brought together most of the various New York City suffrage clubs under the banner of the Woman Suffrage Party. Catt organized New York City politically into wards and precincts to push for passage of woman suffrage. Her work was not sufficient to secure passage of the New York State suffrage referendum in 1915 against powerful vested interests, but Catt's extraordinary organizing abilities, powerful speaking style, and talent for fundraising brought her to the forefront of the movement again. (Suffrage passed in New York in 1917.) She returned to lead the NAWSA in 1915.

The third leader to emerge was Alice Paul. . . . She, too, had been personally active in the British suffrage movement. Along with her militant British counterparts, Paul had been arrested and sent to jail where she went on hunger strikes and was force-fed while pressuring the government to grant woman suffrage.

On returning to the United States, Paul recognized the need for intensive Congressional lobbying to secure votes for women. In late 1912, Paul persuaded the staid NAWSA, headquartered in New York, to permit her to organize a lobbying arm in Washington, D.C. Known as the Congressional Union, its sole purpose was to lobby for a federal woman suffrage amendment. It was agreed, and the NAWSA gave Paul exactly thirteen dollars for her annual lobbying budget!

Alice Paul gathered around her a group of women committed to the suffrage cause. She was determined to jolt Congress and the public into awareness through dramatic, public actions. The first public appearance of the Congressional Union was a suffrage spectacle unequalled in the political annals of the nation's capital. Paul and her strategists took advantage of the festive arrangements and publicity potential surrounding Woodrow Wilson's presidential inauguration in March, 1913. Paul planned a dramatic parade for the day preceding the Inaugural. The city was packed with party operatives and political well-wishers in the hundreds of thousands, most of whom lined Pennsylvania Avenue to watch the parade. Paul, a master of spectacle and street theater, coordinated a march of some 8,000 college women, professional women, working women, and middle-class members of the NAWSA into costumed marching units, each with its own banners.

Leading the parade in flowing white robes, astride a white horse, was the beautiful Inez Milholland (Boissevain). Suffrage floats and marching units followed down Pennsylvania Avenue from the Capitol past the White House. An elaborate suffrage tableau, then much in vogue, was to be held on the steps of the Treasury Building at the climax of the parade.

By the time this parade was staged, woman suffrage had gained political respectability among middle- and upper-class women. Paul counted many politically and socially well-connected women among her supporters. The general public and many male politicians, particularly in the East and the South, however, did not yet support votes for women. The predominantly male crowd watching the parade as it passed down Pennsylvania Avenue jeered, taunted, spat upon, and roughed up the women, disrupting the parade. Police did little to contain the unruly crowd or to protect the women. Fearing a riot, the War Department called in mounted cavalry to restore order. It would prove an omen of things to come.

The mistreatment of many socially prominent women in the parade became an embarrassing debacle for the new Wilson Administration. Congress held hearings into police failure to protect a legitimate political parade, and the District of Columbia's Chief of Police, Richard Sylvester, was dismissed from his position.

Revitalization and Division

Suddenly, however, the issue of suffrage—long thought dead by many politicians—was vividly alive in front-page headlines in newspapers across the country. The dramatic parade—and the ensuing scandal—had succeeded in capturing enormous publicity for the cause. Paul had accomplished her goal—to make woman suffrage a major political issue.

Alice Paul quickly followed this remarkable success with intensive lobbying campaigns. Congress, controlled by the Democratic Party with much of its stronghold in the conservative South, received the women lobbyists, but did little. Deputations of women to President Woodrow Wilson proved an exercise in futility.

By 1916, the suffrage drive experienced a major division that resulted in two primary suffragists' organizations with very different tactics. As Paul intensified her lobbying efforts and escalated confrontational tactics, Catt took over the leadership of the NAWSA. In many ways opposites in political theory and style, Catt and Paul clashed over strategy. Paul's refusal to be limited in her politically confrontational tactics angered many moderate NAWSA members seeking respectable Congressional cooperation. Following the pattern established by the militant British suffrage women, Paul was determined to "hold the party in power responsible,"— the Democratic Party and President Wilson himself—for the failure to pass woman suffrage. On the other hand, Catt's tactic was to woo Wilson to the women's cause, not to enrage him, Congress, or the public by confrontational tactics. Catt feared that the cause would be stigmatized by violence, so she disavowed Paul's actions. A break was inevitable. The Congressional Union withdrew from the NAWSA and, in 1916, formed its own separate organization, the National Woman's Party (NWP), under Paul's leadership. . . .

Picketing the White House

Despite the relentless deputations to President Wilson, he refused to endorse suffrage. Startling the public and Congress, the NWP decided to dramatize their appeal by picketing the White House. They were the first group of citizens in American history to pioneer this form of political protest. In January 1917, the first suffrage pickets, known as "Silent Sentinels," appeared in front of the White House, holding banners with provocative political slogans or demanding the right to vote. In an atmosphere dominated by war hysteria and concerns for national unity in World War I, the women pickets were considered disloyal Americans by large segments of the public.

Unruly crowds often harassed the women, attacking them and destroying their banners. By June 1917, arrests of the women pickets began. While they had violated no law, and their picketing had always been peaceful, police arrested hundreds of women on trumped-up charges of "obstructing sidewalk traffic." In August 1917, a banner appeared decrying the hypocrisy of a President who himself was abroad advocating a policy to "make the world safe for democracy" while abridging civil liberties and suppressing self-determination at home. "Kaiser Wilson . . ." the banner began.

When the Woman's Party pickets came to trial, many, including Alice Paul, were convicted and sentenced to prison terms of up to six months in the District of Columbia Jail and the Occoquan Workhouse in Virginia. . . . Paul and others demanded to be treated as political prisoners—imprisoned for their beliefs and not for any criminal act—and went on hunger strikes. . . . Paul was sent to the psychiatric ward where she was subjected to grueling interrogations by doctors from the District of Columbia's institution for the mentally insane, in an abortive effort to impugn her sanity and discredit her leadership of the suffrage movement.

Escalating the Pressure

The National Woman's Party members remained un-
daunted in the face of political repression and brutal treatment. In fact, it seemed to embolden them to escalate further their confrontational tactics. While many of their
number continued to lobby Congress and the President,
others persisted in picketing the White House, lighting suffrage "watchfires" in Lafayette Park and in front of the
White House, and burning copies of the President's hypo-
critical speeches about democracy and self-government. At
the same time, the NAWSA continued its pointed but non-
confrontational lobbying, and submitted petitions from state
suffrage leagues.

As newspapers and magazines increased their reporting of
the women's demand, public opinion began to turn in favor
of the suffragists. Public and congressional outcry at the
harsh treatment of the women escalated; respected public
leaders demanded their release from jail. In an effort to end
political embarrassment, the Administration ordered the
women pardoned and released from prison. Ever the strategists, the NWP turned their members' jailing to their political advantage. Women released from jail, dressed in prison
garb, garnered publicity by riding a train, called "The Prison
Special," on a speaking tour throughout the country. Women
also conducted automobile petition drives throughout the
West and, as the vehicles made their way across the country,
they stopped in cities and towns along the route where hundreds of thousands of women and men added their signatures
to the suffrage petitions to be delivered to Congress. . . .

A Martyr for Suffrage

Inez Milholland's participation in two major suffrage parades,
one in New York City in 1912, the other in the Washington,
D.C., parade in March 1913, fixed her firmly in American
suffrage imagery as the breathtaking figure of the herald. She
is remembered by the descendants of the women's movement
as "The Woman on a Horse." As the leader of both parades,
Milholland had distinct cultural echoes of Joan of Arc, who
had become the patron saint of the British suffrage move-

Courage and Determination

Linda G. Ford, a history professor at Keene State College in Keene, New Hampshire, is the author of Iron-Jawed Angels: The Suffrage Militancy of the National Woman's Party, 1919– 1920. *In the following passage, Ford describes the militant suffragists' nonviolent protests.*

The National Woman's Party militancy was applied feminism; more specifically, their suffrage militancy was applied political feminism. NWP feminist demonstrators, as in Judith Stiehm's description, had "no access to weapons" except for the potent weapon of their own "moral" action: public displays of female, defiant, resistant strength versus male, heavy-handed, authorized power. The NWP's action-oriented progressive feminists directly applied their egalitarian feminist ideology. Their militant tactics to win suffrage reflected their belief that women were worthy of political power both because of their shrewd use of women's existing political leverage and their obvious courage and iron-willed determination. Increasingly resentful of the men who held power over them, NWP suffragists would use graduated militant actions against an unyielding government. At the same time, they sharpened their feminist critique. They slowly shifted from just insisting on a greater democracy which included women, to a condemnation of an oppressive, autocratic, patriarchal society. In the context of this critique of male-run society, NWP demonstrators made a conscious effort to show the "women's" militancy of picketing and civil disobedience was different from, and highly superior to, the manifestation of "men's" militancy—war. . . . Paradoxically, the Woman's Party used the weapon of nonviolence very effectively to illustrate their enormous strength as women.

Linda G. Ford, *Iron-Jawed Angels: The Suffrage Militancy of the National Woman's Party, 1919–1920*, 1991.

ment. Militant, yet godly, the figure represented moral authority and suggested martyrdom for a righteous cause, both strong themes in the NWP's ideology. . . .

In addition to portraying the herald, Milholland was also a lawyer and social activist whose true interest was reform causes. She enthusiastically worked long hours for the suffrage cause, to the point where, after several years of constant campaigning, her health began to suffer. Despite this, Milholland undertook a strenuous speaking tour in 1916 for the NWP to rally women in the enfranchised states of the West. While in Los Angeles speaking for suffrage and against President Wilson, Milholland collapsed while delivering a suffrage address. The last words ringing from her lips were: "Mr. President, how long must women wait for liberty?" With her death ten weeks later, the American woman suffrage movement lost a talented leader and its own martyr.

The memorial service for Milholland was a brilliantly staged pageant of suffrage symbolism. The NWP wasted no time in elevating her to sainthood and glorifying her death for the cause. On Christmas Day in 1916, Milholland was honored and eulogized in the first memorial service ever held for a woman in the U.S. Capitol. Suffragist Maude Younger of California delivered the memorial address, eulogizing Milholland as ". . . the flaming torch that went ahead to light the way—the symbol of light and freedom. . . ."

After Milholland's death, the NWP circulated an idealized poster of her, a herald clad in flowing white robes, with gold helmet and star, riding a white horse and carrying a banner with the legend, "Forward Into Light." This classic poster became the official logo of the NWP that continues to the present, rendered in purple, on all official NWP correspondence.

"Jailed for Freedom"

Another militant image, that of a woman breaking free, emerging from her imprisoned role, was the "Jailed for Freedom" pin. With its representation of a prison gate secured with a heart-shaped lock, this pin was presented to all members of the NWP who served prison sentences for picketing the White House on behalf of suffrage. The prison door symbol was modeled after Sylvia Pankhurst's Holloway

Brooch, representing the portcullis gate of Holloway Prison where British suffragists were incarcerated. The "Jailed for Freedom" pin was used exclusively by the NWP and suggests its origins in that militant group: a small cadre of committed, disciplined, militant women, set apart from mainstream suffragists, who were willing to go to prison for suffrage.

The Ratification of the Nineteenth Amendment

Sara Hunter Graham

In the 1910s, the women's movement rededicated itself to the attempt to pass a federal suffrage amendment. The Nineteenth Amendment, also called the Susan B. Anthony Amendment, was passed by the U.S. Senate in 1919 and then went to the states for ratification. In the following excerpt from *Woman Suffrage and the New Democracy*, Sara Hunter Graham examines the suffragists' campaign to win ratification in two-thirds of the states, as is necessary for the adoption of a constitutional amendment. In particular, Graham describes the efforts of the National American Woman Suffrage Association (NAWSA), which used all the political tools at its disposal and mobilized activists throughout the United States. She points out that although NAWSA believed that the southern states could not be counted on to ratify the amendment, eventually the deciding battle was held in Tennessee. Graham provides a vivid account of the surprising victory that occurred when the Tennessee House of Representatives unexpectedly approved the amendment by only one vote. Graham, a history professor at Louisiana State University in Baton Rouge, died in 1996 shortly before the publication of her book.

When the United States Senate passed the woman suffrage amendment on June 4, 1919, the twentieth-century suffrage movement entered the final, or ratification, stage of its campaign. Histories of the movement have tended to gloss over the ratification campaign, focusing instead on the decades-long battle for state and congressional approval. Ratification, in contrast, was accomplished in a little more than a year and a half—a relatively short period when compared to the congressional fight. To many readers, ratification by the states seems almost an afterthought, easily accomplished after the gripping congressional drama was played out. In fact, this was far from true. Arguably, ratification was the most difficult political test the National American Woman Suffrage Association (NAWSA) activists would face, and it posed a new and challenging set of problems for suffrage strategists.

Ratification required a shift in focus for those who masterminded the congressional campaign. For the amendment to take effect, it had to be approved by thirty-six state legislatures; in each state, suffragists had to grapple with different political agendas, coalitions, and personalities. Suffrage was not the only item before many legislatures, and unrelated and conflicting goals and factions sometimes threatened to postpone ratification indefinitely. Problems within the suffrage camp also disrupted the ratification process: states' rights suffrage associations refused to support the federal amendment, societies impatient with the slow federal route clamored for state amendment campaigns, and militants vied with NAWSA activists for control in several states. Moreover, the antisuffragists, sensing Armageddon, redoubled their efforts to defeat the amendment.

Given these difficulties, it is quite remarkable that ratification was achieved so quickly, or, perhaps, at all. The importance of NAWSA's ratification campaign, however, does not lie solely in its rapid resolution. Without NAWSA's suffrage machine operating at the federal, state, and local levels, the woman suffrage amendment might easily have gone the way of its late-twentieth-century offspring, the Equal Rights Amendment. Ratification was the ultimate test for the suffrage machine, and it reflects the strategy, political power, and ideology of NAWSA at the culmination of its great campaign.

NAWSA's Ratification Plan

The leaders of NAWSA had anticipated many of the problems inherent in the ratification process when they began planning for the final stage of the campaign in early 1918. That April the Executive Council had met in Indianapolis to make long-range plans for ratification. One idea adopted by the group was for a massive petition campaign to commence at once: state and local suffragists would collect signatures of those favoring speedy action on the part of their legislators and would post the documents in public locations to advertise the strong support for the amendment. After the amendment passed in the U.S. Senate, the petitions would be forwarded to the appropriate legislature to further the impression that a large prosuffrage constituency demanded immediate action. Suffragists also petitioned trade unions, women's clubs, and other reform groups and passed the results on to the state legislatures. "The sentiment of the country is with us," Carrie Chapman Catt explained to activists, "our duty is merely to secure its expression."

In addition to petitions, the ratification plan adopted in Indianapolis called for the formation of suffrage ratification committees, composed of representatives from each suffrage society within the state. . . .

With the favorable Senate vote in June 1919, NAWSA's ratification campaign began in earnest. . . .

Difficulties in the South

Many of the forty-eight state legislatures were slated to meet in fall 1919, and twenty-two were expected to ratify easily. A few states would need to call special sessions if ratification were to be obtained before the elections of 1920. Of the remainder, NAWSA strategists calculated that at least ten would require strenuous efforts on the part of state activists to ensure victory, and the Deep South states were considered all but hopeless. The Executive Board had been loath to abandon the South altogether. In response to the pleadings of a delegation of Dixie activists in spring 1919, the Executive Board allocated funds to support suffrage schools and professional organizers for each state. Moreover, Catt planned to hold a series of conferences throughout the region to train new workers and bolster support for suffrage. In return, southern suffragists agreed to furnish workers to act under the direction of the NAWSA organizers, to create speakers' bureaus, and to embark on petition drives in support of ratification. By fall 1919, however, the South had done little to fulfill its part in the agreement. Trained organizers came and went, but only one state out of thirteen took control of the work after they departed. No speakers' bureaus were set up, and of the three states that attempted petition work, none had completed the task. The proposed conferences had failed to take place as one state after another refused to participate. Two state associations neglected to respond to the NAWSA board's letters in time to schedule the events, nine never scheduled conferences, and two more failed to reply at all. In October, the Executive Board fired off a sharp remonstrance to the southern state presidents and essentially abandoned hope that Dixie would ratify the federal amendment.

Without the southern and border states, NAWSA could afford to lose only two of the remaining states. Suffragists instead pinned their hopes on the West, a region where women had voted for decades and could bring pressure for quick ratification. The West, ironically, was so accustomed to woman suffrage that western women and their representatives felt little urgency. Most western suffrage societies had disbanded; NAWSA had to press for legislative action without the customary organization at the state level. . . .

Oklahoma became the thirty-third state to ratify the federal amendment, and when the governors of West Virginia and Washington signed those states' ratification proclamations in late February and early March of 1920, NAWSA leaders realized that the end was in sight. But which state would provide the thirty-sixth vote? . . .

The Showdown in Tennessee

In June 1920, NAWSA was gratified to learn that both parties had endorsed ratification of the federal amendment at their national conventions. When Democrat Carter Glass read the pro-ratification plank to the party delegates, he added, "And if there is anything else the women want, we are for it!" With the additional support of the national conventions, along with a host of congressmen and governors, Catt and the NAWSA board readied themselves for a showdown in the most unlikely of states: Tennessee.

When suffragists realized that the last battle for the vote would be fought in Tennessee, few were optimistic. Although the legislature that had granted presidential and municipal suffrage to the state's women the previous year would also act on ratification, there were other factors that canceled these advantages. Both the Democratic and Republican parties in the state were split into opposing factions, a rift that was duplicated within the Tennessee suffrage movement. As one state suffragist exclaimed in frustration, "Ratification was an insignificant pawn in the local chess game." Party factionalism also threatened to postpone ratification indefinitely because Governor Albert H. Roberts was reluctant to call the legislature into special session without legislative consensus. Moreover, many legislators insisted in abiding by an archaic provision in the state constitution that required the election of a new legislature before the state could ratify a federal amendment.

In addition to these problems, suffragists quickly learned that state representatives were equally divided on the question and would require extensive lobbying to ensure passage of the amendment. This process was made more difficult by the geographic contours of the state. As a National Woman's Party (NWP) organizer explained in a letter to Alice Paul: "Many of the counties in the mountains and hills of the eastern and middle sections are almost inaccessible, with no railroad facilities and bad dirt roads. . . . There are ninety-seven counties and one hundred and thirty-two members of the legislature [to lobby]. . . . The presidential bill received only a bare majority so that the loss of any Republican votes or of any votes because of states' rights opposition would cost us ratification." In an attempt to overcome one obstacle, NAWSA leaders resolved to contest the Tennessee constitution's provision regarding ratification of federal amendments. Long before the battle had shifted to Tennessee, Helen Hamilton Gardener had persuaded President Woodrow Wilson to request a judgment on the provision from the Justice

Department, which ruled that a recent Supreme Court decision rendered the constitutional point invalid. Wilson then telegraphed the governor, who at last relented and called the Tennessee legislature into special session on August 9, 1920. With the promise of a special session, suffragists and antisuffragists converged on the state capital to lobby legislators and publicize their respective positions on the upcoming ratification procedure. Throughout July, both groups toured the state, speaking in rural villages and urban centers. . . .

For two hot weeks, the Tennessee legislature debated the woman suffrage amendment. The resolution quickly passed the senate, but house members remained divided on the issue. Catt refused to attend the debates; instead she sat alone in her hotel room, listening to the distant sounds of cheering and applause that drifted out of the capitol windows. Meanwhile, suffragists constantly polled the representatives at the statehouse and patrolled the nearby railway station to intercept fleeing antisuffrage legislators who intended to break quorum by boarding trains for hillside hideaways. "[The legislators] were threatened with loss of jobs, ruined careers," Tennessee activist Mrs. Guilford Dudley recalled later, "and they fell away from us like autumn leaves in a high wind." In an effort to counteract the antisuffragists' maneuvers, suffragists spirited favorable legislators away to movies and drives in the country. "With all the political pressure, it ought to be easy," Catt wrote to a friend on August 15, "but the opposition of every sort is here fighting with no scruple desperately. Women . . . are here appealing to Negrophobia and every other cave man's prejudice. Men, lots of them, are here. What they represent, God only knows. We believe they are buying votes. I've been here a month. It's hot, muggy, nasty, and the last battle is desperate. Even if we win, we who have been here will never remember it with anything but a shudder. Verily the way of the reformer is hard.". . .

"The Hour Has Come!"

At the end of two weeks of stormy debate, the speaker of the Tennessee House of Representatives at last called out, "The hour has come!" Tension grew as a poll of the house revealed that the amendment fell two votes short. Speaker Seth Walker, an antisuffragist, called for a roll call vote to table the amendment. Suffrage onlookers drew a sigh of relief when the move to table was stymied by a tie vote. One pro-suffrage supporter had been brought from the hospital to cast his vote, and another legislator, Banks Turner, unexpectedly defected from the antisuffrage ranks. Refusing to accept the tie vote, Speaker Walker quickly called for reconsideration. As the names were called, suffragists watched in horrified silence as the speaker left his seat and approached Representative Turner. Throwing his arms about the startled legislator, Walker pleaded with him to vote against the amendment as the roll call proceeded. At last, Turner's name was called, and a tension-filled silence descended on the chamber; onlookers leaned forward in the gallery, all eyes were riveted on the scene below. Suddenly, Turner shook himself free of the speaker's embrace, rose from his seat, and shouted, "Nay!"

Moments later, the vote to table stood tied; with no choice left but to decide the matter once and for all, the final vote was ordered. Would one representative change his vote to "aye" to break the deadlock? Or would some hesitant soul heed the antisuffragists' siren song and vote to defeat the federal amendment? To the crowds in the gallery, defeat seemed imminent; if victory was to be theirs, who would provide the one needed vote? Unobserved by the suffragists, first-term representative Harry Burn sat musing in his seat below. Minutes before, Burn had voted to table the amendment, and antisuffragists therefore felt confident of his negative vote. To symbolize his antisuffrage stand, the young politician sported a red rose—the antisuffragists' trademark—in his lapel. But as Burn listened to the roll call, he recalled a promise he had made to his elderly suffragist mother. Although his constituency was strongly opposed to woman suffrage, Burn had vowed to his mother that he would cast his vote for suffrage under one condition: if, and only if, ratification hinged on one vote, he would provide that vote. Suddenly, Harry Burn was roused from his reverie: the speaker was calling his name to vote. Rising from his seat, he cast his rose to the floor and shouted out "Aye!" Suffragists in the gallery sat in stunned silence; the needed vote had miraculously appeared, the tie had been broken. Seconds later, deafening applause rained down on the young legislator as the speaker called in vain for order. Within minutes after the demonstration subsided, the federal woman suffrage amendment passed the house, and Tennessee became the thirty-sixth state to ratify.

Victory

A week later the ratification certificate reached Washington, D.C., and was taken by special courier to the secretary of state for his signature. On August 26, 1920, when a weary but exultant Carrie Catt arrived in the city, she quickly placed a call to the secretary of state's office. Harriet Taylor Upton and Maud Wood Park stood beside her as she asked whether the certificate had been received. After a moment of silence, Catt turned to her friends and quietly said, "The Secretary has signed the proclamation." "So quietly as that," Park recounted years later, "we learned that the last step in the enfranchisement of women had been taken and the struggle of more than seventy years brought to a successful end."

Chapter 6

The Impact of the Nineteenth Amendment

Turning | Points

IN WORLD HISTORY

The Immediate Outcome of Women's Suffrage

Mildred Adams

The Nineteenth Amendment, which granted women the right to vote, became law in 1920. As Mildred Adams explains in the following selection, the suffragists had high expectations for women's suffrage: They believed that women would immediately use their new political power to work for societal reforms and to raise the level of morality in politics and government. However, Adams writes, the activists underwent a rude awakening as they realized that the women of the younger generation were too busy ushering in the Roaring Twenties and testing their freedom from old moral standards to be concerned with reform work or politics. They also discovered to their dismay that cleaning up government would be much harder than they had expected, the author notes. On the other hand, she maintains, the former suffragists did institute some important innovations, such as the League of Women Voters, which was one of the first political organizations to take a nonpartisan stance. Adams had a long career as a freelance journalist, writer, and translator; her books include *The Right to Be People*, from which the following is excerpted.

The Nineteenth Amendment, which Susan B. Anthony herself had framed back in 1875, reads as follows:

1. The right of citizens of the United States to vote shall not be denied or abridged by the United States or by any State on account of sex.
2. Congress shall have the power to enforce this Article by appropriate legislation.

The language is definite and leaves no room for doubt or equivocation. Susan had learned hard lessons and had put them in precise words. Little was said, but since those words were chosen it had taken forty-five years to make them official. Much was hoped, but she who had started the amendment on its way did not live to see it made law. Nevertheless, she had known exactly what she wanted, and the first step was now completed.

What They Won

In the passage of this Amendment by the Congress and its subsequent ratification by thirty-six states, the women of the United States won the right to vote in any kind of public election: local, county, state, or national. Or to put it in the negative form, they won the right never to be kept from voting on the ground that they were women, never to be publicly disgraced and punished for casting a ballot in an election as Susan B. Anthony had been, half a century earlier.

They had won the right to be people, political people, voting people in a democracy where government draws its strength from the consent of the governed. They could now give their consent officially, or withhold it. Their opinion had value. Henceforth they would legally be people in the eyes of the federal government as men were people; in the states, the federal government's word about voting rights set the legal pattern for even the most backward.

The women had won their long campaign for the ballot. At the same time, the brighter of them knew that the ballot was only the beginning. The vote was to them a tool. With it in hand, they could more effectively work for all the other points of equality. But they would have to work.

In the long battle women had won other gains. Most of them were better educated than their mothers had a chance to be. They had a better knowledge of government and how it functioned, an experienced skill in organization, a sense of feminine solidarity and of their power, as women and as citizens, to get what they wanted if they wanted it badly enough and worked for it hard enough. The years to come would tell how well they would remember and apply the lessons they had learned. . . .

The League of Women Voters

Certain collateral gains—that feeling of ability in public affairs, that sense of feminine solidarity, those organizational and political skills that the suffrage fight left with its participants as a legacy—took tangible shape in the form of the League of Women Voters. . . . The League was, of course, the deliberately created heiress of the National American Woman Suffrage Association. It was brought into being at St. Louis in March of 1919, when the old organization held a Jubilee Convention that was expected to be its last, and it was baptized in 1920 at its first convention, held jointly with the final one of the suffrage association. . . .

The League was the dream and, to a considerable extent, the creation of Carrie Chapman Catt, who combined many of the instincts of a military commander with those of a first-rate civilian administrator. She had analyzed the strengths and the weaknesses of her followers too well to have any illusions about the likelihood that they could hold to an agreed course of action in a field so unaccustomed for women as was politics unless they had a sound and active organization to furnish them with programs, support, and continuity. She had built the scattered and frequently warring suffrage forces into an organization that for skill and efficiency had not been matched among women's voluntary groups. Like hundreds who recognized its peculiar virtues, she could not bear to see the members become scattered and ineffective the moment the vote was won. Trained women now had the vote. They would now get at the long-planned reforms. Outside the suffrage forces, the ignorance of the untrained concerning the duties expected of a citizen in this democracy was little short of abysmal. There would be action; there must also be education.

Mrs. Catt had therefore proposed in her opening speech at St. Louis that the NAWSA found a League of Women Voters to "finish the fight," and that they then "use their new freedom to make the country safer for their children and their children's children." She had urged a program of nonpartisan political leadership and education, with an expansion of the suffrage schools for citizenship that had been important factors in the fight for the vote and could be even more important in training new citizens. She hoped that the new League would avoid both religious and race bias, that it would work to free women from whatever legal discriminations against them still remained in state and national laws, that it would aid the women of other countries to obtain equal rights. Nor were women to be the only benefactors of League effort. A determined fight against "the world's oldest enemy, corrupt reaction" in government was to infuse its efforts with new energy.

Nonpartisan and All-Partisan

The essence of the League, its pride and at times its stumbling block, lay in that word "nonpartisan." To work for political purposes outside the political parties was a new and revolutionary idea. It startled some of the suffragists who, having worked with or against political parties during the suffrage fight, had taken them for granted as the mechanisms that made political action possible. It shocked the parties which, though notably lagging in their support of suffragists, had assumed that they would reap the benefit of the woman's vote as soon as the women got it. When the argument for and against the League's involvement with parties raged hottest, Mrs. Catt, sitting in the role of Solomon, said firmly,

> There are two kinds of partisanship: one kind has led the world onward, the other kind blinds the sight and paralyzes the judgment. In the League of Women Voters we have an anomaly; we are going to be a semi-political body. We want political things, we want legislation, so we are going to educate for citizenship. We have to be non-partisan and all-partisan. Democrats from Alabama and Republicans from New Hampshire must work for the same things.

She encouraged women as individuals to join the party of their individual choice, while in their work within the League they would take no party stand.

This was in the minds of many an ambivalent, not to say a schizophrenic attitude. It has brought down on the League wave after wave of criticism from disappointed politicians who wanted to organize all women for their own purposes. It lost the League many potential members. At the same time, it has proved to be a continuing source of League power and a source of strength to the parties insofar as they profit from League training of women who choose to work as party members. . . .

Changes in the Culture

Until she got the vote, woman's political influence like her influence in many other fields was indirect. She might be able to persuade men to pass a law or to elect a representative of her choice, or she might not. This indirect influence was highly praised by romantic novelists and by antisuffragists. It was thought to be woman's special gift, a dower bestowed on the weak.

Old status symbols proved remarkably resistant to change, but observers noted that the cherished word "lady" began to lose caste and become quaint. Meanwhile, the word "woman," which replaced it, took on a new set of illusions and started to develop new myths.

This is not to say that the suffrage leaders themselves desired such changes. Their own high ideals were as firm as was their distress when the next generation failed to live up to them. Let no one mistake their moral configuration: they were indubitably ladies, metaphorically as well as literally, and in parades they did ride white horses. They did think themselves engaged in a moral crusade, they did expect to raise the moral tone of politics from New York to San Francisco.

The word "moral," as they used it, had wide implications. If, as they thought, women possessed by nature a real "moral" superiority over men, this referred to a strict code of behavior. It upheld what was then known as the sanctity of marriage. It frowned on sex irregularities in any form. It frowned on gambling, on drunkenness, sometimes on smoking, on lying, bribery, and corruption, on pool rooms, and in some ultrastrict circles on dancing and card-playing.

That ladies did not indulge in any of these "vices" may have been a myth, but all through the campaign that myth had played an important part in suffrage thinking. Susan B. Anthony had been quite sure that there was a real moral difference between the sexes, and that superior virtues lay with the women; so had Carrie Chapman Catt; so, although a shade less volubly as became a younger woman, had [New York suffragist] Gertrude Foster Brown.

The changes of which these women were a moving part proved hard on them. After 1915 their belief in the moral superiority of women began to falter. Skirts that had swept the ground during the nineteenth century shrank upward. Ankles appeared. Women were pictured with a glass of wine in the hand, then with a cigarette. Even in matters as fundamental as sex relations there were changes, excused, perhaps, as exceptions, but admitted, however regretfully.

The Loss of Political Illusions

In the political field, the argument that dealt a hard blow to feminine claims to moral superiority went something like this: men knew politics to be a dirty game. If women now wanted to come down from their Victorian pedestals and engage in the dirt, the dust, the rabbit-punching of the political arena, perhaps they were not as untouchable as they had appeared. That they probably never had been was beside the point. It was a matter of symbols. For women to demand voting equality meant that the symbol goddess-on-a-pedestal was developing political clay feet. Perhaps, in the Irish phrase, she was "no better than she should be." Perhaps she could even be used in political bargaining, as men could be used.

If women newly become voters lost among the politicians a certain old-fashioned moral glamor, they themselves lost, as they ventured into the political world, a host of political illusions. Having spent years of hard, grinding effort in the attempt to raise the moral tone of politics, they were not prepared, as more of them made their way into the political arena, to find conditions none the better for their entry.

What they had had in mind was the older ideal of representative government in which they desired to play an honorable part. What they got was the right of entry into a political world where certain manifestations appalled them. That world was growing bigger, the power of the individual vote was shrinking (they themselves were cutting it in two) and becoming less personal. Some of them were convinced by their own experience that the fate of the country was being handed over to private business interests more interested in making money than in upholding abstract and noble aims. Mrs. Catt, who wrote *Woman Suffrage and Politics* after the fight for suffrage was over, described "those invisible influences that were controlling elections; that invincible and invisible power that for forty years kept suffragists waiting for the woman's hour: . . . the power that made Republican leaders hesitate to fulfill their promises to early suffragists, that restrained both parties from endorsing woman suffrage."

But representative government in the older sense of the term was long gone and democratic government, with all its faults of commission and omission, was there for them to enter and take part in. Could they afford to shrink from it now that they had won a place in it?

The Flapper Generation

With the ending of the fight, women lost certain political illusions and a ringing clarity of faith in democracy. . . .

The most serious loss, however, was the loss of the young. This was borne in on the suffragists very slowly. They had always been sure that they were working not only for their own right to vote, but for the rights and the welfare of future generations of women. And so they were, but the first of the future generations seemed little interested. . . .

[It was not] simply the usual healthy rebellion of the young against their parents. It also had in it an important factor of disappointment and disillusion. Suffragist mothers and aunts, swept into hyperbole by their own enthusiasms, had talked too high and promised too much. Too little of what they said would happen came true. The vote proved to be not the key to heaven, not even the key to a good, sure job. That it was a privilege the young admitted. More im-

The Legacy of Female Disfranchisement

Most historians agree that the women's rights movement lost its initiative and political momentum from shortly after the passage of the Nineteenth Amendment until the beginnings of the women's liberation movement in the 1970s. According to Anna L. Harvey, this occurrence is understandable; she argues that a great deal of time was required for women to overcome their long history of disfranchisement and to learn to work effectively within existing political organizations. Harvey is a professor of politics at New York University and the author of Votes Without Leverage: Women in American Electoral Politics, 1920–1970.

Women in the United States have labored under the long shadow cast by a history of disfranchisement. Even after approximately seventy years of organized efforts simply to win the vote, efforts that finally paid off with the passage of constitutional female suffrage in 1920, American women were to endure fifty more years of the consequences of not having had that right in the first place. In what we can now identify as a predictable sequence of events, women's exclusion from the suffrage created conditions that were to lead to distinctive patterns of postsuffrage female electoral politics. Those unique electoral dynamics can in turn ultimately be held responsible for the oft noted decline in the political influence of women's organizations by the mid-1920s, a decline that would last until 1970. Only by this latter date would a significant feature of the institutional context of women's electoral politics have changed sufficiently to allow women's organizations once again to exercise influence over the course of public policy.

These are relatively startling findings, particularly after decades of scholarship in which the difficulties of women's organizations in the political arena were ascribed to the allegedly timid, self-effacing, and unambitious characteristics of women themselves. For too long scholars assumed that because men and women possessed equal rights to vote after 1920, they possessed equal opportunities to influence political outcomes.

Anna L. Harvey, *Votes Without Leverage: Women in American Electoral Politics, 1920–1970*, 1998.

pressively, it was dinned into them as a duty, and in the roaring twenties duties were not what they sought.

The counterreaction of their elders was one of shock and disbelief. Was it for these pert flappers that they had campaigned the country, sacrificed their sleep, listened to endless legislative oratory, incurred the boredom if not the displeasure of their loving husbands? They could not understand why young women showed so little interest in their exploits and in the possibilities offered by the newly won position of women. . . .

This careless acceptance of the long battle and the hard-won and potentially fruitful victory was a bitter blow to the older suffragists. They had assumed that victory would be followed not only by applause but by gratitude. They had seen independence and the right to vote in classic suffrage terms that would make it possible for women to reform political ways of which they disapproved. Or perhaps it is fairer to say that they were moving in the current of thought of their time, and honestly believed that a kind of earthly paradise was within reach if only a little more education could be dispensed, a little more sense of responsibility instilled. That this did not at the moment seem to be working out, and that the young apparently did not care, was a wound that did not heal.

Disappointment and Disapproval

Carrie Chapman Catt, long after she had seen suffrage victorious, said in private conversation that she was greatly disappointed that younger women were doing so little with the political rights so hardly gained for them. Gertrude Foster Brown went even further. She was railing one evening at the young females of the younger generation for whom she and her suffrage companions had done so much, and who showed so little sense of their obligations as new voters and new citizens. She mentioned their flagrant drinking of illegal cocktails, the freedom with which they smoked long cigarettes in longer holders, the shocking shortness of their skirts, the uncorseted abandon of their gymnastic contortions on the dance floor. She thought these flappers were a disgrace to the female sex, and she said so in no uncertain terms.

Stopping just long enough to catch a breath, she was startled to hear her husband say gently, "You did all this, you know. You wanted independence, you wanted rights. Now you've got 'em, and you can't complain if women don't choose to use them as you thought they would."

A Lasting Affirmation of Democracy

Robert Cooney

In the following article, Robert Cooney decries the lack of attention that has been paid to the women's suffrage movement since the passage of the Nineteenth Amendment. According to Cooney, the story of women's long and valiant struggle to win the ballot began to vanish from public awareness almost immediately after 1920. Moreover, he argues, far too many historians and textbook writers have ignored the suffrage movement, relegating it to a brief sentence that leaves out any mention of the women and men who spent entire lifetimes fighting for women's right to vote. By glossing over this heroic and important nonviolent political movement, these historians have done a great disservice to all Americans, Cooney maintains. The women's suffrage movement represents a lasting affirmation of what it means to live in a democracy, he concludes, and has enduring relevance for modern Americans, both women and men. Cooney is the director of the Woman Suffrage Media Project and the creator of a photographic history and slide show called "Winning the Vote: Iconography of the Woman Suffrage Movement." He is also the coeditor of *The Power of the People: Active Nonviolence in the United States.*

Women vote today because of the woman suffrage movement, a courageous and persistent political campaign which lasted over 72 years, involved tens of thousands of women and men, and resulted in enfranchising one-half of the citizens of the United States. Inspired by idealism and grounded

Excerpted from "Taking a New Look: The Enduring Significance of the American Woman Suffrage Movement," by Robert Cooney, available at www.inform.umd. edu/EdRes/Topic/WomensStudies/ReadingRoom/History/Vote/enduringsignificance.html, 1995. Reprinted with permission from the author and the National Women's History Project.

in sacrifice, the suffrage campaign is of enormous political and social significance, yet it is virtually unacknowledged in the chronicles of American history.

Had the suffrage movement not been so ignored by historians, women like Lucretia Mott, Carrie Chapman Catt and Alice Paul would be as familiar to most Americans as Thomas Jefferson, Theodore Roosevelt or Martin Luther King, Jr. We would know the story of how women were denied the right to vote despite the lofty words of the Constitution, how women were betrayed after the Civil War, defeated and often cheated in election after election, and how they were forced to fight for their rights against entrenched opposition with virtually no financial, legal or political power.

If the history of the suffrage movement was better known, we would understand that democracy for the first 150 years in America included half of the population. And we would realize that this situation changed only after the enormous efforts of American citizens in what remains one of the most remarkable and successful nonviolent efforts to change ingrained social attitudes and institutions in the modern era.

For women *won* the vote. They were not given it, granted it, or anything else. They won it as truly as any political campaign is ultimately won or lost. And they won it, repeatedly, by the slimmest of margins, which only underscores the difficulty and magnitude of their victories. In the successful California referendum of 1911, the margin was one vote per precinct! In the House, suffrage passed the first time by exactly the number needed with supporters coming in from the hospital and funeral home to cast their ballots. In the Senate it passed by two votes. The ratification in Tennessee, the last state, passed the legislature in 1920 by a single vote, at the very last minute, during a recount.

Without Violence and Death

Women were a poor, unarmed and disenfranchised class when they first organized to gain political power in the mid-1800s. The struggle for the ballot took over 70 years of constant, determined campaigning, yet it didn't take a single life, and its achievement has lasted. Compare this with male-led independence movements. Without firing a shot, throwing a rock, or issuing a personal threat, women won for themselves rights that men have launched violent rebellions to achieve. This deliberate rejection of violence may be one of the reasons the movement has not received the attention lavished on other, bloody periods of American history—or on the suffrage movement in Britain. But it should not deceive us; this struggle was waged every bit as seriously as any struggle for equality, and we would do well to consider how women were able to do what men have rarely even tried, changing society in a positive and lasting way without violence and death.

The movement's many nonviolent strategies deserve closer inspection particularly because they repeatedly offered suffragists the way out of strategic binds, dead ends, discouragements and immobility. The nonviolent approach was a logical strategy as a remarkable number of prominent suffrage leaders, from Lucretia Mott to Alice Paul, were Quakers and pacifists, exponents of nonresistance and opponents of war and violence. They were clear about their goals: not victory over men, but equality; not constant war, but reconciliation.

Like the now-celebrated civil rights movement, woman suffrage records the recent and useful experiences of ordinary citizens forced to fight for their own rights against tremendous odds and social inequities. Here are models of political leadership, of women organizers and administrators, activists and lobbyists. Here are the first women lawyers and doctors and ministers, the first women candidates, the first office-holders. Here are stories of achievement, of ingenious strategies and outrageous tactics used to outwit the opponents and make the most of limited resources. Here are new definitions and images of women in our national life which give a more accurate picture of the past and which help explain the way American women are treated today.

The suffrage movement included many Americans whose talents and abilities would have made them prime candidates for national office had the political system and their opportunities been equal. Women like Elizabeth Cady Stanton,

Susan B. Anthony, Lucy Stone, Frances Willard, Jane Addams, Louise Bowen, Ida W. Wells-Barnett, Carrie Chapman Catt, Mary Church Terrell, Alice Paul and others proved themselves, even without the franchise, to be politically competent, highly influential and widely respected leaders with few equals among their male contemporaries.

The suffrage movement offers a unique window onto the emergence of women into American political life. This is where many of the intelligent, active, politically oriented women of the time, denied the right to participate directly in national politics, went. They put their energy into attacking social problems directly and organizing among themselves, locally and nationally, for their own rights.

The Best and the Brightest

Yet despite all of this, the suffrage movement has been routinely and consistently ignored, and when it has not been ignored it has been substantially misrepresented. The result is the misconception today—when there is any conception at all—of the suffrage movement as being essentially an old, passive, white, upper-class, naive, inconsequential cause, one hardly worthy of attention, much less respect. It is treated as a lone curiosity with nothing to teach us, or worse, as a target for clever academics to critique. Fortunately, there are some notable exceptions, but this attitude and the lack of accurate information available lie at the heart of the problem.

A new look at the American woman suffrage movement reveals an entity far different from any popular conception. Not a dour, old-woman cause benevolently recognized by Congressional gods, but a movement of female organizers, leaders, politicians, journalists, visionaries, rabble rousers, and warriors. It was an active, controversial, multi-faceted, challenging, passionate movement of the best and brightest women in America, from all backgrounds, who, in modern parlance, boldly went where no woman had ever gone before.

But rather than acknowledging this, and recognizing that women had to fight for their rights because for the first 150 years American "democracy" actually included half of the population, many academics and historians have chosen to ignore, discount, marginalize, ridicule and/or dismiss the entire 72-year, nationwide, *successful* suffrage movement. In many history textbooks, the entire movement is summed up in one sentence: "In 1920, Congress gave women the right to vote."

Eleanor Flexner noted this censorship in her landmark book *Century of Struggle: The Woman's Rights Movement in the United States*, and quoted the late historian Arthur Schlesinger chiding his colleagues back in 1928 for neglecting women. Schlesinger wrote:

> An examination of the standard histories of the United States and of the history textbooks in use in our schools raises the pertinent question whether women have ever made any contributions to American national progress that are worthy of record. If the silence of the historians is to mean anything, it would appear that one-half of our population have been negligible factors in our country's history . . . any consideration of woman's part in American history must include the protracted struggle of the sex for larger rights and opportunities, a story that is in itself one of the noblest chapters in the history of American democracy.

After Schlesinger wrote this, the civil rights movement added another "noble chapter" to American history, and helped create a new context and vocabulary with which to analyze earlier movements for social change.

"Obliterated the Whole Story"

The suffrage movement stands as a lasting affirmation of our country's democratic promise, for it re-emphasizes the importance of the most fundamental democratic value, the right to vote. Flexner wrote of this in 1975:

> Recently there has been a tendency to low-rate the winning of woman suffrage as something less than the great achievement it seemed to those who carried on the struggle. . . .

> Yet full political citizenship was, for women as for any other group arbitrarily deprived of it, a vital step toward winning full human dignity and the recognition that women, too, are endowed with the faculty of reason, the power of judgment,

the capacity for social responsibility and effective action. As a matter of fact, the opposition to woman suffrage itself bears witness, in a perverse kind of way, to its significance; nothing unimportant would have been so bitterly resisted. If one thinks of those, white and black, who laid down their lives only a few years ago in order that southern black men and women could register to vote, and then actually *vote*, it seems clear that their efforts and sacrifices were no idle exercise in gallantry and that, without the vote, no social or legal reform was either possible, or lasting.

The achievement of the vote for women was extraordinarily difficult, infinitely more so than most people realize, since those who ought to have included it in the history of this country simply obliterated the whole story.

So completely and so quickly was the story lost that it was virtually unknown to the next generation. Suffrage leader Gertrude Foster Brown tells of interviewing one of the women who persuaded the Illinois legislature to grant presidential suffrage in 1913, a key breakthrough in the struggle for national suffrage. She ends her article with this anecdote:

As I sat with Mrs. Booth and her husband some years ago and they told me the tale of the winning of Illinois, he, strangely enough, remembering better than she the details of the long struggle, it was the listening young people who marked for us how far the world has moved since then. Their son and daughter, then grown, sat round-eyed and enthralled by the story. They had never heard it. Did women, just because they were women, ever have to fight against such incredible odds? And was it their mother who had played the leading role on such a stage? Like most young people they had always taken her for granted—retiring, thoughtful, quiet and kind, just a mighty nice mother—and suddenly they saw her a general, a heroine in one of the great dramas of the world. For this Illinois victory was the turning point in the enfranchisement of twenty-five millions of women.

You need not be a feminist, female, or even political to enjoy learning about the suffrage movement. For while the subject is woman suffrage, the larger story is about democracy, and how a powerless class in America won concessions and guarantees from those in power without threatening them with violence or death. We approach this topic not as women or men but as students of American history. We see the woman suffrage movement as a topic of its own, worthy of study and rich with content, apart from the whole field of women's history, notable women, women of achievement, feminist theory or other more general topics where it has previously resided.

Men were suffragists. The suffrage movement both included men as supporters and depended on men for their votes. Even when state measures were lost, the suffrage question often received tens of thousands of male votes of approval, and ultimately, a virtually all-male Senate and House had to approve the amendment, along with 36 virtually all-male state legislatures. Courageous men risked ridicule and worse to actively support women's rights, and they offer far better role models today than many better-known political and military figures.

The suffrage movement also offers us a new cultural heritage, covering not only historical figures and events, but extraordinary personalities, intense relationships, colorful experiences and legendary exploits. Students will find a new view of American history, fuller and richer with new heroes. Next to George Washington and his cherry tree we can set young Carrie Chapman Catt driving a wagon across the prairie by "dead reckoning" or brave Lucretia Mott trusting her own safety to a member of the mob roused against her. We can honor Sojourner Truth no less than Patrick Henry, and Alice Paul no less than Woodrow Wilson.

The suffrage movement holds a particular relevance now as it has helped lead us as a country and a people to where we are today. It celebrates rights won and honors those who helped win them. It is both an example of history suppressed and misunderstood and a lesson of history triumphant. It puts women back into our national history as participants. It reminds us of the necessity of progressive leaders, organizers, and visionaries in every local community. It is the origin of the yet-unpassed Equal Rights Amendment. It exposed the misplaced fears and prejudices of anti-suffragists, and offers a sobering reminder that too many of these same foolish, reactionary attitudes of 100 years ago still exist today. Clearly the wider goal of women's true equality and freedom has not yet been achieved, but the victorious woman suffrage movement offers a new generation of activists a solid base on which to build the future.

Harriot Stanton Blatch summarized the movement's legacy best when she wrote: "Perhaps some day men will raise a tablet reading in letters of gold: 'All honor to women, the first disenfranchised class in history who unaided by any political party won enfranchisement by its own effort alone, and achieved the victory without the shedding of a drop of human blood. All the honor to the women of the world!'"

The Wave of the Future

Nancy Y. Bekavac

Nancy Y. Bekavac, a former lawyer and law professor, is the president of Scripps College in Claremont, California. In the following essay, Bekavac describes her interaction with the young women who attend Scripps College in order to illustrate what she asserts are the changing attitudes of women toward their rights and duties as citizens. According to Bekavac, the women of the upcoming generation believe that their responsibilities as citizens are not only equal to but identical to those of men. For example, she writes, during the Gulf War, these women typically expressed the view that as voting citizens, they have the same obligation to serve as soldiers—and even be subject to a military draft—as do men. Furthermore, she explains, the women of this generation fully expect women to actively take part in politics and are confident that they will see more than one female president in their lifetime. This generation's sense of entitlement to political and social equality is a direct result of the women's suffrage movement, Bekavac concludes.

Ever since I became president of Scripps College in 1990, I have been privileged to view women's participation in politics from a particular vantage point. At Scripps, a women's residential liberal arts college in Southern California, I speak daily with women whose collegiate experience by and large coincides with their eligibility to vote as well as with their initial experience of living away from their families.

The first five years of the 1990s marked a tumultuous time in American politics: we experienced the collapse of the Soviet Union, the Gulf War, continued debates over abor-

Excerpted from "Imagining the Real Future," by Nancy Y. Bekavac, in *A Voice of Our Own: Leading American Women Celebrate the Right to Vote*, edited by Nancy M. Neuman. Copyright ©1996 by Jossey-Bass, Inc. Publishers. Reprinted with permission from the publisher.

tion funding and access, the presidential election of 1992, and the "Republican Revolution" of the 1994 congressional election. . . . For young women, . . . these are challenging and often confusing times.

The Confidence of Young Women

Seventy-five years after passage of the constitutional amendment guaranteeing American women the right to vote, the members of the new generation of women clearly feel confident in their potential to be effective and full citizens of the United States. I cannot hope to speak for these young women; they speak eloquently enough for themselves. But I would like to pass along some of my observations as a member of the baby boomer generation about the experiences and possibilities the women in this new generation will carry into their political maturity and about some of their shared assumptions. Their experiences are sufficiently different from those of the baby boomers and the generations preceding them to give us pause in inferring a clear and certain future. Two sets of incidents will demonstrate the source of my concerns.

The first took place during discussions in the residence halls on the third or fourth day of the Gulf War. A small group of students, mostly Caucasian but including Chicanas, African Americans, and Asian Americans, gathered for a discussion about the war with the dean of faculty and me. Their opinions on the war ranged from fervent support to dismay, confusion, and outright opposition. A number of these students asked about the prospects of conscription—one in particular was concerned about her brother. She did not know, and seemed surprised to learn, that Congress had abolished the draft nearly twenty years before, retaining only vestigial draft registration requirements for men.

Identical Burdens of Citizenship

I was also intrigued by these young women's reactions to what I viewed as one of the most startling aspects of the Gulf War: the deployment of American women military personnel to frontline "support" positions (although what constituted "frontline" was sometimes a difficult issue in this high-tech conflict). I had been particularly struck by the newspaper and television images showing mothers of young children leaving for the war while the fathers held crying infants and talked about assuming child care and other responsibilities. When I asked the students what they thought of these images, they seemed a bit surprised. "They're soldiers. It's their duty; they're trained for it," was the general tone of the replies.

I pressed the issue further, remembering vividly the conundrum of women who loved men—brothers, friends, boyfriends—who faced the draft during the Vietnam War and our coming to terms with the paradox of our own immunity from the threat of conscription, an immunity almost never questioned by anyone in all the endless debates about that war. "Aren't mothers needed at home in a different way than fathers?" I asked. "How would you feel if you were called up and your brothers weren't?" The young women seemed untouched by these questions. Finally, I asked, "Suppose Congress reintroduced the draft. How would you feel about a draft for men and women?" "Fine," they all said. "We vote; we're citizens. It isn't fair to require men to do what we don't have to do." End of discussion.

When I told them that federal law does not require women to register for the draft, they shrugged. When I told them that federal law explicitly bars women from serving in combat, they simply could not dredge up any interest anymore than they wanted to debate bustles or corsets. . . . I had essentially the same discussion four or five times that spring term, including a discussion with some high school seniors who visited the campus.

All of these women, in the spring of 1991, took as an established principle the idea that women bear not only equal but *identical* burdens as citizens, including that responsibility explicitly denied by federal law: to serve equally in their nation's defense in battle.

All of these women grew up during the 1980s when, at least according to many surveys and commentaries, women's rights and advocacy decreased. Moreover, the country failed to ratify the Equal Rights Amendment. Yet these students' deeply rooted conception of their place in the center of national debate and national service was shaped during that same period. Indeed, they formed a conclusion that only the most radical theorists of the 1960s advocated: women have identical rights and obligations in national defense as well as in every other aspect of citizenship.

I believe that such deep assumptions—that women belong in the military, that their family obligations are no different or more special than men's obligations, that the ultimate call of the nation for service in wartime must be met in the same way by both men and women, both single and married people—ultimately will guide this generation's responses to major political issues over time, particularly to the issue of women's right to lead, not just follow, in the public sphere. The older view of women as auxiliaries to men's enterprises was hallowed by tradition and culture; it is found in the federal law that relegates women to military "support" services. I would say that older view has little future. . . .

"The Year of the Woman"

A second event reinforces what I believe is the younger generation's definitively altered view of women's possibilities in public life. On election night 1992, Scripps College set up a very large television screen in an auditorium so that the members of the college community could watch the election results together. We had popcorn and cocoa, blackboards with running totals, and announcements of winners in our own contests for the Scripps class with the highest voter registration percentage and the highest voter turnout. Several faculty and staff along with the usual complement of children, dogs, neighbors, and other passersby were there, a varying crowd of two or three hundred during the course of the evening.

Looking around at a group that was perhaps 75 to 85 percent women, I realized that in all my previous election night vigils, I never had been with so overwhelmingly female a crowd. I knew from the college's comparative data on student attitudes that Scripps students are more idealistic and politically more liberal than their collegiate counterparts generally. So it was no surprise that they cheered most of the early returns showing a Democratic tide. What was striking, however, was the sisterly solidarity that kept welling up. The

The Power of the Ballot

Geraldine Ferraro is a former U.S. representative; in 1984, she became the first woman vice-presidential candidate on a major party ticket. She has also served as an ambassador to the United Nations Human Rights Commission, co-hosted CNN's Crossfire, *and written several books, including* Changing History: Women, Power, and Politics. *The following passage is excerpted from an essay Ferraro wrote to commemorate the 150th anniversary of the Seneca Falls Women's Rights Convention in 1998.*

Women have been able to vote for more than 75 years, but many express the same disturbing indifference to politics as many men. I say this not as chastisement but as a reminder of the power of the ballot box. At Seneca Falls women rejected passivity in favor of action. Voting is an action that asserts that no one is entitled to make decisions for us without considering our opinions. You may doubt the effect voting has on what politicians do but I assure you, my colleagues would be doing cartwheels to win your approval if they knew 85 percent rather than 55 percent of voters would turn out [on] election day. . . .

Even a casual political observer knows that passing legislation is not an easy process. But compared to changing attitudes, sweeping legislative reform is a breeze. To change attitudes in 1848, men had to acknowledge that the rights they enjoyed belonged to their sisters as well as their brothers. And women needed to take the power they claimed, recognizing that passivity would never be as persuasive as organizing. . . .

The work continues. The moral imperatives and practical necessities that have been the underpinnings of the women's movement since Seneca Falls are still vital to our nation today. The celebration of this anniversary is an opportunity to rededicate ourselves to those principles.

Geraldine Ferraro, foreword to *A History of the American Suffragist Movement* by Doris Weatherford, 1998.

crowd responded anxiously, and then enthusiastically, as results from the "Year of the Woman" scrolled across the screen. I particularly remember a sophomore calling out, "I'm from Illinois—I voted for her!" when Carol Moseley-Braun's name blinked on in victory. Women cheered as various returns and predictions were entered on the large maps, but the loudest cheer of all came when the ticker along the bottom of the screen projected Barbara Boxer as well as Dianne Feinstein winning senatorial seats in California—the first time in history any state had elected two women to the U.S. Senate. The reaction was electric; young women danced and hugged and cheered wildly. They stood on chairs and waved. Clearly they felt some part of the victory and some measure of vindication.

The news of California's double election of woman Senators came just as the television cameras were trained on the stage in Little Rock, Arkansas, awaiting candidates Bill Clinton and Al Gore and their wives. Shortly after the four emerged into the spotlight, Bill Clinton turned to his wife and whispered something. Partly because the projected television image was so large, we all clearly saw her take a piece of paper from her pocket and hand it to him; it was from that piece of paper that he spoke. What he said at first was lost in a roar of young women standing up on chairs cheering, not necessarily for President-elect Clinton but for first-lady-to-be Hillary Rodham Clinton. The women were shouting, in unison, "*She* wrote it! *She* wrote it! *She* wrote it!"

I was truly surprised by the reactions—ambushed, as it were, by the passions and emotions I had seen on a campus and during an election that had not seemed particularly involving for the students, even though our surveys showed that more than half of them had registered and voted. Their reactions to women's elections were probably foreseeable, but I was astonished at the reaction to the scene in Little Rock. I saw in that incident a brief insight of intimate partnership, even of wifely dutifulness. The students "read" the clues differently, inferring authorship from Mrs. Clinton's possession of the paper and probably interpreting the relationship differently as well. . . .

A New Set of Expectations

After the last of the concession speeches, I walked back to my house on campus, marveling at what I had seen on those faces and heard in those voices of Scripps women at the beginning of their voting lives. They had a wholly new set of expectations and ambitions: they had just seen, and many had voted for, women elected in record numbers to high office. These students would begin their political maturity expecting not just to be active politically but to see themselves and their fellow students as candidates, as major forces in politics, as Senators and political advisers and forces in their own right.

How different their experience would be from mine. I began my political education watching my mother argue with the television set during the McCarthy-Army Hearings in 1954; there was not a woman on the screen. . . .

In the years after my first vote, I stayed active as a financial contributor, sometime campaign worker, and consistent voter, but many years passed before I had the chance to vote for women candidates seeking high office. I have watched women candidates and officeholders criticized, as their male colleagues and opponents are not, for their clothing and hairstyles and hem lines, for child care and homemaking arrangements, for slips of temper that are commonplace in the masculine world, for daring to speak on topics that some contend are "off limits" to women, and for failing to speak on topics that are "supposed" to be women's issues. Because I know and admire some of these women, I wince and worry and wonder how such biases can be overcome.

Scripps students, by and large, assume these differences do not matter; the differences are unimportant in their view of the world. These young women seem to be blinded or, better yet, looking at facts through polarized lenses that filter out what they do not want to see. While calmly asserting belief in a radical social and political equality, they seem oblivious, or indifferent, to actual inequities: federal laws affecting the military, the gender pay differential in the marketplace, the complex expectations for first ladies, or the double burdens of family and work that women bear every day.

Nevertheless, I hope these Scripps women are not terribly different in their aspirations and assumptions from women their age across the country and across the political spectrum. Almost a century and a half after they helped to mold the abolitionist movement into a great political force, and half again as long after they gained the constitutional right to vote, women are beginning to merge into the electorate and the ranks of political candidates not as valorous heroines or moral avenging angels, not even as political heiresses to great family names or fortunes, but as workaday everyday politicians of pluck and hard work and occasional grandeur.

The women who will dominate the politics of the next fifty to seventy-five years will emerge over the next few years much as other candidates do. And younger women assume these future candidates will experience neither the special barrier of explaining that a woman can do the job nor the special benefits of automatic support because of their gender.

The Legacy of Universal Suffrage

That is, for better or worse (and I must believe it is for better), the legacy of the last seventy-five years. It is the legacy of the women who proposed and campaigned for universal suffrage, and those who took advantage of suffrage to become leaders not just of women but of the nation. Women like Jeannette Rankin, Frances Perkins, Eleanor Roosevelt, Margaret Chase Smith, Rosa Parks, Shirley Chisholm, and Barbara Jordan come to mind. Today's female officeholders are their beneficiaries, who in turn will mark the transition to a new generation that will make the 19th Amendment not so much a signpost as a memorial along a much traveled highway.

The young women who have helped me to understand the interior landscape of assumptions and values on which they map their plans and lives showed me how much has changed from our maps of twenty-five years ago. These women expect, like a friend's daughter who is ten, that by the time they are ready to campaign, they will not be seeking to become the first woman president of the United States but the third or fourth. While their experiences to date have given them a set of assumptions and values far more radically egalitarian, and optimistic, than my generation's, I worry for them. . . .

I believe that many Scripps students underestimate the difficulties that remain; they think I am a victim of old fears. At my most optimistic, I hope they are engaged in that creative enterprise [philosopher] Martin Buber called "imagining the real"—imagining desired goals to shape our actions in a purposeful way so that through our actions, we make those goals concrete. I hope this is what I am seeing, because this is what the world needs so desperately: the informed passions, involvement, talents, genius, and ideals of all of our citizens. That is the goal toward which woman suffrage has helped to move our nation.

Discussion Questions

Chapter 1: The Roots of the Women's Suffrage Movement

1. Doris Weatherford maintains that early American feminists provided the groundwork for the women's suffrage movement. What examples does she present to support her argument? In Weatherford's view, why did early American women want the right to vote?

2. Many founders of the suffrage movement were first involved in abolitionism. According to Eleanor Flexner, what important skills and tactics did women learn in the antislavery movement? In what ways did these abolitionists challenge societal beliefs about women's proper role?

3. The events of the World Anti-Slavery Convention led directly to the formation of the suffrage movement, in Miriam Gurko's opinion. Which issues concerning women's role caused a split in the abolitionist movement? How did this controversy come to a head at the convention?

Chapter 2: Forming the Movement

1. Bill Severn outlines the events leading up to the Seneca Falls Convention and the adoption of the Declaration of Sentiments. According to Severn, which resolution created the most controversy, and why? Cite the text to support your answer.

2. Ellen Carol DuBois contends that suffrage quickly became the primary cause of the fledgling women's movement. What general ideas did early feminists hold about the power and importance of the ballot, in the author's opinion? Why did these feminists place special significance on gaining the vote?

3. According to Alice S. Rossi, the working relationship of Elizabeth Cady Stanton and Susan B. Anthony was of particular importance to the suffrage movement. In her view, what qualities and talents did each woman contribute to their partnership? Do you agree with Rossi's assessment of their significance? Why or why not?

4. African Americans were involved in the suffrage movement from its earliest days. According to Rosalyn Terborg-Penn, how

did the experience of black suffragists differ from that of their white counterparts? What important contributions did African Americans make to the movement?

Chapter 3: Tactics and Disagreements

1. Anne Firor Scott and Andrew MacKay Scott examine the controversy over the Fourteenth and Fifteenth Amendments. In their opinion, how did this controversy both divide and galvanize the suffrage movement? Which two philosophies contributed to the split in the movement?

2. Ellen Carol DuBois discusses the strategic innovation known as the New Departure. What premises underlie the New Departure argument, and what new tactics did it inspire? How did the Supreme Court's rejection of this argument adversely affect the rights of black men, according to the author?

3. Barbara Hilkert Andolsen traces the adoption of racist arguments by many white suffragists. What factors caused white suffragists to employ racist rhetoric? In Andolsen's view, how did this tactic affect the moral legacy of the women's suffrage movement?

Chapter 4: The Antisuffragists

1. Anastatia Sims maintains that antisuffragists anticipated many radical consequences of women's suffrage that the suffragists missed. Do you find her argument convincing? Cite the text to defend your answer.

2. Aileen S. Kraditor provides examples of different types of antisuffrage arguments. In what ways do these arguments contradict each other? What premises do they share?

3. According to Susan E. Marshall, in what ways did the antisuffrage movement evolve over the years? What advantages did the suffrage movement possess that the antisuffragists lacked? How did these differences between the movements affect the antisuffragists' effectiveness?

Chapter 5: The Final Push for Women's Suffrage

1. Christine A. Lunardini describes the "New Suffragists" of the early 1900s. What characteristics and life experiences did this generation share? How did they differ from the experiences of earlier generations of suffragists? How did these factors affect the new generation's approach to the suffrage movement?

2. The militant suffragists adopted a variety of new tactics in the 1910s, according to Edith Mayo. How did these tactics differ from those favored by the older suffrage organizations? What were the drawbacks and the advantages of the radical tactics, in Mayo's opinion?

3. Sara Hunter Graham depicts the final campaign for ratification of the Nineteenth Amendment. According to Graham, what difficulties did the suffragists face in the ratification process? How did the leaders of the movement meet these challenges?

Chapter 6: The Impact of the Nineteenth Amendment

1. In Mildred Adams's opinion, what gains did the newly enfranchised suffragists receive? What losses did they incur? According to the author, which loss was the most serious, and why?

2. Robert Cooney argues that the women's suffrage movement has not received the attention it deserves. In his opinion, what misconceptions still exist about the movement and its participants? How have these misconceptions influenced the historical assessment of the movement?

3. Nancy Y. Bekavac explores the legacy of suffrage and its relevancy to modern women. According to the author, what political and societal assumptions do young women share? How do their attitudes differ from those of the previous generation? Do you agree with Bekavac that these women's lives have been affected by the ongoing legacy of the suffrage movement? Why or why not?

Appendix of Documents

Document 1: Man and Wife Are One Person

Much of early American law was based on English legal theories and practices. The following passage is taken from an anonymous essay published by an English legal scholar in 1632. The author sets forth the argument that in the eyes of the law, a married woman is considered one person with her husband and therefore has no right to a separate vote. Variations of this argument were used by antisuffragists in the United States as late as the 1910s.

In this consolidation which we call wedlock is a locking together. It is true, that man and wife are one person; but understand in what manner. When a small brooke or little river incorporateth with Rhodanus, Humber, or the Thames, the poor rivulet looseth her name; it is carried and recarried with the new associate; it beareth no sway; it possesseth nothing during coverture. A woman as soon as she is married, is called *covert*; in Latine *nupta*, that is, "veiled"; as it were, clouded and overshadowed; she hath lost her streame. I may more truly, farre away, say to a married woman, Her new self is her superior; her companion, her master. . . . See here the reason of that which I touched before,—that women have no voice in Parliament. They make no laws, they consent to none, they abrogate none. All of them are understood either married, or to be married, and their desires are to their husbands. I know no remedy, that some can shift it well enough. The common laws here shaketh hand with divinitye.

Anonymous, *The Lawes Resolutions of Women's Rights; Or, the Lawes Provisions for Women*. London, 1632.

Document 2: Remember the Ladies

In 1776, John Adams was attending the Second Continental Congress, at which the American colonies decided to declare their independence from England. On March 31, 1776, his wife Abigail wrote the following letter urging him and the other delegates to place fewer legal restrictions on women. Although she did not specifically ask for the right to vote, she did assert that without more rights, women would rebel—a statement that would prove to be prophetic.

I long to hear that you have declared an independancy—and by the way in the new Code of Laws which I suppose it will be necessary for you to make I desire you would Remember the Ladies, and be more generous and favourable to them than your ancestors. Do not put such unlimited power into the hands of the Husbands. Remember all Men would be tyrants if they could. If perticuliar care and attention is not paid to the Laidies we are determined to foment a Rebelion, and will not hold ourselves bound by any Laws in which we have no voice, or Representation.

That your Sex are Naturally Tyrannical is a Truth so thoroughly established as to admit of no dispute, but such of you as wish to be happy willingly give up the harsh title of Master for the more tender and endearing one of Friend. Why then, not put it out of the power of the vicious and the Lawless to use us with cruelty and indignity with impunity. Men of Sense in all Ages abhor those customs which treat us only as the vassals of your Sex. Regard us then as Beings placed by providence under your protection and in immitation of the Supreem Being make use of that power only for our happiness.

L.H. Butterfield, ed., *The Adams Papers: Adams Family Correspondence*, vol. I. Cambridge, MA: Harvard University Press, 1963.

Document 3: An Early Feminist Text

The following passage is excerpted from Mary Wollstonecraft's A Vindication of the Rights of Woman, *first published in 1792. Wollstonecraft was an English author, but her book was the most prominent of several feminist texts written during this era and was widely read in the United States. Her work had a lasting impact on many of the women who became involved in the American suffrage movement.*

Women . . . have now perhaps more power than they would have if the world, divided and subdivided into kingdoms and families, were governed by laws deduced from the exercise of reason; but in obtaining it . . . their character is degraded, and licentiousness spread through the whole aggregate of society. The many become pedestal to the few. I, therefore, will venture to assert that till women are more rationally educated, the progress of human virtue and improvement in knowledge must receive continual checks. . . .

Let not men then in the pride of power . . . fallaciously assert that woman ought to be subjected because she has always been so. But, when man, governed by reasonable laws, enjoys his natural freedom, let him despise woman, if she do not share it with him; and, till that glorious period arrives, in descanting on the folly of the sex, let him not overlook his own.

Women, it is true, obtaining power by unjust means, by practising or fostering vice, evidently lose the rank which reason would assign them, and they become either abject slaves or capricious tyrants. They lose all simplicity, all dignity of mind, in acquiring power, and act as men are observed to act when they have been exalted by the same means.

It is time to effect a revolution in female manners—time to restore to them their lost dignity—and make them, as a part of the human species, labour by reforming themselves to reform the world.

Mary Wollstonecraft, *A Vindication of the Rights of Woman*. New York: Penguin Books, 1992.

Document 4: The Pastoral Letter

In the early 1800s, a number of American women became involved in the campaign to abolish slavery. At a time when it was considered scandalous for women to participate in public affairs, these abolitionists gave lectures, circulated petitions door to door, and attended anti-slavery conventions. Many people were offended by such "unladylike" behavior, as evidenced in the following pastoral letter issued by the General Association of Massachusetts Congregational Churches in 1837.

The power of woman is in her dependence, flowing from the consciousness of that weakness which God has given her for her protection, and which keeps her in those departments of life that form the character of individuals and of the nation. There are social influences which females use in promoting piety and the great objects of Christian benevolence which we cannot too highly commend. We appreciate the unostentatious prayers and efforts of woman in advancing the cause of religion at home and abroad; in Sabbath-schools; in leading religious inquirers to the pastors for instruction; and in all such associated effort as becomes the modesty of her sex; and earnestly hope that she may abound more and more in these labors of piety and love.

But when she assumes the place and tone of man as a public reformer, our care and protection of her seem unnecessary; we put ourselves in self-defence against her; she yields the power which God has given her for protection, and her character becomes unnatural. . . . We cannot, therefore, but regret the mistaken conduct of those who encourage females to bear an obtrusive and ostentatious part in measures of reform, and countenance any of that sex who so far forget themselves as to itinerate in the character of public lecturers and teachers. We especially deplore the intimate acquaintance and promiscuous conversation of females with regard to things "which ought not to be named"; by which that modesty and delicacy which is the charm of domestic life, and which constitutes the true influence of woman in society is consumed, and the way opened, as we apprehend, for degeneracy and ruin.

The General Association of Massachusetts Congregational Churches, "Pastoral Letter," *New England Spectator*, July 12, 1837.

Document 5: A Female Abolitionist Responds to Criticism

Raised in a southern slaveholding family, sisters Sarah and Angelina Grimké moved to New England in the 1820s and became fervent abolitionists. In the 1830s, they rose to prominence as anti-slavery lecturers, becoming two of the first American women to speak in front of "mixed" audiences of both men and women. Although the General Association's pastoral letter—which condemned women's participation in public reforms—did not mention the Grimkés by name, it was directly aimed at the sisters. Sarah Grimké responded to the attack with this eloquent defense of women's rights.

I am persuaded that the rights of woman, like the rights of slaves, need only be examined to be understood and asserted, even by some of those, who are now endeavoring to smother the irrepressible desire for mental and spiritual freedom which glows in the breast of many, who hardly dare to speak their sentiments. . . .

The Lord Jesus defines the duties of his followers in his Sermon on the Mount. He lays down grand principles by which they should be governed, without any reference to sex or condition.—"Ye are the light of the world. A city that is set on a hill cannot be hid. Neither do men light a candle and put it under a bushel, but on a candlestick, and it giveth light unto all that are in the house. Let your light so shine before men, that they may see your good works, and glorify your Father which is in Heaven" [Matt. 5:14–16]. I follow him through all his precepts, and find him giving the same directions to women as to men, never even referring to the distinction now so strenuously insisted upon between masculine and feminine virtues: this is one of the anti-christian "traditions of men" which are taught instead of the "commandments of God." Men and women were CREATED EQUAL; they are both moral and accountable beings, and whatever is *right* for man to do, is *right* for woman.

But the influence of woman, says the Association, is to be private and unobtrusive; her light is not to shine before man like that of her brethren; but she is passively to let the lords of the creation, as they call themselves, put the bushel over it, lest peradventure it might appear that the world has been benefitted by the rays of *her* candle. So that her quenched light, according to their judgment, will be of more use than if it were set on the candlestick. "Her influence is the source of mighty power." This has ever been the flattering language of man since he laid aside the whip as a means to keep woman in subjection. He spares her body; but the war he has waged against her mind, her heart, and her soul, has been no less destructive to her as a moral being. How monstrous, how anti-christian, is the doctrine that woman is to be dependent on man! . . .

We are told, "the power of woman is in her dependence, flowing from a consciousness of that weakness which God has given her for her protection." If physical weakness is alluded to, I cheerfully concede the superiority; if brute force is what my brethren are claiming, I am willing to let them have all the honor they desire; but if they mean to intimate, that mental or moral weakness belongs to woman, more than to man, I utterly disclaim the charge. Our powers of mind have been crushed, as far as man could do it, our sense of morality has been impaired by his interpretation of our duties; but no where does God say that he made any distinction between us, as moral and intelligent beings.

Sarah Grimké, *Letters on the Equality of the Sexes and the Condition of Woman.* Boston: Isaac Knapp, 1838.

Document 6: The Debate at the World Anti-Slavery Convention

The World Anti-Slavery Convention was held in London, England, in 1840. American abolitionist societies elected several women to serve as delegates, but when they arrived, many of the male participants protested their involvement. In the ensuing debate, Massachusetts abolitionist George Bradburn argued in support of the women's right to participate; his speech is quoted here. However, Bradburn and the other advocates of the women were ultimately outvoted.

We are told that it would be outraging the customs of England to allow women to sit in this Convention. I have a great respect for the customs of old England. But I ask, gentlemen, if it be right to set up the customs and habits, not to say prejudices of Englishmen, as a standard for the government on this occasion of Americans, and of persons belonging to several other independent nations. I can see neither reason nor policy in so doing. Besides, I deprecate the principle of the objection. In America it would exclude from our conventions all persons of color, for there customs, habits, tastes, prejudices, would be outraged by *their* admission. And I do not wish to be deprived of the aid of those who have done so much for this cause, for the purpose of gratifying any mere custom or prejudice. Women have furnished most essential aid in accomplishing what has been done in the State of Massachusetts. . . . And shall such women be refused seats here in a Convention seeking the emancipation of slaves throughout the world? What a misnomer to call this a World's Convention of Abolitionists, when some of the oldest and most thorough-going Abolitionists in the world are denied the right to be represented in it by delegates of their own choice.

Elizabeth Cady Stanton, Susan B. Anthony, and Matilda Joslyn Gage, eds., *History of Woman Suffrage*, vol. I. Rochester, NY: Charles Mann, 1889.

Document 7: The Declaration of Sentiments

The Declaration of Sentiments that follows was written in July 1848 by the organizers of the first women's rights convention in Seneca Falls, New York. It is primarily the work of Elizabeth Cady Stanton, who modeled it closely on the Declaration of Independence. Its blistering condemnation of men's historical treatment of women became a rallying cry for the fledgling women's movement.

When, in the course of human events, it becomes necessary for one portion of the family of man to assume among the people of the earth a position different from that which they have hitherto occupied, but one to which the laws of nature and of nature's God entitle them, a decent respect to the opinions of mankind requires that they should declare the causes that impel them to such a course.

We hold these truths to be self-evident: that all men and women are created equal; that they are endowed by their Creator with certain inalienable rights; that among these are life, liberty, and the pursuit of happiness; that to secure these rights governments are instituted, deriving their just powers from the consent of the governed. Whenever any form of government becomes destructive of these ends, it is the right of those who suffer from it to refuse allegiance to it, and to insist upon the institution of a new government, laying its foundation on such principles, and organizing its powers in such form, as to them shall seem most likely to effect their safety and happiness. Prudence, indeed, will dictate that governments long established should not be changed for light and transient causes; and accordingly all experience hath shown that mankind are more disposed to suffer, while evils are sufferable, than to right themselves by abolishing the forms to which they were accustomed. But when a long train of abuses and usurpations, pursuing invariably the same object evinces a design to reduce them under absolute despotism, it is their duty to throw off such government, and to provide new guards for their future security. Such has been the patient sufferance of the women under this government, and such is now the necessity which constrains them to demand the equal station to which they are entitled.

The history of mankind is a history of repeated injuries and usurpations on the part of man toward woman, having in direct object the establishment of an absolute tyranny over her. To prove this, let facts be submitted to a candid world.

He has never permitted her to exercise her inalienable right to the elective franchise.

He has compelled her to submit to laws, in the formation of which she had no voice.

He has withheld from her rights which are given to the most ignorant and degraded men—both natives and foreigners.

Having deprived her of this first right of a citizen, the elective franchise, thereby leaving her without representation in the halls of legislation, he has oppressed her on all sides.

He has made her, if married, in the eye of the law, civilly dead.

He has taken from her all right in property, even to the wages she earns.

He has made her, morally, an irresponsible being, as she can commit many crimes with impunity, provided they be done in the presence of her husband. In the covenant of marriage, she is compelled to promise obedience to her husband, he becoming, to all intents and purposes, her master—the law giving him power to deprive her of her liberty, and to administer chastisement.

He has so framed the laws of divorce, as to what shall be the proper causes, and in case of separation, to whom the guardianship of the children shall be given, as to be wholly regardless of the happiness of women—the law, in all cases, going upon a false supposition of the supremacy of man, and giving all power into his hands.

After depriving her of all rights as a married woman, if single, and the owner of property, he has taxed her to support a government which recognizes her only when her property can be made profitable to it.

He has monopolized nearly all the profitable employments, and from those she is permitted to follow, she receives but a scanty remuneration. He closes against her all the avenues to wealth and distinction which he considers most honorable to himself. As a teacher of theology, medicine, or law, she is not known.

He has denied her the facilities for obtaining a thorough education, all colleges being closed against her.

He allows her in Church, as well as State, but a subordinate position, claiming Apostolic authority for her exclusion from the ministry, and, with some exceptions, from any public participation in the affairs of the Church.

He has created a false public sentiment by giving to the world a different code of morals for men and women, by which moral delinquencies which exclude women from society, are not only tolerated, but deemed of little account in man.

He has usurped the prerogative of Jehovah himself, claiming it as his right to assign for her a sphere of action, when that belongs to her conscience and to her God.

He has endeavored, in every way that he could, to destroy her confidence in her own powers, to lessen her self-respect, and to make her willing to lead a dependent and abject life.

Now, in view of this entire disfranchisement of one-half the people of this country, their social and religious degradation—in view of the unjust laws above mentioned, and because women do feel themselves aggrieved, oppressed, and fraudulently deprived of their most sacred rights, we insist that they have immediate admission to all the rights and privileges which belong to them as citizens of the United States.

In entering upon the great work before us, we anticipate no small amount of misconception, misrepresentation, and ridicule; but we shall use every instrumentality within our power to effect our object. We shall employ agents, circulate tracts, petition the State and National legislatures, and endeavor to enlist the pulpit and the press in our behalf. We hope this Convention will be followed by a series of Conventions embracing every part of the country.

Elizabeth Cady Stanton, Susan B. Anthony, and Matilda Joslyn Gage, eds., *History of Woman Suffrage*, vol. I. Rochester, NY: Charles Mann, 1889.

Document 8: The Beginnings of a Grand Movement

Born a slave, Frederick Douglass escaped to the North and became a leading abolitionist. He attended the first women's rights convention at Seneca Falls in July 1848 and was impressed by the speeches made by the women. Shortly after the convention, he published the following editorial describing the proceedings and expressing his support for the new movement.

One of the most interesting events of the past week, was the holding of what is technically styled a Woman's Rights Convention at Seneca Falls. The speaking, addresses, and resolutions of this extraordinary meeting were almost wholly conducted by women; and although they evidently felt themselves in a novel position, it is but simple justice to say that their whole proceedings were characterized by marked ability and dignity. . . . Several interesting documents setting forth the rights as well as grievances of women were read. Among these was a Declaration of Sentiments, to be regarded as the basis of a grand movement for attaining the civil, social, political, and religious rights of women. We should not do justice to our own convictions, or to the excellent persons connected with this infant movement, if we did not in this connection offer a few remarks on the general subject which the Convention met to consider and the objects they seek to attain. . . .

While it is impossible for us to go into this subject at length, and dispose of the various objections which are often urged against such a doctrine as that of female equality, we are free to say that in respect to political rights, we hold woman to be justly entitled to all we claim for man. We go farther, and express our conviction that all political rights which it is expedient for man to exercise, it is equally so for woman. All that distinguishes man as an intelligent and accountable being, is equally true of woman; and if that government only is just which governs by the free consent of the governed, there can be no reason in the world for denying to woman the exercise of the elective franchise, or a hand in making and administering the laws of the land. Our doctrine is that "right is of no sex." We therefore bid the women engaged in this movement our humble Godspeed.

Frederick Douglass, "The Rights of Women," *North Star*, July 28, 1848.

Document 9: Unwomanly and Wrong

Frederick Douglass's ringing support of the early women's movement was not a majority view. Instead, most Americans reacted to the news with amusement or dismay. More typical of the responses in the press is this anonymous 1848 editorial from the Mechanic's Advocate, *a periodical published in Albany, New York. The author ridicules the convention participants and warns that the reforms they want would wreak havoc on society.*

We are sorry to see that the women in several parts of this State are holding what they call "Woman's Rights Conventions," and setting forth a formidable list of those Rights in a parody upon the

Declaration of American Independence. . . .

The women who attend these meetings, no doubt at the expense of their more appropriate duties, act as committees, write resolutions and addresses, hold much correspondence, make speeches, etc., etc. They affirm, as among their rights, that of unrestricted franchise, and assert that it is wrong to deprive them of the privilege to become legislators, lawyers, doctors, divines, etc., etc.; and they are holding Conventions and making an agitatory movement, with the object in view of revolutionizing public opinion and the laws of the land, and changing their relative position in society in such a way as to divide with the male sex the labors and responsibilities of active life in every branch of art, science, trades, and professions.

Now, it requires no argument to prove that this is all wrong. Every true hearted female will instantly feel that this is unwomanly, and that to be practically carried out, the males must change their position in society to the same extent in an opposite direction, in order to enable them to discharge an equal share of the domestic duties which now appertain to females, and which must be neglected, to a great extent, if women are allowed to exercise all the "rights" that are claimed by these Convention-holders. Society would have to be radically remodelled in order to accommodate itself to so great a change in the most vital part of the compact of the social relations of life; and the order of things established at the creation of mankind, and continued *six thousand years*, would be completely broken up. The organic laws of our country, and of each State, would have to be licked into new shapes, in order to admit of the introduction of the vast change that it contemplated. In a thousand other ways that might be mentioned, if we had room to make, and our readers had patience to hear them, would this sweeping reform be attended by fundamental changes in the public and private, civil and religious, moral and social relations of the sexes, of life, and of the Government.

But this change is impracticable, uncalled for, and unnecessary. *If effected*, it would set the world by the ears, make "confusion worse confounded," demoralize and degrade from their high sphere and noble destiny, women of all respectable and useful classes, and prove a monstrous injury to all mankind. It would be productive of no positive good, that would not be outweighed tenfold by positive evil. It would alter the relations of females without bettering their condition. Besides all, and above all, it presents no remedy for the *real* evils that the millions of the industrious, hard-working, and much suffering women of our country groan under and seek to redress.

"Women Out of Their Latitude," *Mechanic's Advocate*, July/August 1848.

Document 10: Temperance Reform and the Power of the Vote

Many early suffragists were also involved in the temperance movement, which was predominately female in composition. As temperance advocate and author Mary C. Vaughan explains here, she initially opposed women's suffrage but soon changed her mind. In her letter to the editor of the Lily, *a temperance periodical, Vaughan writes that she realized women could use the ballot to bring about social reforms that would otherwise be beyond their reach.*

My thoughts have of late been much turned to the subject of woman's influence upon the cause of temperance, and I am convinced that she can do little except through the medium of the ballot box. True, there is the powerful though quiet influence she exerts at home, as an educator, but beyond the precincts of her own family circle, what is she accomplishing toward the arrest of this formidable evil? Alas, very, *very* little. . . .

Less than a year since, . . . the idea that women should go to the polls, was utterly repugnant to me. But when once convinced that she could act in no other way to any extent in the Temperance reform, there came a complete change over my feelings upon that subject. I am not ashamed to change opinions when convinced that those heretofore held are erroneous—as in this case I am, most sincerely. But then comes the thought if she should enjoy the right of voting for Temperance measures, why not for every reform? why not for all things that affect the public weal, if she choose to use that right? I for one have no ambition at present to approach the ballot-box, except for cast into it a vote which might have its bearing upon Temperance. Yet while I feel that I have a right, which, though withheld, is not the less mine, to do that, I cannot deny that I have the same right to vote on other questions.

Mary C. Vaughan, *Lily*, October 1851.

Document 11: Asking for an Amendment

After the Civil War and the emancipation of the slaves, Congress began considering constitutional amendments designed to protect the rights of African Americans, including the right to vote. Most suffragists hoped that Congress would also grant voting rights to women. When they learned that the proposed Fourteenth Amendment specifically limited suffrage to "male citizens," they were outraged. In 1865, Elizabeth Cady Stanton, Susan B. Anthony, and many other suffragists signed the following petition to Congress, demanding their right to vote.

The undersigned women of the United States, respectfully ask an amendment of the Constitution that shall prohibit the several States from disfranchising any of their citizens on the ground of sex.

In making our demand for Suffrage, we would call your attention to the fact that we represent fifteen million people—one-half the entire population of the country—intelligent, virtuous, native-born American citizens; and yet stand outside the pale of political recognition. The Constitution classes us as "free people," and counts us *whole* persons in the basis of representation; and yet are we governed without our consent, compelled to pay taxes without appeal, and punished for violations of law without choice of judge or juror. The experience of all ages, the Declarations of the Fathers, the Statute Laws of our own day, and the fearful revolution [the Civil War] through which we have just passed, all prove the uncertain tenure of life, liberty, and property so long as the ballot—the only weapon of self-protection—is not in the hand of every citizen.

Therefore, as you are now amending the Constitution, and, in harmony with advancing civilization, placing new safeguards round the individual rights of four millions of emancipated slaves, we ask that you extend the right of Suffrage to Woman—the only remaining class of disfranchised citizens—and thus fulfill your constitutional obligation "to guarantee to every State in the Union a Republican form of Government." As all partial application of Republican principles must ever breed a complicated legislation as well as a discontented people, we would pray your Honorable Body, in order to simplify the machinery of Government and ensure domestic tranquillity, that you legislate hereafter for persons, citizens, tax-payers, and not for class or caste. For justice and equality your petitioners will ever pray.

Elizabeth Cady Stanton, Susan B. Anthony, and Matilda Joslyn Gage, eds., *History of Woman Suffrage*, vol. II. Rochester, NY: Charles Mann, 1881.

Document 12: A Feeble Clamor

With suffragists loudly protesting the proposed Fourteenth Amendment, Congress considered the issue of women's suffrage during the mid-1860s. In the following excerpt from an 1866 congressional debate, Senator George H. Williams of Oregon argues that relatively few women want the right to vote.

To extend the right of suffrage to the negroes in this country I think is necessary for their protection; but to extend the right of suffrage to women, in my judgment, is not necessary for their protection. . . .

When women ask Congress to extend to them the right of suffrage it will be proper to consider their claims. Not one in a thousand of them at this time wants any such thing, and would not exercise the power if it was granted to them. Some few who are seeking notoriety make a feeble clamor for the right of suffrage, but they do not represent the sex to which they belong. . . .

Women do not bear their proportion and share, they cannot bear their proportion and share, of the public burdens. Men represent them in the Army and in the Navy; men represent them at the polls and in the affairs of the Government; and though it be true that individual women do own property that is taxed, yet nine tenths of the property and the business from which the revenues of the Government are derived are in the hands [of] and belong to and are controlled by the men. Sir, when the women of this country come to be sailors and soldiers; when they come to navigate the ocean and to follow the plow; when they love to be jostled and crowded by all sorts of men in the thoroughfares of trade and business; when they love the treachery and the turmoil of politics; when they love the dissoluteness of the camp and the smoke and the thunder and the blood of battle better than they love the affections and enjoyments of home and family, then it will be time to talk about making the women voters; but until that time, the question is not fairly before the country.

Congressional Globe, December 11, 1866.

Document 13: Keep It Stirring

As it became increasingly clear that women would be excluded from the Fourteenth and Fifteenth Amendments, the suffrage movement began to split apart. Some suffragists actively worked against the passage of the amendments, but others felt it was wrong to oppose measures that would protect the civil rights of black men. Sojourner Truth was one of the few suffragists in the midst of this controversy who spoke out for black women. In the following excerpts from an 1867 speech, Truth advocates equal rights for all, regardless of gender or race.

There is a great stir about colored men getting their rights, but not a word about the colored women; and if colored men get their rights, and not colored women theirs, you see the colored men will be masters over the women, and it will be just as bad as it was before. So I am for keeping the thing going while things are stirring; because if we wait till it is still, it will take a great while to get it going again. . . . I want women to have their rights. In the courts women have no right, no voice; nobody speaks for them. I wish woman to have her voice there among the pettifoggers. If it is not a fit place for women, it is unfit for men to be there.

I am above eighty years old; it is about time for me to be going. I have been forty years a slave and forty years free, and would be here forty years more to have equal rights for all. I suppose I am kept here because something remains for me to do; I suppose I am yet to help to break the chain. . . . I suppose I am about the only colored woman that goes about to speak for the rights of the colored women. I want to keep the thing stirring, now that the ice is cracked. . . . I have been in Washington about three years, seeing about these colored people. Now colored men have the right to vote. There ought to be equal rights now more than ever, since colored people have got their freedom.

Elizabeth Cady Stanton, Susan B. Anthony, and Matilda Joslyn Gage, eds., *History of Woman Suffrage*, vol. II. Rochester, NY: Charles Mann, 1881.

Document 14: A Deliberate Insult to American Women

Most white suffragists who opposed the Fourteenth and Fifteenth Amendments did not think in terms of black women's right to vote. Many suffragists—even those who had previously been ardent abolitionists and social reformers—began to use racist, classist, and anti-immigrant language in their arguments. In this 1869 speech, Elizabeth Cady Stanton rails against the fact that the Fifteenth Amendment would give immigrants and former slaves the right to vote while denying it to educated, native-born women.

When "manhood suffrage" is established from Maine to California, woman [will have] reached the lowest depths of political degradation. So long as there is a disfranchised class in this country, and that class its women, a man's government is worse than a white man's government with suffrage limited by property and educational qualifications, because in proportion as you multiply the rulers, the condition of the politically ostracised is more hopeless and degraded. . . . If American women find it hard to bear the oppressions of their own Saxon fathers, the best orders of manhood, what may they not be called to endure when all the lower orders of foreigners now crowding our shores legislate for them and their daughters. Think of Patrick and Sambo and Hans and Yung Tung, who do not know the difference between a monarchy and a republic, who can not read the Declaration of Independence or Webster's spelling-book, making laws for Lucretia Mott, Ernestine L. Rose, and Anna E. Dickinson. . . . This manhood suffrage is an appalling question, and it would be well for thinking women, who seem to consider it so magnanimous to hold their own claims in abeyance until all men are crowned with citizenship, to remember that the most ignorant men are ever the most hostile to the equality of women, as they have known them only in slavery and degradation. . . .

It is an open, deliberate insult to American womanhood to be cast down under the iron-heeled peasantry of the Old World and the slaves of the New, as we shall be in the practical working of the Fifteenth Amendment, and the only atonement the Republican party can make is now to complete its work, by enfranchising the women of the nation. . . .

Now, when the attention of the whole world is turned to this question of suffrage, . . . shall American statesmen, claiming to be liberal, so amend their constitutions as to make their wives and mothers the political inferiors of unlettered and unwashed ditch-diggers, boot-blacks, butchers, and barbers, fresh from the slave plantations of the South, and the effete civilizations of the Old World? While poets and philosophers, statesmen and men of science are all alike pointing to woman as the new hope for the redemption of the race, shall the freest Government on the earth be the first to establish an aristocracy based on sex alone? to exalt ignorance above education, vice above virtue, brutality and barbarism above refinement and religion? . . . On all the blackest pages of history there is no record of an act like this, in any nation, where native born citizens, having the same religion, speaking the same language, equal to their rulers in wealth, family, and education, have been politically ostracised by their own countrymen, outlawed with savages, and subjected to the government of outside barbarians. Remember the Fifteenth Amendment takes in a larger population than the 2,000,000 black men on the Southern plantation. It takes in all the foreigners daily landing in our eastern cities, the Chinese crowding our western shores, the inhabitants of Alaska, and all those western isles that will soon be ours. . . . [But] women of wealth and education, who pay taxes and obey the laws, who in morals and intellect are the peers of their proudest rulers, are thrust outside the pale of political consideration with minors, paupers, lunatics, traitors, idiots, with those guilty of bribery, larceny, and infamous crimes.

Elizabeth Cady Stanton, Susan B. Anthony, and Matilda Joslyn Gage, eds., *History of Woman Suffrage*, vol. II. Rochester, NY: Charles Mann, 1881.

Document 15: Concentrating on Suffrage

The Fourteenth and Fifteenth Amendments were not the only issues that divided the women's rights movement after the Civil War. While some members of the movement continued to speak on a wide variety of topics concerning women, others decided that they needed to narrow their focus to suffrage, avoiding controversial social issues such as divorce reform. In January 1870, longtime suffragist Henry Blackwell published this editorial promoting the latter view.

The great necessity of the cause of WOMAN SUFFRAGE in America is an efficient organization in which every friend of the movement can work freely and without the need of protest.

To effect such an organization is not as easy as may at first appear. The advocates of woman's political equality differ utterly upon every other topic. Some are abolitionists; others, hostile to the equality of races. Some are evangelical Christians; others, Catholics, Unitarians, Spiritualists or Quakers. Some hold the most rigid theories with regard to marriage and divorce; others are latitudinarian on these questions. Some are Republicans, others Democrats. In short, people of the most opposite views agree in desiring to establish Woman Suffrage, while they anticipate very different results from the reform, when effected.

Now the union of all these people is essential to success. But their diversities of opinion are only compatible with union, provided the question of Woman's legal and political equality is made *sole* and *paramount*. Unfortunately, many well-meaning people cannot, or will not so regard it. They insist upon dragging in their peculiar views upon theology, temperance, marriage, race, dress, finance, labor and capital—it matters not what. They demand a free platform and unlimited latitude of expression.

We have had quite enough of this unlimited range of discussion, this confusion of ideas which have no logical connection. No one can estimate the damage the cause of Woman's enfranchisement has already sustained, by the failure of its advocates to limit themselves to the main question. For ourselves, we propose to begin our reform at this very point. As advocates of equal rights, we protest against loading the good ship "Woman Suffrage" with a cargo of irrelevant opinions. . . .

If it be objected that to limit the question to Suffrage alone is to narrow the platform of Woman's Rights, we reply that in practical questions which involve the united action of masses of men, distinctness and definiteness are primary conditions of success. A certain narrowness and precision are as essential to practical action as are breadth and comprehensiveness to theoretical speculation. This is the law of all political organizations. And Woman Suffrage *is* a political question. . . . In order to command the universal support which is essential to political success, Woman Suffrage must cease to be treated as a symbol of social innovations. It must be urged as a purely political question upon its own merits.

Henry Blackwell, *Woman's Journal*, January 8, 1870.

Document 16: An Antisuffrage Petition

Before the Civil War, there had been no organized opposition to the women's rights movement. However, during the years immediately after the war, women's suffrage became such a pressing issue that antisuffragists felt the need to make their opinions known. In the summer of 1870, the following petition to the U.S. Congress was circulating among antisuffrage women in New York and other cities.

We, the undersigned, do hereby appeal to your honorable body, and desire respectfully to enter our protest against an extension of suffrage to women; and in the firm belief that our petition represents the sober convictions of the majority of the women of the country.

Although we shrink from the notoriety of the public eye, yet we are too deeply and painfully impressed by the grave perils which threaten our peace and happiness in these proposed changes in our civil and political rights longer to remain silent.

Because, Holy Scripture inculcates a different, and for us, higher sphere, apart from the public life.

Because, as women we find a full measure of duties, cares and responsibilities devolving upon us, and we are therefore unwilling to bear other and heavier burdens, and those unsuited to our physical organizations.

Because, we hold that an extension of suffrage would be adverse to the interest of the working women of the country, with whom we heartily sympathize.

Because, these changes must introduce a fruitful element of discord in the existing marriage relation, which would tend to the infinite detriment of children, and increase the already alarming prevalence of divorce throughout the land.

Because, no general law, affecting the condition of all women, should be framed to meet exceptional discontent.

For these and many more reasons, do we beg of your wisdom that no law extending suffrage to women may be passed, as the passage of such a law would be fraught with danger so grave to the general order of the country.

Lana Rakow and Cheris Kramarae, eds., *The Revolution in Words: Righting Women, 1868–1871.* New York: Routledge, 1990.

Document 17: Women Have the Right to Vote

The flamboyant and controversial Victoria Woodhull—notorious for her unconventional views on sexual freedom—was briefly a prominent member of the women's suffrage movement. On January 11, 1871, she became the first woman ever to address the Judiciary Committee of the House of Representatives. In the following excerpt from her address, Woodhull asserts that as citizens of the United States, women inherently possess the right to vote.

Women constitute a majority of the people of this country—they hold vast portions of the nation's wealth and pay a proportionate share of the taxes. They are intrusted with the most vital responsibilities of society; they bear, rear, and educate men; they train and mould their characters; they inspire the noblest impulses in men; they often hold the accumulated fortunes of a man's life for the safety of the family and as guardians of the infants, and yet they are debarred from uttering any opinion by public vote, as to the management by public servants of these interests; they are the secret counselors, the best advisers, the most devoted aids in the most trying periods of men's lives, and yet men shrink from trusting them in the common questions of ordinary politics. Men trust women in the market, in the shop, on the highway and railroad, and in all other public places and assemblies, but when they propose to carry a slip of paper with a name upon it to the polls, they fear them. Nevertheless, as citizens, women have the right to vote; they are part and parcel of that great element in which the sovereign power of the land had birth; and it is by usurpation only that men debar them from this right. The American nation, in its march onward and upward, can not publicly choke the intellectual and political activity of half its citizens by narrow statutes. The will of the entire people is the true basis of republican government, and a free expression of that will by the public vote of all citizens, without distinctions of race, color, occupation, or sex, is the only means by which that will can be ascertained. As the world has advanced into civilization and culture; as mind has risen in its dominion over matter; as the principle of justice and moral right has gained sway, and merely physical organized power has yielded thereto; as the might of right has supplanted the right of might, so have the rights of women become more fully recognized, and that recognition is the result of the development of the minds of men, which through the ages she has polished, and thereby heightened the lustre of civilization.

Elizabeth Cady Stanton, Susan B. Anthony, and Matilda Joslyn Gage, eds., *History of Woman Suffrage*, vol. II. Rochester, NY: Charles Mann, 1881.

Document 18: Susan B. Anthony's Trial

In 1872, Susan B. Anthony went to the polls and cast her ballot; she was arrested shortly thereafter for voting illegally. Her trial was held on June 17, 1873, presided over by Judge Ward Hunt. The judge refused to allow Anthony to testify during the trial. He also dismissed the jury before they could vote on the case, handing down a guilty verdict himself. On the next day, at her sentencing, Anthony finally managed to speak to the court.

The Court: The prisoner will stand up. Has the prisoner anything to say why sentence shall not be pronounced?

Miss Anthony: Yes, your honor, I have many things to say; for in your ordered verdict of guilty, you have trampled underfoot every vital principle of our government. My natural rights, my civil rights, my political rights, are all alike ignored. Robbed of the fundamental privilege of citizenship, I am degraded from the status of a citizen to that of a subject; and not only myself individually, but all of my sex, are, by your honor's verdict, doomed to political subjection under this so-called Republican government.

Judge Hunt: The Court can not listen to a rehearsal of arguments the prisoner's counsel has already consumed three hours in presenting.

Miss Anthony: May it please your honor, I am not arguing the question, but simply stating the reasons why sentence can not, in justice, be pronounced against me. Your denial of my citizen's right to vote is the denial of my right of consent as one of the governed, the denial of my right of representation as one of the taxed, the denial of my right to a trial by a jury of my peers as an offender against law, therefore, the denial of my sacred rights to life, liberty, property, and—

Judge Hunt: The Court can not allow the prisoner to go on.

Miss Anthony: But your honor will not deny me this one and

only poor privilege of protest against this high-handed outrage upon my citizen's rights. May it please the Court to remember that since the day of my arrest last November, this is the first time that either myself or any person of my disfranchised class has been allowed a word of defense before judge or jury—

Judge Hunt: The prisoner must sit down; the Court can not allow it.

Miss Anthony: All my prosecutors, from the 8th Ward corner grocery politician, who entered the complaint, to the United States Marshal, Commissioner, District Attorney, District Judge, your honor on the bench, not one is my peer, but each and all are my political sovereigns; and had your honor submitted my case to the jury, as was clearly your duty, even then I should have had just cause of protest, for not one of those men was my peer; but, native or foreign, white or black, rich or poor, educated or ignorant, awake or asleep, sober or drunk, each and every man of them was my political superior; hence, in no sense, my peer. Even, under such circumstances, a commoner of England, tried before a jury of lords, would have far less cause to complain than should I, a woman, tried before a jury of men. Even my counsel, the Hon. Henry R. Selden, who has argued my cause so ably, so earnestly, so unanswerably before your honor, is my political sovereign. Precisely as no disfranchised person is entitled to sit upon a jury, and no woman is entitled to the franchise, so, none but a regularly admitted lawyer is allowed to practice in the courts, and no woman can gain admission to the bar—hence, jury, judge, counsel, must all be of the superior class.

Judge Hunt: The Court must insist—the prisoner has been tried according to the established forms of law.

Miss Anthony: Yes, your honor, but by forms of law all made by men, interpreted by men, administered by men, in favor of men, and against women; and hence, your honor's ordered verdict of guilty, against a United States citizen for the exercise of "that citizen's right to vote," simply because that citizen was a woman and not a man. But, yesterday, the same man-made forms of law declared it a crime punishable with $1,000 fine and six months' imprisonment, for you, or me, or any of us, to give a cup of cold water, a crust of bread, or a night's shelter to a panting fugitive as he was tracking his way to Canada. And every man or woman in whose veins coursed a drop of human sympathy violated that wicked law, reckless of consequences, and was justified in so doing. As then the slaves who got their freedom must take it over, or under, or through the unjust forms of law, precisely so now must women, to get their right to a voice in this Government, take it; and I have taken mine, and mean to take it at every possible opportunity.

Judge Hunt: The Court orders the prisoner to sit down. It will not allow another word.

Miss Anthony: When I was brought before your honor for trial, I hoped for a broad and liberal interpretation of the Constitution and its recent amendments, that should declare all United States citizens under its protecting aegis—that should declare equality of rights the national guarantee to all persons born or naturalized in the United States. But failing to get this justice—failing, even, to get a trial by a jury *not* of my peers—I ask not leniency at your hands—but rather the full rigors of the law.

Judge Hunt: The Court must insist—(Here the prisoner sat down.)

Judge Hunt: The prisoner will stand up. (Here Miss Anthony arose again.) The sentence of the Court is that you pay a fine of one hundred dollars and the costs of the prosecution.

Miss Anthony: May it please your honor, I shall never pay a dollar of your unjust penalty.

Elizabeth Cady Stanton, Susan B. Anthony, and Matilda Joslyn Gage, eds., *History of Woman Suffrage*, vol. II. Rochester, NY: Charles Mann, 1881.

Document 19: A Working Woman's View

The suffrage movement had a solid base among middle-class housewives, but it also attracted factory workers and other women who worked outside the home. In this passage from 1874, Ella A. Little, a shoemaker in Lynn, Massachusetts, maintains that working women want and need the right to vote.

Some ladies say they have no desire to go to the ballot-box. They have good husbands and pleasant homes, and have all the rights they desire. I admit this may be so in many instances; but you who are favored and surrounded by luxury, and can recline on your velvet cushions and feel wholly indifferent to this important subject, do little know or imagine the sorrows of oppression which other females have to contend with, and the want and woe which daily and yearly stare them in the face, and of the temptations which lurk in the path of those who are obliged to go forth alone to battle with temptation and earn their livelihood, working far beyond their strength for meagre pay. . . .

I contemplate with joy the future, and look forward to the

"good time coming" as not far distant when woman shall have her rights and all professions shall be open to her as to man; when she shall occupy positions which males occupy now, but which rightly belong to her; and hope soon woman's voice shall echo in senate chambers and halls of representatives.

Ella A. Little, *Lynn Record*, February 28, 1874.

Document 20: The Need for Better Voters

Toward the end of the nineteenth century, suffragists began to focus less on arguments concerning women's equality with men. Instead, they embraced the theory that women were morally superior to men—and argued that women therefore deserved the right to vote. In the following piece, African-American suffragist Frances Watkins Harper contends that women would use their votes to improve society.

Through weary, wasting years men have destroyed, dashed in pieces, and overthrown, but to-day we stand on the threshold of woman's era, and woman's work is grandly constructive. In her hand are possibilities whose use or abuse must tell upon the political life of the nation, and send their influence for good or evil across the track of unborn ages.

As the saffron tints and crimson flushes of morn herald the coming day, so the social and political advancement which woman has already gained bears the promise of the rising of the full-orbed sun of emancipation. The result will be not to make home less happy, but society more holy; yet I do not think the mere extension of the ballot a panacea for all the ills of our national life. What we need to-day is not simply more voters, but better voters. To-day there are red-handed men in our republic, who walk unwhipped of justice, who richly deserve to exchange the ballot of the freeman for the wristlets of the felon; brutal and cowardly men, who torture, burn, and lynch their fellow-men, men whose defenselessness should be their best defense and their weakness an ensign of protection. More than the changing of institutions we need the development of a national conscience, and the upbuilding of national character. Men may boast of the aristocracy of blood, may glory in the aristocracy of talent, and be proud of the aristocracy of wealth, but there is one aristocracy which must ever outrank them all, and that is the aristocracy of character; and it is the women of a country who help to mold its character, and to influence if not determine its destiny; and in the political future of our nation woman will not have done what she could if she does not endeavor to have our republic stand foremost among the nations of the earth, wearing sobriety as a crown and righteousness as a garment and a girdle. In coming into her political estate woman will find a mass of illiteracy to be dispelled. If knowledge is power, ignorance is also power. The power that educates wickedness may manipulate and dash against the pillars of any state when they are undermined and honeycombed by injustice.

May Wright Sewall, ed., *The World's Congress of Representative Women*. Chicago: Rand McNally, 1894.

Document 21: Sexism and Suffrage

The following is excerpted from Carrie Chapman Catt's speech to the 1902 convention of the National American Woman Suffrage Association. Catt identifies "sex-prejudice" (sexism) as one of the main roadblocks to achieving women's suffrage.

In the United States, at least, we need no longer argue woman's intellectual, moral and physical qualification for the ballot with the intelligent. The Reason of the best of our citizens has long been convinced. The justice of the argument has been admitted, but sex-prejudice is far from conquered.

When a great church official exclaims petulantly, that if women are not more modest in their demands men may be obliged to take to drowning female infants again; when a renowned United States Senator declares no human being can find an answer to the arguments for woman suffrage, but with all the force of his position and influence he will oppose it; when a popular woman novelist speaks of the advocates of the movement as the "shrieking sisterhood;" when a prominent politician says "to argue against woman suffrage is to repudiate the Declaration of Independence," yet he hopes it may never come, the question flies entirely outside the domain of reason, and retreats within the realm of sex-prejudice, where neither logic nor common sense can dislodge it.

Carrie Chapman Catt, *President's Annual Address*. Washington, DC: Hayworth Publishing, 1902.

Document 22: The Experiment Is a Failure

In 1893, Colorado became the second state to allow women to vote. By 1910, when Colorado suffragist Mrs. Francis W. Goddard wrote the following letter to the U.S. House of Representatives, she had changed her mind about the usefulness of women's suffrage. Goddard complains that women voters have not brought about sweeping social reforms and calls her former support of suffrage a mistake.

I have voted since 1893. I have been a delegate to the city and State conventions, and a member of the Republican State Committee from my county. I have been a deputy sheriff and a watcher at the polls. For twenty-three years I have been in the midst of the woman suffrage movement in Colorado. For years I believed in woman suffrage and have worked day in and day out for it. I now see my mistake and would abolish it tomorrow if I could.

No law has been put on the statute book of Colorado for the benefit of women and children that has been put there by the women. The child labor law went through independently of the women's vote. The hours of working-women have not been shortened; the wages of school-teachers have not been raised; the type of men that got into office has not improved a bit.

Frankly, the experiment is a failure. It has done Colorado no good. It has done woman no good. The best thing for both would be if tomorrow the ballot for women could be abolished.

Grace Duffield Goodwin, *Anti-Suffrage: Ten Good Reasons.* New York: Duffield, 1913.

Document 23: Rebelling Against Injustice

While many of the suffragists who walked the picket lines at the White House were young, some older radicals also took part, facing arrests and prison time with the younger women. In 1917, sixty-year-old Lavinia L. Dock of the National Woman's Party wrote this spirited defense of the tactics of the new generation.

If any one says to me: "Why the picketing for Suffrage?" I should say in reply, "Why the fearless spirit of youth? Why does it exist and make itself manifest?"

Is it not really that our whole social world would be likely to harden and toughen into a dreary mass of conventional negations and forbiddances—into hopeless layers of conformity and caste, did not the irrepressible energy and animation of youth, when joined to the clear-eyed sham-hating intelligence of the young, break up the dull masses and set a new pace for laggards to follow?

What is the potent spirit of youth? Is it not the spirit of revolt, of rebellion against senseless and useless and deadening things? Most of all, against injustice, which is of all stupid things the stupidest?

Such thoughts come to one in looking over the field of the Suffrage campaign and watching the pickets at the White House and at the Capitol, where sit the men who complacently enjoy the rights they deny to the women at their gates. Surely, nothing but the creeping paralysis of mental old age can account for the phenomenon of American men, law-makers, officials, administrators, and guardians of the peace, who can see nothing in the intrepid young pickets with their banners, asking for bare justice but common obstructors of traffic, naggers—nuisances that are to be abolished by passing stupid laws forbidding and repressing to add to the old junk-heap of laws which forbid and repress? Can it be possible that any brain cells not totally crystallized could imagine that giving a stone instead of bread would answer conclusively the demand of the women who, because they are young, fearless, eager, and rebellious, are fighting and winning a cause for all women—even for those who are timid, conventional, and inert?

A fatal error—a losing fight. The old stiff minds must give way. The old selfish minds must go. Obstructive reactionaries must move on. The young are at the gates!

Lavinia L. Dock, "The Young Are at the Gates," *Suffragist*, June 30, 1917.

Document 24: Hunger Strike

Jailed for picketing in front of the White House in October 1917, several National Woman's Party members went on a hunger strike to emphasize their demands to be treated as political prisoners. The prison authorities responded by forcibly tube feeding the women. In these notes smuggled out of jail, Rose Winslow describes the procedure.

Alice Paul is in the psychopathic ward. She dreaded forcible feeding frightfully, and I hate to think how she must be feeling. I had a nervous time of it, gasping a long time afterward, and my stomach rejecting during the process. I spent a bad, restless night, but otherwise I am all right. The poor soul who fed me got liberally besprinkled during the process. I heard myself making the most hideous sounds. . . . One feels so forsaken when one lies prone and people shove a pipe down one's stomach.

Yesterday was a bad day for me in feeding. I was vomiting continually during the process. The tube has developed an irritation somewhere that is painful.

Never was there a sentence like ours for such an offense as ours, even in England. No woman ever got it over there even for tearing down buildings. And during all that agitation we were busy saying that never would such things happen in the United States. The men told us they would not endure such frightfulness.

The same doctor feeds both Alice Paul and me. Don't let them tell you we take this well. Miss Paul vomits much. I do too. It's the nervous reaction, and I can't control it much. We think of the coming feeding all day. It is horrible. The doctor thinks I take it well. I hate the thought of Alice Paul and the others if I take it well.

All the officers here know we are making this hunger strike so that women fighting for liberty may be considered political prisoners; we have told them. God knows we don't want other women ever to have to do this over again.

Doris Stevens, *Jailed for Freedom: American Women Win the Vote*, ed. Carol O'Hare. Troutdale, OR: NewSage Press, 1995.

Document 25: The Nineteenth Amendment

On August 26, 1920, the Nineteenth Amendment to the U.S. Constitution was signed into law, granting women the right to vote.

The right of citizens of the United States to vote shall not be denied or abridged by the United States or by any State on account of sex.

Congress shall have power to enforce this article by appropriate legislation.

Chronology

1647
Margaret Brent, the executrix of the colonial governor of Maryland, appears before Maryland's legislative assembly to demand the right to vote. Her petition is denied.

1776
New Jersey's new constitution grants suffrage to "all free inhabitants," not specifying gender.

1792
British author Mary Wollstonecraft publishes *A Vindication of the Rights of Women*.

1807
New Jersey repeals women's right to vote.

1837
Abolitionists Sarah and Angelina Grimké start to address large mixed audiences of both men and women.

June 12–20, 1840
At the World Anti-Slavery Convention in London, women delegates are not allowed to participate, and all female attendees are required to remain in segregated seating. Lucretia Mott and Elizabeth Cady Stanton agree to hold a women's rights convention.

1848
The first women's rights convention is held on July 19 and 20 in Seneca Falls, New York. A second convention takes place on August 2 in Rochester, New York.

1850
The First National Woman's Rights Convention is held in Worcester, Massachusetts, on October 23 and 24. Subsequently, national conventions are held every year but one until the beginning of the Civil War. Many regional conventions are also organized in various states and territories.

1851
In March, Stanton meets temperance activist Susan B. Anthony. Over the next few years, they begin to work closely together for the cause of women's rights.

1853
Pauline Wright Davis begins publication of the *Una*, the first newspaper of the women's rights movement.

1857
Lucy Stone refuses to pay taxes in protest of her inability to vote.

1860
On March 19, Stanton addresses the New York legislature, asking for women's suffrage.

1861
The Civil War breaks out in April, disrupting suffrage activities as women concentrate on aiding the war effort.

1865
The Civil War ends with the South's surrender on April 9.

1866
In April, the Fourteenth Amendment—which excludes women from suffrage—is proposed. The Eleventh National Woman's Rights Convention, the first since the beginning of the war, convenes in New York City in May. The attendees found the American Equal Rights Association, dedicated to obtaining universal suffrage regardless of race or sex. In October, Stanton becomes the first female candidate for Congress.

1867
Kansas becomes the first state to hold a referendum on women's suffrage. Despite intense campaigning by Anthony, Stanton, Stone, and other suffragists, the measure is voted down.

1868
In January, Anthony and Stanton begin publishing the *Revolution*, a newspaper advocating women's suffrage and progressive reforms. The Fourteenth Amendment is adopted in July. In December, the first federal amendment for women's suffrage is proposed in Congress.

1869
The Fifteenth Amendment is proposed in Congress in February. In May, the American Equal Rights Association dissolves; Stanton and Anthony establish the radical National Woman Suffrage Association (NWSA). Stone forms the more conservative American Woman Suffrage Association (AWSA) in November. On December 10, the Wyoming Territory becomes the first to give women unrestricted suffrage.

1870

In January, AWSA begins publication of the *Woman's Journal*. The Utah Territory enfranchises women in February. The Fifteenth Amendment is ratified on March 30.

1871

On January 11, Victoria Woodhull addresses the Judiciary Committee of the U.S. House of Representatives, arguing that women have a constitutional right to vote under the Fourteenth Amendment. Opponents to women's suffrage organize the Anti-Suffrage Party.

1872

Woodhull becomes the first woman to run for president of the United States. On November 5, Anthony casts her vote in the national elections; on November 28, she is arrested.

1873

Anthony stands trial on June 17 and is found guilty of voting illegally.

1875

In March, the U.S. Supreme Court hands down its decision in the case of *Minor v. Happersett*, declaring that the Fourteenth and Fifteenth Amendments do not give women a constitutional right to vote and that women's political rights fall under the jurisdiction of the individual states.

1878

Senator A.A. Sargent of California introduces a new women's suffrage amendment in Congress, which eventually becomes known as the Susan B. Anthony amendment.

1883

The legislature of the Washington Territory grants women the right to vote.

1887

The Senate votes for the first time on the federal suffrage amendment; it is defeated. The Supreme Court repeals women's suffrage in the Washington Territory, and Congress disfranchises women in the Utah Territory.

1890

On February 18, after several years of negotiations, the two divisions of the suffrage movement reunite to form the National American Woman Suffrage Association (NAWSA). On July 23,

Wyoming is admitted to the Union as the first state with voting rights for women.

1893
Colorado holds a referendum on women's suffrage; the measure is approved, making Colorado the second state to give women the right to vote. New Zealand becomes the first nation to grant women unrestricted suffrage.

1896
Idaho approves women's suffrage in a state referendum. Utah is admitted to the Union; its new constitution reinstates women's right to vote.

1900
Anthony resigns as the president of NAWSA and is succeeded by Carrie Chapman Catt.

1903
In England, suffragette Emmeline Pankhurst founds the radical Women's Social and Political Movement; the group's militant tactics influence many young American suffragists.

1904
Catt resigns from the presidency of NAWSA and is succeeded by Anna Howard Shaw.

1907
Harriot Stanton Blatch forms the Equality League of Self-Supporting Women, later renamed the Women's Political Union.

1908
The National College Women's Equal Suffrage League is founded. Maud Malone and British suffragette Bettina Borrmann Wells organize a small suffrage parade in New York City.

1909
In October, Catt launches the Woman Suffrage Party.

1910
Blatch and the Women's Political Union organize the first large-scale women's suffrage parade, held in New York City on May 21. Women's suffrage passes in a state referendum in Washington.

1911
Women's suffrage is approved in a state referendum in California. The National Association Opposed to Woman Suffrage (NAOWS) is formed.

1912

Women's suffrage is granted in Arizona, Kansas, and Oregon.

1913

On March 3, the day prior to President Woodrow Wilson's inauguration, Alice Paul organizes a suffrage parade of several thousand women in Washington, D.C. On April 13, Paul and Lucy Burns form the Congressional Union. Kate Gordon founds the Southern States Woman Suffrage Conference, which works only for the enfranchisement of white women. The Alaska Territory gives women the vote.

1914

On March 19, the Senate votes on the Susan B. Anthony amendment for the first time since 1887, but the measure fails to pass. Montana and Nevada grant women suffrage.

1915

On January 12, the House of Representatives votes on the Susan B. Anthony amendment for the first time; the amendment is rejected. Shaw is pressured to resign as president of NAWSA and is replaced by Catt.

1916

In June, the Congressional Union formally separates from NAWSA and organizes the National Woman's Party. At NAWSA's convention in September, Catt announces her "winning plan" to achieve national women's suffrage. Representative Jeanette Rankin of Montana becomes the first woman to be elected to the U.S. Congress.

1917

On January 10, the National Woman's Party begins picketing the White House. The United States enters World War I on April 6. On June 22, the first arrests of the White House protesters occur. Demanding recognition as political prisoners, some picketers begin a hunger strike on November 5. On November 27 and 28, all the picketers are released from prison. New York's state referendum on women's suffrage passes.

1918

President Wilson issues a statement in support of the federal suffrage amendment on January 9. World War I ends on November 11. Michigan, South Dakota, and Oklahoma grant women suffrage.

1919

The House of Representatives approves the federal amendment on May 21. The Senate passes the amendment on June 4 and sends it to the states for ratification. Between June and December, twenty-two states ratify the Nineteenth Amendment.

1920

Between January and March, thirteen states ratify the Nineteenth Amendment. On August 18, Tennessee ratifies the amendment, giving it the required two-thirds majority of the states. On August 26, Secretary of State Bainbridge Colby signs the proclamation, certifying the final adoption of the Nineteenth Amendment to the U.S. Constitution.

For Further Research

Collections of Original Documents Pertaining to Women's Suffrage

Mari Jo Buhle and Paul Buhle, eds., *The Concise History of Woman Suffrage.* Urbana: University of Illinois Press, 1978.

Elizabeth Frost and Kathryn Cullen-DuPont, eds., *Women's Suffrage in America: An Eyewitness History.* New York: Facts On File, 1992.

Dawn Keetley and John Pettegrew, eds., *Public Women, Public Words: A Documentary History of American Feminism*, 2 vols. Madison, WI: Madison House, 1997–2000.

Michael S. Kimmel and Thomas E. Mosmiller, eds., *Against the Tide: Pro-Feminist Men in the United States, 1776–1990: A Documentary History.* Boston: Beacon Press, 1992.

Winston E. Langley and Vivian C. Fox, eds., *Women's Rights in the United States: A Documentary History.* Westport, CT: Greenwood Press, 1994.

Martha M. Solomon, ed., *A Voice of Their Own: The Woman Suffrage Press, 1840–1910.* Tuscaloosa: University of Alabama Press, 1991.

General Histories of the Women's Suffrage Movement

Olivia Coolidge, *Women's Rights: The Suffrage Movement in America, 1848–1920.* New York: E.P. Dutton, 1966.

Margaret Finnegan, *Selling Suffrage: Consumer Culture and Votes for Women.* New York: Columbia University Press, 1999.

Robert Gallagher, "I Was Arrested, of Course," *American Heritage*, February 1974.

Janet Zollinger Geile, *Two Paths to Women's Equality: Temperance, Suffrage, and the Origins of Modern Feminism.* New York: Twayne, 1995.

Ann D. Gordon, ed., *African American Women and the Vote, 1837–1965.* Amherst: University of Massachusetts Press, 1997.

Linda J. Lumsden, *Rampant Women: Suffragists and the Right of Assembly.* Knoxville: University of Tennessee Press, 1997.

Judy Monroe, *The Nineteenth Amendment: Women's Right to Vote.* Springfield, NJ: Enslow, 1998.

David Morgan, *Suffragists and Democrats: The Politics of Woman Suffrage in America.* East Lansing: Michigan State University Press, 1972.

Ross Evans Paulson, *Women's Suffrage and Prohibition.* Glenview: Scott, Foresman, 1973.

Sylvia Strauss, *"Traitors to the Masculine Cause": The Men's Campaigns for Women's Rights.* Westport, CT: Greenwood Press, 1982.

Sally Roesch Wagner, *A Time of Protest: Suffragists Challenge the Republic, 1870–1887.* Carmichael, CA: Sky Carrier Press, 1988.

Marjorie Spruill Wheeler, ed., *One Woman, One Vote: Rediscovering the Woman Suffrage Movement.* Troutdale, OR: NewSage Press, 1995.

Studies of Regional Suffrage Activities

Beverly Beeton, *Women Vote in the West: The Woman Suffrage Movement, 1869–1896.* New York: Garland, 1986.

Steven M. Buechler, *The Transformation of the Woman Suffrage Movement: The Case of Illinois, 1850–1920.* New Brunswick, NJ: Rutgers University Press, 1986.

Susan Englander, *Class Conflict and Class Coalition in the California Woman Suffrage Movement, 1907–1912: The San Francisco Wage Earners' Suffrage League.* Lewiston, NY: Edwin Mellen Press, 1992.

Elna C. Green, *Southern Strategies: Southern Women and the Woman Suffrage Question.* Chapel Hill: University of North Carolina Press, 1997.

Marjorie Spruill Wheeler, *New Women of the New South: The Leaders of the Woman Suffrage Movement in the Southern States.* New York: Oxford University Press, 1993.

The Antisuffragists

Anne M. Benjamin, *A History of the Anti-Suffrage Movement in the United States from 1895 to 1920: Women Against Equality.* Lewiston, NY: Edwin Mellen Press, 1991.

Jane Jerome Camhi, *Women Against Women: American Anti-Suffragism, 1880–1920.* Brooklyn, NY: Carlson, 1994.

Thomas J. Jablonsky, *The Home, Heaven, and Mother Party: Female*

Anti-Suffragists in the United States, 1868–1920. Brooklyn, NY: Carlson, 1994.

Mara Mayor, "Fears and Fantasies of the Anti-Suffragists," *Connecticut Review*, April 1974.

Women's Suffrage Movements Outside the United States

Catherine Lyle Cleverdon, *The Woman Suffrage Movement in Canada.* Toronto: University of Toronto Press, 1974.

Patricia Grimshaw, *Women's Suffrage in New Zealand.* Auckland, NZ: Auckland University Press, 1987.

Audrey Oldfield, *Woman Suffrage in Australia: A Gift or a Struggle?* New York: Cambridge University Press, 1992.

Sophia A. van Wingerden, *The Women's Suffrage Movement in Britain, 1866–1928.* New York: St. Martin's Press, 1999.

Biographies of Suffrage Leaders

Margaret Hope Bacon, *Valiant Friend: The Life of Lucretia Mott.* New York: Walker, 1980.

Kathleen Barry, *Susan B. Anthony: A Biography of a Singular Feminist.* New York: New York University Press, 1988.

Elisabeth Griffith, *In Her Own Right: The Life of Elizabeth Cady Stanton.* New York: Oxford University Press, 1984.

Andrea Moore Kerr, *Lucy Stone: Speaking Out for Equality.* New Brunswick, NJ: Rutgers University Press, 1992.

Nell Irvin Painter, *Sojourner Truth: A Life, a Symbol.* New York: W.W. Norton, 1996.

Jacqueline Van Voris, *Carrie Chapman Catt: A Public Life.* New York: Feminist Press, 1987.

Geoffrey C. Ward, *Not for Ourselves Alone: The Story of Elizabeth Cady Stanton and Susan B. Anthony: An Illustrated History.* New York: Knopf, 1999.

Index